VICTOR LUSTIG

THE MAN WHO
CONNED THE WORLD

VICTOR
LUSTIG

CHRISTOPHER SANDFORD

The
History
Press

First published 2021

The History Press
97 St George's Place, Cheltenham,
Gloucestershire, GL50 3QB
www.thehistorypress.co.uk

British Library Cataloguing in Publication Data.
A catalogue record for this book is available from the British Library.

ISBN 978 0 7509 9367 8

Typesetting and origination by The History Press
Printed and bound in Great Britain by TJ Books Limited, Padstow, Cornwall.

MIX
Paper from
responsible sources
FSC® C013056

Trees for LYfe

To Fred and Cindy Smith

'Worth [goes] on foot, and rascals in a coach.'

John Dryden

Victor Lustig's 'Ten Commandments of the Con':

1. Be a patient listener (it is this, not fast talking, that gets a con-man his coups).

2. Never look bored.

3. Wait for the other person to reveal any political opinions, then agree with them.

4. Let them reveal religious views, then have the same ones.

5. Hint at sex talk, but don't follow it up unless the other fellow shows a strong interest.

6. Never discuss health, unless some special concern is shown.

7. Never pry into a person's personal circumstances (they'll tell you eventually).

8. Never boast; just let your importance be quietly obvious.

9. Never be untidy.

10. Never get drunk.

CONTENTS

ACKNOWLEDGEMENTS

Victor Lustig used to observe that writers always say they're aiming to entertain the widest possible audience but they're in fact in it chiefly for their own amusement. In this context I should immediately acknowledge that the book you're now holding was largely written during the great lockdown of 2020–21, and as such gave me a daily purpose in life other than obsessing about the correct use of face masks or the latest protocol on social distancing. Even so, I hope you won't find the story that follows to be entirely without wider merit. Perhaps one of the consolations of getting on a bit is that you tend to clarify in your own mind what's good and what's not, and I thus brazenly offer the opinion that this book at least avoids any conspicuous falling off from the modest standards of its predecessors. In fact, further throwing caution to the wind, I can nominate it as my personal favourite. Nonetheless, it goes without saying that none of the names listed below can be blamed for the shortcomings of the text. They are mine alone.

For archive material, input or advice I should thank, professionally: AbeBooks; Alcatraz Archives; Alibris; *America*; *Atlantic Monthly*; Bonham's; Book Depository; Bookfinder; the British Library; the British Newspaper Library; Central Lutheran; *Chronicles*; Common Ground; the *Cricketer International*; the Cricket Society; the *Daily Mail*; the Davenport Hotel; Emerald Downs; the FBI's Freedom of Information Division; Dominic Farr; Garden Court Hotel; the General Register Office; Grumbles; *Hansard*; *Hedgehog Review*; The History Press; Michael Hurley; Jane Jamieson; Barbara Levy; the Library of Congress; Sue Lynch; Christine McMorris; Missouri State Department of Health; the Mitchell Library, Glasgow; *Modern Age*; the National Archives; the National Gallery; *National Review*; the 1976 Coalition; the *Oldie*; Tim Reidy; Renton Public Library; Rebecca Romney; Jane Rosen; St Mary's Hospital, Paddington; Sandy Cove Inn, Oregon; Seaside Library, Oregon; Seattle C.C.; Seattle Mariners; the *Seattle Times*; the *Spectator*; Liz Street; Andrew Stuart; US National Archives/Records of the Bureau of Prisons; Unity Museum, Seattle; University of Montana; University of Washington; Vital Records; Douglas Williford; *Wisden Cricket Monthly*; Qona Wright; and Simon Wright.

And personally: Tony An; Rev. Maynard Atik; Pete Barnes; Carlos Beltran; Alison Bent; Rob Boddie; Geoff and Emma Boycott; Robert and Hilary Bruce; Jon Burke; John Bush; Lincoln Callaghan; Don Carson; Steve Cropper; Celia Culpan; the Daudet family; Monty Dennison; Ted Dexter; Chris Difford; Micky Dolenz; the Dowdall family; Barbara and the late John Dungee; Jon Filby; Malcolm Galfe; Tony Gill; James Graham; Freddy Gray; Jeff and Rita Griffin; Steve and Jo Hackett; Peter Hain; Nigel Hancock; Hermino; Alastair Hignell; Charles Hillman; Alex Holmes; Jo Jacobius; Mick Jagger; Julian James; Robin B. James; Jo Johnson; Lincoln Kamell; Aslam Khan; Imran Khan; Carol Lamb; Terry Lambert; Belinda Lawson; Eugene Lemcio; Todd Linse; the Lorimer family; Nick Lowe; Robert Dean Lurie; Les McBride; Dan McCarthy; Charles McIntosh; Dennis McNally; the Macris; Lee Mattson; Jim Meyersahm; Jerry Miller; Sheila Mohn; Yvette Montague; the Morgans; Harry Mount; Colleen and the late John Murray; Greg Nowak; Chuck Ogmund; Phil Oppenheim; Valya Page; Peter Parfitt; Robin and Lucinda Parish; Owen Paterson; Bill Payne; Rick Pearson; Peter Perchard; Marlys and the late Chris Pickrell; Pat Pocock,

Roman Polanski; Debbie Poulsen; Robert and Jewell Prins; the Prins family; the late Christopher Riley; Neil Robinson; Ailsa Rushbrooke; Debbie Saks; Sam; the late Sefton Sandford; Sue Sandford; Peter Scaramanga; the late Dennis Silk; Silver Platters; Pat Simmons; the Smith family; Chris Spedding; Debbie Standish; the Stanley family; David Starkey; the late Thaddeus Stuart; Jack Surendranath; Belinda and Ian Taylor; Millie Thompson; Hugh Turbervill; Derek Turner; the late Ben and Mary Tyvand; Diana Villar; Ross Viner; Lisbeth Vogl; Phil Walker; Edward Welsch; Alan and Rogena White; Debbie Wild; the Willis Fleming family; the late Aaron Wolf; Heng and Lang Woon; the Zombies.

My deepest thanks, as always, to Karen and Nicholas Sandford.

C.S.
2021

LIST OF ILLUSTRATIONS

While every effort has been made to trace or contact all copyright holders, the publishers would be pleased to rectify at the earliest opportunity any errors or ommissions brought to their attention.

I

THE AGE OF ILLUSION

The period either side of the First World War was a golden age for the confidence man. When you add an inflamed sense of patriotism to heightened levels of anxiety about personal survival, you have conditions uniquely receptive to both the acknowledged masters of reality manipulation and to others experienced in squeezing a defenceless victim in a tight spot. 'A new kind of entrepreneur is stirring amongst us,' *The Times* wrote in March 1919. 'He is prone to the most detestable tactics, and is a stranger to charity and public spirit. One may nonetheless note his acuity in separating others from their money.'

Arthur John 'Maundy' Gregory was one of those men who quickly came to appreciate the unintended consequences of the war. 'He was a compulsive extortionist of the sort prevalent in the 1920s,' the *Daily News* once noted. In time Gregory combined active service in the Irish Guards with a sideline in wistful, snobbish journalism and freelance espionage work against what he saw as the rising threat of worldwide Bolshevism. In practice this meant that he arranged payments to the ruling Liberal party in exchange for peerages, published his own newspaper, and collected information about the sex lives of his political foes for the purpose of blackmailing or otherwise fleecing them. Gregory particularly cultivated the company of the deposed royals who haunted Europe in the post-war years, once touching the exiled crown prince of Greece for a loan secured by the proceeds of a non-existent Bolivian goldmine, and similarly interesting the Empress Maria Fyodorovna, mother of the last Tsar, in a perhaps fanciful scheme to breed pigs for the purpose of pitting them in public mud-wrestling contests against human opponents. Gregory was described as a plump, middle-sized man who always wore an exquisite dove-grey suit and made use of a chauffeured, production-model Bentley saloon. He may conceivably have had something to do with the disappearance of his sworn enemy, the radical politician Victor Grayson, who, receiving a phone call while dining with friends in London's Leicester Square one evening in September 1920, told his companions that he had to go on a matter of urgency to a nearby hotel, but would be back shortly. He never returned. Gregory himself lived long enough to be declared bankrupt and to move to Paris, where he had the ill luck to be captured by the invading Germans in June 1940. He died in an internment camp the following year, aged 64.

Gregory's was far from the only case of personal duplicity or commercial opportunism to take place in the pendulum years around the time of the Great War. There was the sad story of Mabel Edith Scott, for example, who married the second Lord Russell in 1890 but went on to spend much of the next decade locked in increasingly bitter litigation with her estranged husband over matters involving his unusual bedroom practices and other intimate conjugal details. In time the unhappy lady was able to divorce Russell and enter into a second marriage with an individual describing himself as Arthurpold Stuart de Modena, an Austrian prince who for never fully explained reasons found himself living above a greengrocer's shop in Portsmouth. In reality, the groom turned out to be a recently discharged naval rating and sometime valet named Bill Brown, and Lady Russell was not his only wife. 'He was not inattentive to me,' in the measured words of one lady read out in court, 'but he presumed on my generosity.'

At about the same time there was one Stephane Otto, who, posing as a member of the Belgian royal family, got as far as pinning the Order of Leopold on the lapel of the commanding officer of the American Army of Occupation of the Rhine, but who later went to jail in Crewe after being convicted of obtaining 12s 6d from a clergyman. Similarly there was the case of Netley Lucas, a Croydon drifter who set himself up as a displaced Rumanian count and best-selling author in post-war London, until he received eighteen months at the Old Bailey for obtaining £225 by false pretences. 'There must be a trace of insanity in my brain,' he confessed disarmingly. Or, across the Atlantic, there was the so-called Jerome Tarbot, who enjoyed a comfortable living as a decorated combat veteran and visiting lecturer on the horrors of the Somme, until War Department investigators outed him as a convicted swindler and serial bigamist named Al Dubois Jr, a draft dodger who had in fact been stealing cars in California at the time he claimed to have been in the killing fields of France.

The above list is far from comprehensive. What strikes the observer today is just how many men and women could be so restlessly inventive in their pursuit of the brazen personal imposture or the deft financial shakedown. The whole concept of the creative extraction of funds was one that was painfully familiar to a generation coming of age in the early years of the twentieth century. Such was the range and variety of the scams that it sometimes seems surprising that anyone could have emerged from the era with his wallet intact.

Perhaps the most colourful and long-running hoax of the day wasn't a narrowly commercial one at all, although it could be argued that, over time, whole fortunes were made and lost as a result. It began, instead, at a meeting of immaculately dark-suited and apparently sober-minded men held at the Geological Society in London on 18 December 1912, when a 48-year-old lawyer and amateur paleontologist named Charles Dawson claimed to have discovered bone fragments at a gravel pit near his home at Piltdown, West Sussex, and that these had 'terrific significance' for our understanding of man's evolution.

At the same meeting, Arthur Smith Woodward, curator of the geological department at the British Museum, announced that a reconstruction of the fragments had been prepared, and that a resulting 'human-like' skull, thought to be some 600,000 years old, was all but indistinguishable from that of a modern chimpanzee. Dawson and Woodward went on to claim that 'Piltdown Man' represented no less than a genetic missing link between apes and humans, and by extension a denial of the biblical story of creation, a thesis much of the more progressive element of the press was happy to accept.

It would be forty-one years before new scientific dating techniques conclusively proved that Dawson's find was a hoax. The Piltdown fossils 'could not possibly form an integral whole', *The Times* reported in November 1953. Instead, they consisted of a human skull of medieval age, the jawbone of an eighteenth-century orangutan, and several assorted modern baboon teeth. There was also a bone chip determined to have come from an extinct species of elephant unique to the plains of Tunisia. Only a brief microscopic examination was required to show that several jaw fragments presented by Dawson had been filed down to give them a shape associated with that of a human. A sculpted bone found at the original site in Sussex, and said by the *New York Times* to be 'a wonderfully preserved Neanderthal hunting or sporting tool' – a sort of primitive cricket bat – had in fact been carved with an 'implement like a Swiss army knife' in the years around 1911 or 1912. In short order, Piltdown Man was unceremoniously removed from display and consigned to a metal box in the basement of London's Natural History Museum. Perhaps the ultimate lesson of the whole escapade is that, as Harry Houdini, himself something of a past master of artifice, once observed: 'As a rule, I have found the greater brain a man has, and the better he is educated, the easier it is to dupe him.'

The commercial possibilities of the time were captivating, and it was remiss of men not to exploit them to the full, a former British

Horace Ridler, aka the Great Omi or 'Zebra Man'.

army officer named Horace Ridler later wrote when reflecting on his appearance in the pages of *Tatler* in 1921, and his subsequent life as a paid guest in the upper echelons of London society. After the war he had gone to the tattooist 'Professor' George Burchett in his premises behind Waterloo station and had himself engraved from head to toe with black and white stripes, a protracted and painful business that had taken nearly a year to complete. In time Ridler launched himself on the world as 'The Great Omi: The Zebra Man', claiming to have been forcibly disfigured under the most barbaric circumstances by native bushmen in New Guinea. He would tell theatrical booking agents that the best time to reach him direct in his office was between 1 and 2 p.m. every weekday while his secretary was at lunch. Ridler would give them the number of a public phone box in Millwall, and ensconce himself in it for an hour each afternoon heedless of other waiting customers. He went on to become a popular lay preacher and to tour with the Ringling Brothers circus, but was turned down when he tried to re-enlist with the army in 1940. He retired at the height of his fame to Ripe, a small village in Sussex, where he died in 1969 at the age of 77.

In broadly the same pseudo-anthropological vein, there was the long, often tragicomic saga of the Cottingley fairies. It began one hot afternoon in July 1917, when 16-year-old Elsie Wright and her 10-year-old cousin Frances Griffiths disappeared with a camera into the glen behind the Wrights' terraced home in West Yorkshire, and returned with an image that among other things seemed to show Frances leaning on the side of a small hill on which four miniature people were dancing. 'It is a revelation', no less an authority than the spiritualist-minded author Sir Arthur Conan Doyle wrote, when hearing of the affair two years later. There were to be several further twists and turns to the story, but the immediate result was that in 1920 Conan Doyle went into print in a widely syndicated article entitled 'The Evidence for Fairies'.

The reaction to this was mixed. While many in the worldwide spiritualist movement that sprang up after the First World War championed the two young girls, the newspaper *Truth* expressed a more widely held view when, in January 1921, it wrote, 'For the real explanation of these fairy photographs, what is wanted is not a knowledge of occult phenomena but a knowledge of children.' Even this was mild compared to some of the popular jokes that did the rounds, including the one where Doyle was said to have appeared at the climax of his friend James Barrie's *Peter Pan* to lead the audience in a chorus of 'I do believe in fairies!' Other wisecracks were less elevated.

Although Conan Doyle went to his grave stubbornly believing in what he called the 'miracle' of Cottingley, in 1983 the then elderly women at the heart of the affair admitted that 'most' of their original pictures had been faked. The two cousins had cut out illustrations from *Princess Mary's Gift Book*, a 1914 annual (in which Doyle himself had published a story) and propped them up with hatpins in the grassy banks behind the Wrights' house. Frances Griffiths added that the girls had 'not wanted to embarrass the great men' who had swallowed their tale, and had been horrified to see it take root for the next sixty years.

Of a more base, sordidly commercial character, there was the sensational case first published in the *News of the World* on 3 January 1915. It concerned the sorry fate of 38-year-old Margaret Lloyd, née Lofty, a vicar's daughter who had been married only two weeks earlier. Her 42-year-old husband John, apparently a successful land agent, had discovered her lifeless body in the bath of their lodgings at Bismarck Road in north London. The couple's landlady testified that she had been ironing in her kitchen that evening when the sound of splashing came from the bathroom above. This was followed by the 'queer noise of hands rubbing [or] slapping a firm surface', and then by a deep sigh. A few moments later, she had heard the mournful strains of someone playing 'Nearer My God, to Thee' on the organ in the Lloyds' sitting room. The hymn had ominous associations: legend insists that the ship's band had been playing the same tune as the RMS *Titanic* sank into the Atlantic.

Mr Lloyd then came down the stairs and went out, only to ring at the front door a few minutes later, explaining that he had forgotten his key. 'I've bought some tomatoes for Mrs. Lloyd's supper,' he announced. 'Is she down yet?' Margaret's death was quickly recorded as misadventure, and her grieving widower collected the £700 life insurance policy he had thoughtfully taken out for her on the day of their wedding. It later emerged that Lloyd, whose real name was George Joseph Smith, had been in the habit of entering into bigamous marriages and disposing of his brides in this manner. He was tried and hanged at Wandsworth Prison for one of what were thought to be as many as six murders.

On a more spiritual if not always charitable level, there were those who exploited the public's post-war fascination with the idea of a visible afterlife, promising, for only a modest fee, to reunite the living and the dead. It took Houdini himself to put an end to the career of one popular London medium who began her séances by standing nude in a bowl of flour so that she was unable to move around the room without leaving incriminating tracks.

'She has a tube for her vagin [*sic*] in which she stashes a pair of silk stockings,' he explained. 'When the lights are out, as it is impossible to quit the floor without leaving footprints, she reaches in and gets the silk stockings, puts them on her feet, steps out of the bowl of flour [and] is able to walk around without besmirching the floor or leaving prints. After the materialisation she goes back, takes off her stockings, conceals her load, and – presto! – steps back into the bowl of flour.'

Working much the same angle were the Washington DC-based Julius and Ada Zancig, a husband-and-wife sometime-vaudeville team who in the immediate post-war years advertised themselves

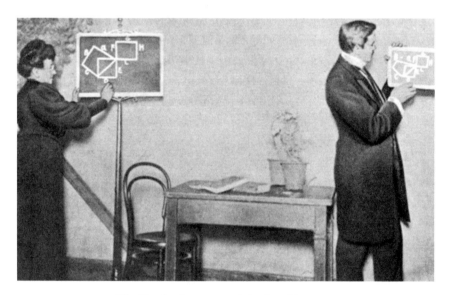

The Zancigs demonstrate their telepathic powers.

as 'Professional astrologers, tea leaf readers, crystal ball seers, diviners and palmists'. Conan Doyle went to the Zancigs' home and came away convinced that the couple possessed telepathic powers. Houdini was less impressed, writing that the Zancigs used a system of codes rather than any supernatural gifts to achieve their results, and that even these had been developed only after extended rehearsal. When the first Mrs Zancig had died, her widower 'took a teenaged street-car conductor from Philadelphia and broke him into the duo,' Houdini noted. Some acrimony had arisen when the young man later defected from the team and began offering his own mindreading routine, using a trained monkey as a foil. He was replaced by a conjuror known professionally as 'Syko the Psychic', who in turn left the act. 'At that stage, Prof. Zancig came to me for an assistant and I introduced him to an actress,' Houdini wrote. 'He said he would guarantee to teach her the code inside a month, but they never came to an agreement on financial matters.' Where Doyle found Zancig to be a 'remarkable man [who] undoubtedly enjoyed paranormal or divine powers', Houdini saw only an old circus sideshow stooge whose new act 'reflects the modern rage for mediumistic bunco.'

A lesser occultist than Zancig, but as great a fraud, was Horatio Bottomley, an English journalist, financier and Liberal politician who in 1912 was bankrupted with liabilities of £233,000, or about £6 million in modern money. He had recently added to his losses when, after bribing all six jockeys in a race at Brighton to finish in a certain order, a heavy sea mist had rolled in and the suddenly blinded riders had failed to follow instructions. Undeterred, Bottomley successfully stood for parliament as an Independent in December 1918 and began offering the public Victory Bonds at the heavily discounted price of £1 each, promising subscribers the chance to enter in an annual draw for prizes – up to £20,000, he said – from the accrued interest. The response to this offer was overwhelming, and Bottomley would have had his hands full had he ever tried to properly administer the scheme. Instead he

Horatio Bottomley addresses a wartime recruiting rally in London.

lavished the funds on luxury cars and thoroughbred racehorses, as well as on mistresses whom he visited in several discreet flats around London. He was eventually sent for trial at the Old Bailey. Even then he conducted himself with a certain élan, securing the judge's agreement to a fifteen-minute adjournment each day so that he, Bottomley, could drink a pint of champagne, ostensibly for medicinal purposes. Sentenced to seven years, he emerged to launch himself on the London music hall stage of the 1930s, but failed to prosper in his new role. Bottomley died in a charity ward on 26 May 1933, at the age of 73. One obituary called him 'more a series of public attitudes than a person'.

Following in the same long if not distinguished line as Gregory, Bottomley and the rest was Artur Alves Reis, an impoverished Lisbon undertaker's son who forged himself a diploma from Oxford University and, posing as an accredited government finance ministry official, persuaded a printer to issue him with 200,000 Portuguese banknotes. Reis bought himself old masters, three farms, a taxi fleet and expensive French couture for his wife and numerous mistresses on the proceeds. A contemporary account describes him 'stroll[ing] the Rua do Salite in a businessman's double-breasted grey suit, with three-pointed white handkerchief on display in the breast pocket, Malacca cane in hand'. Arrested in December 1925 and sentenced to twenty years, on his release Reis was offered a job advising the state bank on security. He died of a heart attack in June 1955, aged 58.

The equal of them all was Ivar Kreuger, the Swedish-born match-stick king of the post-war world who built himself a marble-floored, 125-room Stockholm office complex as he all but cornered the market for phosphorus-based household combustibles. By 1922 Kreuger had sufficient cash on hand to allow him to lend money to several foreign governments, and was in the habit of transferring funds from one holding company to another with what a judge later called 'little or no formality'. Some of it went into non-existent client accounts, but more was spent on beautiful women and expensive houses. Kreuger's penchant for gambling his investors' money on the foreign exchange markets proved disastrous, however, and he apparently shot himself in March 1932, aged 52, although rumours persist that he was murdered for reasons buried amongst the chaos of his reign as Europe's most notorious rogue trader.

In the years following the First World War, a lady might have discreetly availed herself of a small mechanical device known as a Pulsocon. Looking rather like a hand-cranked rotary egg whisk, it was officially described as a 'blood circulator, able to relieve pain, rheumatism, deafness, gout, and many other ailments', but seems to have been most popular as a prototype vibrator. It was the brainchild of an Irish-born showman called Gerald Macaura. Macaura gave himself the title 'Doctor', but he had no medical qualification; nor had he served in the trenches, as he often claimed. Jailed in Paris for practising without a licence, he returned to his native country to promote the merits of his new invention the O'Lectron, which 'produces both mechanical and magnetic oscillations', giving man 'control over the circulation of his blood and the very atoms of which he is composed'. It sold in impressive numbers, allowing Macaura to buy large houses on both sides of the Atlantic, as well as to underwrite a brass band and a first-ever cinema in his home town. Strong, sly, charming, decisive and intolerant of criticism, over the years he successfully sued a number of newspapers and once forced the *New York Times* to publish a front-page apology for having aired doubts about the O'Lectron. How did he do it? 'Gerry told them to shut up, so they shut up,' one Irish justice ministry official explained.

Consumers in the 1920s became accustomed to the miracle health cure or the sure-fire investment opportunity. In the era of dissimulation, it was all part of their daily routine. Perhaps no one was more emblematic of the age than the Italian-born Carlo 'Charles' Ponzi (1882–1949), who for a few heady years bestrode the financial malpractice world with his 'scheme' to buy up stocks of the humble international reply coupon – a voucher to allow someone in one country to send it to a correspondent in another country – and sell them at a 400 per cent profit. By June 1920 investors were cheerfully paying some $1 million a day to be allowed to participate. In the classic tradition, Ponzi bought himself a fabulous Boston estate, which he staffed with numerous live-in servants and a pack of Doberman guard dogs. One biographer writes: 'He had an enormous limousine specially built for him, driven by a chauffeur with a footman beside him, both in plum uniforms to match the car.' It seemed Ponzi had positioned himself exactly where he wished to be – poised to profit from either the naked greed or the naïve enthusiasm of the American consumer of the 1920s.

Charles Ponzi.

Alas, the scheme collapsed just as quickly as it had risen. Later in the summer of 1920 the *Boston Post* began asking pointed questions about Ponzi's cash machine, noting that he would have needed to control a minimum of 160 million international reply coupons to have covered his investments. As there were only 27,000 such certificates in worldwide circulation, 'there would seem to be doubts about the soundness of his basic proposition', in the *Post*'s measured words. It all came crashing down for Ponzi later in August 1920 when the same paper revealed that the 'modern-day King Midas' was one and the same as the young Montreal bank clerk who had recently been released from a Canadian prison after being convicted of forgery. He was eventually indicted on eighty-six counts of fraud, and served three-and-a-half years of a five-year sentence. It was thought that Ponzi's investors had collectively lost some $20 million (roughly $500 million today) as a result of his activities. On his release the Massachusetts officials promptly arrested him again for grand larceny.

While awaiting trial, Ponzi moved to Florida and offered investors parcels of 'prime oceanside real estate' on which he promised a 200 per cent return within sixty days. In reality it was a scam that sold practically worthless swampland. Following that, Ponzi shaved his head, grew a moustache, and tried to flee the country disguised as a crewman on a merchant ship, but was returned to serve seven more years in jail before emigrating to Brazil. On his death his final estate was valued at $62, which proved just enough to provide a third-class funeral in Rio's municipal cemetery.

Broadly speaking, there are two distinct kinds of confidence artist: those who aspire to the single, big score, or at least who work one basic angle and then repeat it, with little or no variation, to the bitter end; and others who go in for variety, perhaps truer to the spirit of the scam as an expression of rebellion, of reinvention, and of scandalising the respectable. An example of the former would be Arthur Orton, aka Thomas Castro, the young butcher's assistant from Wagga Wagga in New South Wales by way of Wapping, east London, who famously came forward claiming to be Roger Tichborne, the shipwrecked heir to the wealthy baronetcy of Tichborne Park in Hampshire. Although the claimant's manner and bearing were unrefined and he appeared to have both doubled in weight and lost a number of distinguishing tattoos during the years he had wandered around the Australian bush, he gathered support and duly sailed to England. Lady Tichborne initially accepted him as her lost son, although other family members were sceptical that the obese and barely literate Orton might be one and the same as the slight and well-educated Roger Tichborne. Extensive civil and criminal proceedings followed, at the end of which the claimant was tried for perjury under the name of Thomas Castro and sentenced to fourteen years' imprisonment. He died on April Fool's Day, and was given a pauper's grave without a headstone. It seems

Orton wasn't so much a career confidence man per se as someone who saw his opportunity, however misguided, and took it.

Much the same could be said of Anna Anderson, the young woman who in 1922 emerged from a Berlin mental ward to insist that she was the Grand Duchess Anastasia, youngest daughter of the last Tsar of Russia, who conventional wisdom believed had been murdered by Red Guards along with the rest of her family four years earlier in the basement of a house in the foothills of the Ural mountains 900 miles from Moscow. The German courts were unable to decide Anderson's claim one way or another, and, after forty years of deliberation, ruled that her case was 'neither established nor refuted'. Most modern scholars are agreed that she was probably one Franziska Schanzkowska, a wartime Polish factory worker with a history of mental illness.

Perhaps both Orton and Anderson were simply clever and unusually tenacious frauds, or possibly they could be seen as more timeless figures – social anarchists, masters of imposture, the ultimate inappropriate persons. In any case, they surely anticipate our modern celebrity culture, which relentlessly teaches us that we can break free from the mundane or unpalatable reality of our lives and instead be whatever we choose.

By contrast, there are serial grifters such as the Irish-born but truly international man of mystery Michael Dennis Corrigan, who enlivened the legal pages of the world's press in the 1920s and '30s. Hailing, like Gerald Macaura, from Cork, he posed successively as a general in the Mexican army, a Chinese warlord, the Soviet Union's commissar for trade, and an apparently authorised representative of the Rumanian government, mandated to enter into commercial agreements with foreign powers. To call Corrigan the David Bowie of the early twentieth-century flimflam world is to confer a flattering sense of consistency on a man whose personal changes of status were so rapid and extreme that there was only the simple, unifying theme of deceit running as a throughline to confirm that he was the same person. Described as a 'stolid man of military bearing',

Corrigan went bankrupt while living in London in 1928 with debts of £108,882 and assets of £30. That same year he sold a French businessman sight unseen 550 crates of supposedly high-grade rifles and ammunition, but which turned out on closer inspection to contain only sawdust and bricks. On another occasion, Corrigan played the part of a chief inspector in the Royal Canadian Mounted Police seconded to London, and persuaded a Mayfair jeweller to lend him his stock for a day in order to trap a gang of international thieves. At the time of his eventual arrest he was living in a luxurious Chelsea penthouse, employing a butler and a chauffeur, and apparently happily married to a woman whose own mother he had taken for several thousand pounds in a share fiddle. Facing up to twenty years for fraud, Corrigan hanged himself in his cell with an Old Etonian tie. He left a note for his solicitor saying, 'I deserve everything for being such a greedy fool … I don't think I can pay this price.'

An interesting fact about many of the scams seen above, whether of the habitual or more specialised kind, is the almost touching gratitude displayed by at least some of the victims. Horatio Bottlomley's career is evidence not only of personal *chutzpah* on a grand scale but of the extent to which the public will always be charmed by a plausible rogue. 'I like this man,' one man told his family after being fleeced of his life savings. 'I have heard him speak. I won't have you say a word against him. Anyone who utters a breath against Bottomley I will quarrel with. I am not sorry I lent [*sic*] him the money, and I would do it again.'

It was the same story with Charles Ponzi. Even in prison he continued to receive Christmas cards from dozens of his defrauded customers, as well as requests from many others to take more of their money. When the French police first came for Gerald Macaura they were attacked by a large crowd of men and, more particularly, women gathered in the street, so sure were they of their hero's innocence. The obituary in the daily *News Chronicle* attempted to make sense of Michael Corrigan's life in a long notice that wasn't uncritical of Corrigan's habitual attempts to hoodwink the public. The paper's final conclusion, nevertheless, was that the deceased had been 'at heart a thoroughly credible and strangely likeable character who [had] targeted well-heeled institutions and governments rather than the common man'. The lesson seems to be that one mistake in public life can often lead to oblivion, but that even today many of us find the crooked charmer such as Macaura or Bottomley a rather endearing figure.

Another theme observable in the careers of Corrigan and his like is that they rarely seem to end well. At heart the confidence man really deals in the disintegration of lives, his own as well as his victims'. With just a touch of colour, Corrigan once remarked from his cell that, 'Heaven and hell [were] both in evidence during my mortal walk.' The opportunity to travel the world, often in the guise of a visiting foreign dignitary, and be treated with a 'warmth and respect denied the common pilgrim' provided a glimpse of heaven. There was his late 1930s tour of Leningrad, for instance, where he gamely sought to interest the municipal authorities in a heavily discounted consignment of asbestos padding for their new city hall. In between being wined and dined by his Soviet hosts, Corrigan took the time to write in his journal of the 'rustling woods, green fields waving in the wind, spruce white-painted churches and red-roofed, oak-beamed peasant cottages trimmed in shades of pink and ochre'. These were not the typical sights or experiences of the average illegitimately born working-class Irishman of his day.

Hell was provided by Brixton Jail. Corrigan spent some weeks confined there over the winter of 1945–46 while awaiting trial at the Old Bailey. He had finally been incarcerated after being charged with posing as a member of the Guatemalan government visiting London as part of an elaborate scam to supply the Ministry of Defence with 300 tons of 'high-quality native rosewood' for the construction of wartime fighter aircraft. Corrigan had previously secured £2,000 from the King's personal dentist as a loan towards his modest accommodation and travel expenses while concluding the deal. Brixton was a 'squalid and inhumane existence, caged up like a beast 23 hours a day,' he wrote. At one stage the resident of the next cell had been a well-born, 34-year-old American embassy clerk named Tyler Kent. Kent had been picked up in 1940 under the Official Secrets Act, shouting through the letterbox of his London flat to inform the first police on the scene that they were Communists who themselves deserved to be arrested. After breaking down the door and taking the suspect into custody, the authorities had found 1,929 official or semi-official documents, as well as what the Home Office report termed 'a female clad in the most sparing of garments' on the premises. The former included copies of secret cables between Winston Churchill and President Roosevelt that would seem to have been in breach of the strict US neutrality laws. It says something for the inveterate schemer in Corrigan that he went on to persuade both Kent and a number of other Brixton inmates to invest in an apparently legitimate mortgage company, which he marketed under the slogan, 'Own your own house and be a free man'. This, too, ultimately failed to prosper, and there had been 'grim scenes', he admitted, when some of the disgruntled subscribers to Corrigan's project had confronted him about it in the prison showers.

Like all confidence men, Corrigan loathed being alone. As the door of his single cell slammed behind him on the dark night of 15 October 1946 he was left to write of the 'self-imposed hades' of his recent life, adding somewhat oddly that 'these blasted krauts who [had] so terrorised the world surely deserve the rope more than me'. Corrigan could have had no way of knowing that Hermann Göring, the most senior surviving such Nazi official, would commit suicide in his own prison cell some 600 miles away in Nuremberg on the same night he did. It was much the same sorry tale for Maundy Gregory, Horatio Bottomley, Artur Reis, Ivar Kreuger and Charles Ponzi – not to mention George Joseph Smith – as well as many others. For the truly dedicated career confidence man it would seem that disappointment and ultimate self-destruction are the rule, and prolonged professional or personal contentment the exception.

A final generic thought on the times in which most if not all of the above names came to prominence. One of the striking characteristics of the 1920s is the unparalleled rapidity and unanimity with which millions of men and women, on both sides of the Atlantic, opened their wallets to an exceptional number of charlatans and hoaxers. Whether it was the frenzied speculation in worthless American swampland, or the mania in the upper echelons of British society for quack doctors and miracle health cures, the immediate post-war generation seemed to be in thrall to almost every halfway plausible huckster to appear over the horizon. Without delving too far into the briar patch of psychiatry, it's possible to generalise that a disillusioned world fed on war, self-denial and conformity was revolting against the diminished prospects in life it had long been forced to endure. For years people had been spiritually and materially starved. They had seen their ideals and illusions and hopes one by one worn away by the corrosive influence of events and ideas – by the horrors of the war and its aftermath, by scientific doctrines and psychological themes that undermined their religion and shook the guardrails defining the boundaries of acceptable behaviour, by the spectacle of graft in politics and a seemingly daily newspaper diet of smut and murder, and then in turn by a widespread if by no means universal decade of prosperity, during which the businessman was, as the economist Stuart Chase put it, 'the dictator of all our destinies', ousting 'the statesman, the priest, the philosopher, as the creator of standards of ethics and behaviour' and becoming 'the final word on the conduct of our society'.

In short, a large number of people, in all walks of life, were in an unusually febrile mood following the years of sacrifice, and now had unprecedented amounts of cash at their disposal. These were conditions that would seem to have been tailor-made for the type of smooth-talking individual tuned in to the commercial opportunities of the age – the sort of person who understands that it's when we're most emotionally vulnerable, or when the times are most volatile, that we're most grateful for the kind stranger who shows up with the easy solution, and who has both the gall and the resources to carry it all off.

In assessing the career of that ultimate emblematic criminal of the day, Victor Lustig, we should acknowledge that he was one of those marginal figures who, as the police say, had form. In fact, he epitomised the serial offender. By the age of 16, while still at a state-run boarding school in Dresden, Lustig already knew how to hustle an older opponent at billiards, understood both how to lay odds at the local racecourse and rapidly absent himself from the scene if the need arose, was on terms of some familiarity with what he called the 'incurable romantics' who loitered around doorways in the city centre dressed in tight skirts, and, to quote his subsequent arrest file, generally preferred the company of the 'louche and mutant types who [sat] drinking away the afternoon' rather than the more conventional adolescent pursuits of his day.

Despite all this, Lustig could speak fluent German, Italian, Hungarian, French and English while still a schoolboy, loved to watch the opera, and taught himself to play competitive-level chess. As he remarked in a letter he wrote from a prison cell, 'I have a consuming thirst for knowledge, and have always been able to find it, one way or another.' The author Floyd Miller later noted that the man who had gone on to become the quarry of police forces all over the world was 'the cleverest and most resourceful exploiter of human frailty in the history of crime'.

One stormy night in November 1906, the teenaged Lustig took a young girlfriend with him to a production of Wagner's *Rienzi* at the ornate Semperoper theatre in Dresden. The girl was impressed both by her companion's obvious good taste and abundant charm, but she grew uneasy when, following the performance, he silently led her on to a nearby rooftop, grasped her hand tightly as they stood staring down on the city lights and in a voice 'hoarse with passion' began to speak of his hopes and fears for a life that, like that of the fictional Rienzi, he was convinced fate had singled out for the wildest extremes of success and disaster. With his eyes narrowed and the collar of his black opera cloak turned up in the chill night air, he seemed 'almost possessed', wrote the girl, who put an end to their relationship a short time later.

Here is what Lustig's first and most tenacious wife, the former Roberta Noret of Kansas, had to say of him:

> He could be terrible. His dark streak frightened even his friends. And he remembered. He never missed anything you said or did.

But although Lustig had a sort of personal blacklist, Roberta added:

> If, on the other hand, you were on his good side, he treated you like a brother. If you were his friend, nothing was too much trouble. He would only take from those who deserved it. His life's purpose was to rob the rich and help the needy. If you were on his white list, you could do no wrong. There was no grey list. He was incapable of grey. It was always either black or white.

It is debatable how far Lustig's benevolence truly extended beyond himself and his immediate circle. But there's no doubt that he was one of those individuals who opt for a full-blooded approach to life rather than what he termed a 'timid but steady progress [towards] the grave'. When such a character is both supremely intelligent and intensely ambitious and he is, like Lustig, possessed of almost messianic zeal for his life's goal of separating people from their money, matched only by that of the world's police forces for stopping him, then the stage is set for high drama.

2

BOHEMIAN RHAPSODY

Victor Lustig was not born either in New York City or Paris on 4 January 1891. The date and one or other of the locations appear in several records, primarily rap sheets, circulated during his lifetime. Perhaps they help form an appropriately hazy starting point for a career dedicated to the art of deception. He certainly never went out of his way to correct the misapprehension, which arose out of a combination of clerical error and his own reluctance to dwell on his immigrant past or admit his real age. On the day in May 1935 when he was detained in New York, he signed a statement with the inscription: 'Count Robert V. Miller-Lustig, b. Jan 4 '91, NYC', and those details duly appeared in the indictment read out in the federal court proceedings against him later in the autumn, possibly giving him a last sardonic laugh at the expense of the authorities he had so successfully misled for much of the previous twenty-five years.

Victor Lustig wasn't even his real name, of course. Somehow aptly, his parents christened him Robbe, today's Robert, and as a family they generally went by variants of Molnar, Mueller or Miller. A land tax assessment issued to their home in December 1897 is addressed to one 'L. Muller', although in those days spelling was still generally as flexible as in pre-Chaucerian Britain. Perhaps it hardly matters in the case of a man who eventually enjoyed some forty-five different aliases.

Victor Lustig, as we'll call him, was born, the middle of three children, in the small family home in Hostinné, Bohemia, one of those marginal places in central Europe that flit back and forth between countries depending on the fortunes of war. At the time, it was a hamlet of some 6,000 souls, set close to the junction of the Elbe and Čistá rivers in what is now the Czech Republic. In 1841, Hostinné had also been the birthplace of Karel Klíč, the inventor of the photogravure process that in later years made millionaires of several counterfeiters of the world's banknotes, Lustig himself prominently among them. In the late nineteenth century the town was spread out around a number of bustling squares in a haphazard jumble of shops, bazaars, tenements, bungalows, bridges and richly aromatic livestock pens. There was also a Gothic city hall set up on a rocky spur, fronted by a gold-faced clock tower and topped by domes pointed like witches' hats. Visiting Hostinné in 1893, Klíč wrote of the town's striking architectural contrasts, 'a glittering visual patisserie' of soaring medieval spires and 'crude wooden shacks with animal swamps that bubbled and stank like

Hostinné's Gothic city hall by moonlight.

stewing tripe'. Gritty snow hillocks formed every winter along the unpaved streets, and sewage ran raw and braided in the gutters. Many of the town's adult inhabitants were illiterate, or semi-literate at best, and had been born as serfs. In all, it was the kind of place that teaches a boy to be practical while it forces him to dream of other, headier realities. Lustig was born here on the Saturday morning of 4 January 1890. There is no evidence that either he or any of his family were ever granted the title 'Count'.

His father, Ludwig, was of 'low peasant stock', Victor later recalled, although other accounts insist that he served as the mayor of Hostinné. Perhaps both versions are true. It's known that the family lived in a four-roomed stone house on Tyrsovy, a narrow street winding up by the river north of the main market square, and that neither the home itself nor the immediate vicinity had any pretension to elegance. On the day Victor was born the weather broke in a thick shawl of snow. Jugs of river water had to be boiled over a peat fire in the parlour to help with the delivery. At that time of the year, a greasy, yellow fog often descended by day, leaving spectacular rime deposits on Hostinné's streets. At night the Čistá froze solid and the cold seemed to have the pygmy's power of shrinking skin.

Ludwig was a small, squat, cynically humorous man. Whatever his true status in life, he doesn't always make a sympathetic figure in Lustig biographies. We know that he was relatively well groomed, irrepressibly proud of his dark cavalryman's moustache, responsible and apparently honest, but also that he was gruff, bad-tempered and stingy – a 'clenched fist' in one account. Ludwig's granddaughter Betty remembered him as a tradesman, dealing mainly in pipes and tobacco, and adds that he had forced the young Victor to take violin lessons, which he hated. In a distressing scene, she writes that following one clash of wills on the subject, 'Ludwig carefully raised the instrument, pointing to the ceiling, and, with all the force of his more than average strength, every muscle in his body taut, brought it down on the boy's head.'

Ludwig had, it's agreed, a way with women, a talent Victor would inherit from him. Mostly, though, the son consciously tried to be as unlike his father as possible. Where Ludwig was frugal, Victor prided himself on spending money the second he got it, and often even earlier. The boy was told that the novels of Émile Zola and his school were corrupting filth, and at the age of 8 he had to sign a solemn oath that he would abstain from alcohol and faithfully attend the Catholic Church. The elder Lustig was 'used to dominating all scenes in which he appeared,' Betty wrote. Unsurprisingly, Victor never forgot the violin incident: for the rest of his life authority figures would rarely evoke anything but contempt. In later years he complained bitterly that Ludwig had frequently thrashed him 'unmercifully with a bull whip', although in the rural Bohemia of those days severe beatings of children weren't uncommon, being considered good for the soul. The violence apparently extended to Ludwig's docile wife Amelia, known as Fanny, fifteen years younger than her husband, and if true must have made an indelible impression on Victor.

Weighing up the evidence, it seems fair to say that the family were of modest means, certainly, but not the absolute dregs of Habsburg society as it was constituted in the 1890s. Ludwig's granddaughter says that his tobacco business often took him on lucrative trips as far afield as Zürich or Prague. At the age of 7, Victor accompanied his father on the train to Paris, a city that later struck him as exquisite in its central areas, but elsewhere a 'sad, soiled place that slithered around in a sea of immorality', to which in time he duly contributed. Victor was considered bright but wayward as a child. Early on he showed signs of being both self-willed and resistant to the discipline of regular work. He lasted only one day at the Hostinné infants' school, where he was expelled for saying *Leck mich am Arsch'* – roughly translated as 'Kiss my ass' – to his female teacher. After that he transferred to a one-room establishment located 3 miles away down a dirt path in Čermná, which he reached each day on foot. Victor's parents reportedly separated only a year later, when he was 8, although the Habsburg census taken in December 1900 shows all five family members, a mule and a 15-year-old 'idiot-girl' named Klara Muller – possibly a cousin – living together at the Tyrsovy residence.

Even at that early age there was something in the dark-eyed youngster's look that set him apart from his schoolmates. In the form picture that year at Čermná he stands in the centre of the front row, looking several years older than his contemporaries, chin up, frowning. 'We all liked him, but the teachers didn't,' his friend Karl Harrer wrote. 'He had "guts". He could impersonate different people's voices, march[ing] around the play yard shouting mad army commands with a tin saucepan on his head. Somehow he seemed a lot wiser than us. I remember he was the first person who told me in detail about the difference between boys and girls, [which] was very impressive.'

Perhaps reflecting the authorities' less appreciative view, Lustig's July 1902 school report called him 'Retarded morally, an idiot in other respects'. Such things tended to be more bluntly stated than they are today. At 13 he was tall and heavyset with an engaging smile that carried a glint of rebellion. Talented at boxing, he was not otherwise very athletically gifted. From early childhood he was a martyr to his sinuses, sometimes emitting a harsh, guttural snort that Harrer compared to the 'violent peal of a blocked sewer' as he painfully cleared his throat. Although Victor always seemed strong, he was sick a great deal, a reality he hid from his school friends. Migraines continued to plague him, his hands mysteriously swelled up in the summer months, and, on a trip to Prague, he fell and broke his collarbone. Nonetheless, he hated to miss even a day of school, where he had a perfect attendance record. Karl Harrer once watched in wonder as his friend came 'bound[ing] up to the front gate one morning, like a dog off the leash, and then only minutes later, once out of view, slowly shuffled up a muddy back path to the latrine one limping step at a time'.

Harrer himself, who was a year younger, provided – in addition to Lustig's little brother Emil – the necessary audience for the stream of fantasy he poured out. In what way Victor was to express his latent genius was unclear – whether as artist, actor, inventor (he produced elaborate plans for a flying bicycle), boxer or poet – but it was always on his own terms, not as a team player. Socially he was quite precocious. In later and less-reticent times several American ladies would come forward to describe, often in well-remembered detail, how Lustig had so thoroughly corrupted them. Leaving aside his own moral shortcomings, with certain rare exceptions the complainants' principal qualities would seem to have been vapidity, greed and physical beauty. As a 14-year-old schoolboy Lustig apparently once persuaded a village girl of his own age to accompany him back to his empty family home, where he made love to her on the floor in front of a large antique mirror propped up against the wall. Immediately afterwards he found that he wanted to be alone. 'I've got to run,' he announced. Lustig seems not to have understood how cutting his remark was, or that leaving so abruptly might have hurt anyone's feelings, because he reportedly said the same thing to a number of subsequent partners – indeed, it became something of a catchphrase for him later in life.

Betty Lustig writes that when her father was 12 he ran away from home and in due course found himself living 700 miles away in Paris. 'There, for two months, he lodged in various quarters … He even found shelter in a house of prostitution, where the Madam was kind to him and never once let him be harmed. Finally, the police found him and returned him to his father.'

Actually the Paris escapade was in 1904, when Victor was 14 not 12, and according to Karl Harrer lasted 'about a week at the time of the school's Easter holiday'. If Betty's memory was fragile, the story was sturdy, and found its way into the early Lustig legend. Not long afterwards, Ludwig sent his headstrong son off to a subsidised boarding school 150 miles away in Dresden. Victor's daughter loyally insists that he excelled there, and was considered a genius by his teachers. If so, he seems to have also found time for several extracurricular activities. While awaiting trial in New York thirty years later Lustig reminisced to detectives about his street-hustling experiences in Dresden, and in particular the warm spring night he had been scavenging for food outside the kitchen door of a fashionable hotel when an attractive young woman walked by.

'To me, she was a fairy princess,' he recalled. 'She was with a man much older than her. I saw the waiter come and take their order … my mouth began to water, because all I'd had to eat for days had come out of garbage cans.' No sooner had the couple sat down, however, than the man pulled out a thick bankroll and passed it to the woman. The two of them promptly stood up and left their table without eating, presumably to carry on their evening in more intimate surroundings. Neither party had bothered to glance at the schoolboy vagrant loitering by the back door.

Psychologically, the importance of this incident, which Lustig could still vividly recall in middle age, lies in two things. The first is that, 'What I saw that night shattered my faith in women forever.' To him, they now became commodities to be bought and sold like everything else. 'As a poverty-stricken kid,' Lustig wrote, 'I had always looked on the fair sex as goddesses. No more.'

The second important result was that it helped provide the intellectual underpinning for a life devoted almost exclusively to crime. Even in 1945, in the squalor of an American maximum-security prison cell, Lustig was unable fully to turn his back on the ideology that had shaped his whole career. 'The man and the woman both got up, without touching a morsel of that delicious food … At that moment I resolved that there were those among us who didn't deserve their wealth, and that my purpose on earth was to address this.' From that hot spring night onwards, Lustig's life mission combined a sort of morally spurious class struggle against capitalism with more narrowly personal greed. Perhaps he simply found it exhilarating to trade wits with wealthy or resourceful people. They were his adversaries, but they were at least halfway worthy adversaries. 'Victor enjoyed jousting with them,' Floyd Miller wrote. 'It was a chance to perform.'

In late 1905 Lustig suddenly announced that he intended to become either an author or an architect, and over the Christmas holidays that year treated himself to a week in Vienna. Although barely 200 miles from Hostinné, it took him all day to reach the Habsburg capital, in part by a horse-drawn railway carriage. When he finally climbed down from his third-class berth just before midnight he found himself too excited to sleep and instead walked around in circles among the fairy-tale towers of Heldenplatz, 'looking up in awe at the softly-lit rooms of the palace and then down again to the huddled men and women passing by in the rain'. His memory of the scene has an almost theatrical quality: as in a stylised Hollywood film, a young waif stands gazing up in wonder at the splendours he wants to possess. The next morning, Victor walked down to the newly opened State Savings Bank, an imposing eight-storey structure covered in square marble slabs that looked like huge safety deposit boxes. The building appealed to him on both the visual and symbolic levels. 'I walked about, noting my observations – the heavy, barred windows and smooth stone walls, tantalised that such riches lay so close.' He was surprised not to see any armed guards. Lustig later wrote that he had spent hours standing in place there, through sunbreaks and thunderstorms, noting down everything in his florid, looping handwriting – the weather, the passing carriages, the ladies' fashions, 'a sudden cacophony of striking clocks, the smell of the wet cobblestones' – all grouped around his central fascination with the bank itself. 'I realised that on one side were the guardians of wealth and privilege, and on the other members of an oppressed class who were too feeble to redress this imbalance.' Again, there's a sort of cinematic vividness to the scene. The young boy stares up, and the moment is frozen in time as with a sudden insight he realises his true calling in life. Everything that Lustig said or did from the age of 16 reveals that his mind allowed him to broadly sympathise with those he saw as fellow class strugglers against the system, but that he was really in the business of wealth redistribution for himself.

Lustig took a design course at the school in Dresden, turning in an elaborately bound portfolio for the academic year ending in June 1906. The verdict was scathing: 'Basic drawing skills negligible.' When he got the report back in Hostinné, he spent a day complaining to his friend Karl Harrer about the idiocy of his teachers and the academic elite in general. Then he led Harrer into a small grocery shop, walked around a bit, and left again with a bottle of dynamite-strength schnapps tucked under his coat. The two teenagers drank it during the course of an afternoon spent under the shelter of a nearby footbridge. As he passed from the euphoric to the maudlin, Victor began repeating all the laments Harrer had heard so many times before: why didn't the world treat everyone fairly, why were people such idiots, why did they waste their lives pandering to the rich and powerful instead of seizing the moment and making something of themselves?

The further details of Lustig's schooldays are unclear. Several biographies note that he left Dresden before his 17th birthday, while his daughter insisted he was still pursuing his architectural and literary classes 'well into his early twenties'. That was at least one account; but the accounts are as various and confused as the career they claim to describe, and the only certainty is that in October 1907 he sent Karl Harrer his review of Tolstoy's novel *Resurrection*. 'This Napoleonic War, he believes, was so fine that men constantly seek to fight it again, so they can bathe in its virtue, forgetting all the terrible cries and oaths of the afflicted ... Also addresses the folly of our mortal system of justice.' The lines were typical of the adolescent Lustig – precociously sharp observation mixed with a splash of purple prose. Harrer was becoming increasingly uneasy about his old friend, who seemed to take every opportunity to remind him that he, Victor, was living an altogether more rarefied life than the one he left behind in Hostinné. 'Tomorrow I go to the grand opera to see *Lohengrin*, the week after *Tosca*, etc,' he wrote in another card from Vienna. No one seemed to know how Lustig supported himself during these years, although he once wrote that he had 'wandered about' without any fixed abode, and 'came to learn something valuable about human nature' as a result.

Lustig's devoted child Betty would later write of the period:

Victor [now] spoke six languages … Deep inside, however, he knew he would never be the businessman his father wanted him to be. Not knowing what he would do, he began a life of travelling. He developed hobbies: dog races, sailing, gambling, billiards and chess. He mounted butterflies and became an expert at it. He loved birds and all animals … He was a conversationalist on any subject. His genius mind seemed to be as broad as the world, if only he could find his niche in it.

Lustig would do so soon enough.

One hint of Victor's future progress in life came when Karl Harrer wrote to tell him of his plan to apply to Charles University in Prague to study law. Replying to his boyhood friend 'plainly and candidly', Victor declared: 'I would rather be a village leech-collector than a lawyer. Indeed, the older I become, the higher opinion I have of the courage and wit of the man prepared to forego a diploma and proceed through life on his own terms.'

That sharp exchange of December 1907 concluded the old friends' correspondence.

Once again back in Vienna, Lustig seems to have followed an erratic programme of self-education, wandering around the Innenstadt district at night to 'observe' the young women who loitered there. During the day he haunted the central library, scribbling away furiously at a memoir – generally a strategic error while still a teenager – several pages of which survived to be included in his arrest file twenty years later. The long passages of disordered and random youthful erotic daydreams strike an odd note in the context of his later criminal life. If Victor is to be believed, one young lady had advertised herself to him by exposing her 'plump white bosom' as he hurried past on his way back to his room. He had no use for such 'tawdry display' he later told investigators. He prided himself on his self-restraint in general, remarking that in his opinion a glass or two of beer (or even a shared bottle of schnapps) was all right, but that he was appalled that anyone could really let himself go, 'inflicting his random jollity on utter strangers'. His file notes that he was 'not particularly fond of the Bohemian life' as he experienced it in Vienna. He still wore the sack coat and baggy felt cap of the provincial adolescent, and that made him a rare sight among the fashion-conscious pedestrians on the elegant Ringstrasse. Nonetheless, his file notes, 'Victor [was] not afraid. He slid into the criminal life naturally.'

Lustig has never been short of supporters. He was the incorrigible joker whose whole life consisted of a sort of surrealist prank played at the expense of polite society, one of those loveable rogues who later found their fictional apotheosis in Arthur Daley from the television series *Minder*. His US file quotes him in 1939. 'I wasn't going to hurt anyone who didn't deserve it.'

How to reconcile the image of this cheerfully irreverent 'Tricky Vic', as he was known, with his alternative persona as the FBI's 'unscrupulous criminal felon – a character without morals or pity … because of him men's careers were destroyed, women committed suicide'? An earlier biographer thought that Lustig 'was really two people … a day-time Jekyll and a night-time Hyde'. Like all good clichés, it has an element of truth about it.

Imprisoned first by the Austrian police, and then by the Czechs and French, and finally by the forces of almost every other nation he visited, Lustig remained the same courteous, affable man he had always been. He was scrupulously polite, even to his captors. It was as though he lived in his own self-contained world. On the night Britain declared war on Germany in August 1914, Lustig had his own preoccupations. 'Another fine day with a light mist.' Yet beneath the surface charm he could be supremely callous. An 18-year-old starlet whom he later seduced in the guise of a Broadway producer was 'really just asking for it – she'd be far better off back home in Illinois'. Another of his scams led directly to a run on a community bank in rural Kansas, depriving scores of working-class customers of their life's savings. 'Fools,' he remarked. Even in his long, final captivity, when he had time to recognise mistakes and rethink his basic attitude to life, he did nothing of the kind. As the world emerged from another catastrophic war in 1945, Lustig was hard at work in his jail cell on a sequel to an earlier, 20,000-word Peace Plan, which he suggested the victorious powers might wish to adopt when coming to decide how best to administer occupied Germany, an offer the Allies politely declined.

As one of his New York arresting officers remarked of him in 1935: 'The Count prefers to keep private moral judgements private. He [knows] very well of the human price of his actions, but he did what he had to, regardless of the fallout to people's livelihoods and wealth.' Lustig could do the tricky calculus involved in such decisions without losing sleep. Even his daughter struggled to reconcile the doting parent whom she says 'I loved every day of my life, and who loved me tenderly in return' with the man who for the most part saw others as mere props or statistics rather than individuals. 'My father undoubtedly had the learning and talent to accumulate a legitimate fortune,' Betty muses, reproducing Robert Frost's poem 'The Road Not Taken' on the first page of her Lustig biography.

'He was a genuinely charming fellow,' the US Secret Serviceman James Johnson wrote of the man he eventually helped bring to justice. 'But there was a kind of film between him and the rest of the world. He didn't have feelings in the way other people do.' This charming veneer kept out everyone but Lustig's wife and child, and sometimes even them. He was a friendly man with few friends; and perhaps it could hardly have been otherwise in light of the fact that very nearly every man, woman and child he met over the course of thirty years was a potential patsy for one of his schemes.

Lustig had another side to him, of course, and this expressed itself in his knack (perhaps not untainted by a desire to soften them up) of making people feel good. He always seemed to be receptive, or sympathetic. He was popular with women, especially American women, who responded to his polished manner and raffish old-world charm. Both sexes commented on his essential optimism. Nothing seemed to get him down for long. When he emerged from one of his cyclical spells as a guest of the state, he paused long enough only to change his name and then move on to the next money-making play in a new location.

This is what a young woman named Valya Daudet said of the man whom she met in Paris a year or so after the First World War who then called himself Baron Eric von Kessler:

> We were walking one hot autumn day down a street under the shade of the chestnut trees and there was a child of seven or eight years dressed in rags, shoeless, his face blackened with ash, prone in a doorway. The men and women promenading past this piti-ful display of human misery pretended it was invisible to them. But [Lustig] lent down and spoke to the boy at length. I saw him withdraw several banknotes and hand them over to the child. He also wrote copiously in his notebook. I later learned that he had helped to arrange proper shelter for the wretch, and to ensure that he be clothed and fed. I asked my companion why he should take such pains over a total stranger. 'He reminds me of myself,' he answered, and proceeded to tell me most affectingly of growing up with his nine brothers and sisters on the cold streets of Berlin.

In due course Daudet made two other significant discoveries about the man she had at one time believed might propose mar-riage to her. The first was that he habitually wore a heavy dark topcoat, whatever the season, and that on closer inspection she found this to contain multiple interior zips and pockets with a sort of 'portable vault' of high-denomination pounds, francs and half a dozen other currencies sewn into the lining. Still, she knew her friend liked to do business in cash. There was nothing unusual about that in the Europe of that uniquely turbulent era, when a series of banks collapsed amid panic withdrawals and people generally preferred to keep their assets close to hand.

The second revelation possibly reflected less well on Baron Kessler, and indeed proved fatal to the couple's continued relationship. It appeared Kessler's real name was Miller, and that he had recently taken a young American bride who was even then waiting for him elsewhere in Paris as part of the couple's extended European honeymoon.

In the end the adolescent Lustig didn't pursue his plan of becoming a famous architect or great writer. Instead he progressed from shoplifter to pickpocket, to petty thief to card sharp. Already, at 18, Victor was described in the Viennese police files, which also noted that his hands were 'swift [*zugig*] as the west wind'. One victim wrote of him half-admiringly: 'He could make a deck of cards do everything but talk.'

The police in Budapest picked up Lustig on 7 January 1908. He had turned 18 just three days earlier, and the complaint against him said that he had celebrated the event by installing himself in a suite of the Nemzeti Hotel and, sporting expensive new tailoring and a waxed moustache, posing as an apparently well-bred young insurance company executive sent on a continental tour by his associates in London. For only a token fee, he announced, he would be glad to take a piece of any potential client's jewellery, leave behind a receipt, and then have the item professionally appraised by an expert before returning it in the morning. He had walked off in this manner with a Cartier 'tutti frutti' necklace and matching earrings, after introducing himself to their owner as 'Earl Mountjoy' and mentioning that he hoped she might find time later in the spring to join him on his yacht as he cruised the French Riviera. That was the last the lady had seen either of the young lord or her valuables.

When the law came for him, Lustig remained calm. He told them his fiancée was his alibi. She didn't speak Hungarian, though.

The police found the fiancée at the suburban address Lustig gave them, and brought her downtown for questioning. Speaking in a colourful mixture of German and Italian, she told them that the couple had been many miles away exploring the natural beauty of the Baradla caves and the surrounding countryside on Victor's birthday, making it quite impossible for her betrothed to have presented himself that same day in the role of Earl Mountjoy, or any other such fanciful title, in a city centre hotel. He had never been out of her sight. She corroborated all his statements.

The suspect was released.

For the next twelve months, Victor moved back and forth in a roughly 300-mile semicircle, rarely staying in one place for long and coming to shuttle like a human pinball between Prague, Vienna and Budapest in particular. He generally travelled in some style, by first-class train compartment and private horse carriage. As usual no one seemed to know where he got the money to pay for it all. Back in Hostinné, Ludwig was apparently both proud and anxious at the reports of his son's cosmopolitanism. We know that he sent Victor regular letters enquiring at length about the state of his health and finances, asking him for any details of his latest stay. Perhaps he was attempting to live vicariously through him. Reluctant to assert himself against his bossy father, the 18-year-old had 'quietly hated the pressure on me to succeed', and Ludwig was perplexed that his elder son 'never seemed inclined to settle himself, and was so fugitive and changeable'. Somehow Victor did not marry the young woman he had introduced to the Hungarian police as his fiancée.

According to Lustig's later US Justice Department file, 'Miller [also] made his way to Chicago' in late 1908 or early 1909. The file describes him 'as of no fixed trade or occupation', although on unstated evidence 'an associate of larcenous and unsavory individuals'. Lustig himself, in a draft of a letter he wrote in 1941, stated that he had first crossed the Atlantic 'at the age of 20 or 21'. He denied having been involved in any criminal activity at the time. With tongue firmly in cheek, he also later informed the FBI that for years he had not even dared to walk through the doors of an American bank, for fear that this 'would have indicated an impure motive on my part'.

Lustig was evidently back in Vienna in February 1909, because the police came calling for him there on the 21st of the month. They wanted to ask him about a complaint they had received from the manager of the Grand Hotel. Europe as a whole might have been in a state of ferment, but the Grand was a place of the utmost calm and refinement, where conversation in the morning room was officially 'not preferred' and diners ate Romanoff caviar off plates with smart gold crests. The manager had engaged the services of a carpenter to help remodel several of the hotel's rooms. But the workman in question had seemingly strayed beyond the strict letter of his brief. According to the complaint, 'this individual [had] fashioned an invisible sliding panel in one bedroom wall, immediately behind a large oak escritoire'. A guest had innocently laid out his valuables on that same desk before retiring for the night, and in the morning they were gone. The police report goes to some lengths to emphasise this last point. 'The surface of the desk was bare. Our search of it was fruitless. It was devoid of material. There was nothing there.'

Lustig told the police that they could question him all they wanted, but that they should also speak to his 'betrothed – an unimpeachable young lady' on the subject. She would confirm that he had never offered his services anywhere as a carpenter, and what was more could vouch for his movements on both the day and the night in question. 'I'm not refusing you an interview,' Lustig repeated for the record. The police explained that they would be happy to consider his alibi, although they first needed to speak to him privately on the matter. But Lustig's mind had fastened stubbornly on the person of his delicate young fiancée. 'She will be perturbed by these fanciful allegations. I will give you an interview. But you must speak to the young lady once our consultation is over. She will correct your misapprehensions. I trust you will apologise to her for her distress.'

The police did much as Lustig suggested. He denied having ever set foot in the Grand Hotel, and the manager there was unable to positively identify him. Following that, an exquisitely dressed young woman had presented herself for an interview. She confirmed all Lustig's statements, and he was released without charge. 'There is no stain on his character,' the police report concludes, although a sharp-eyed observer might have noted the fact that whereas Victor's alibi of a year earlier in Budapest had been slim and dark-haired with a faint oriental touch about her face, the lady he introduced here was statuesque and blonde, 'with the ruddy complexion of a dish of fruit in a painting'.

When the authorities came to catalogue Lustig's personal belongings following his death, they found a carefully preserved cutting from the *St. Louis Star-Times* of March 1909:

THE CRIMINAL ROMANCE OF 'LORD BARRINGTON'

About to Hang for Murder of a Friend

Life of Crime and Adventure Extending Over Two Continents to End on the Gallows – His Quest for an American Heiress

By affirming the decision of the lower tribunal, the Missouri Supreme Court has sealed the fate of 'Lord' Barrington, one of the most notorious criminals of the age, and he will be hanged for the brutal murder of his friend John P. McCann, nearly three years ago.

'George Frederick Barton, 45, or as he persists in calling himself 'Lord Barrington', has had a most extraordinary criminal career, extending throughout England and half-way across the American continent. His record covers one successful and one attempted murder, five distinct cases of bigamy, innumerable acts of burglary, cheating at cards, bank spoofs, and even common pocket-picking. Through it all 'Barrington' has stoutly maintained that he is an Englishman of high birth, with a brilliant army record and a father whose estate and title he would succeed. Not one of these statements is founded on truth.

In fact, Barton was a prolific career criminal, from a working-class home in Tunbridge Wells, who invented a title for himself when he first sailed to New York in 1891. He had soon married a wealthy young woman named Celestine Miller, stolen all her money, and vanished. Shortly afterwards he had been given twelve years by a court in Lewes, Sussex, for armed robbery. Back in America following his release, Barton left and reconciled with his next heiress wife several times, took a succession of mistresses, moved around New England and various luxury resorts in Florida, often leaving no forwarding address, and eventually fell out with his business partner McCann to the extent that he beat him to death. In the end Barton's capital sentence was commuted to one of life imprisonment. During his confinement in the Missouri state penitentiary he stridently maintained his role as Lord Barrington, insisting that his conviction was all a ghastly mistake. A report in the *Brooklyn Eagle* of September 1938 has him 'sailing involuntarily' back to England, where on arrival he was asked by immigration officials to fill in a card stating his personal details. In the box for 'Occupation' Barton wrote 'Self-employed'.

Could it have been that in 1909 'Count' Victor Lustig already saw a sort of foreshadowing of his own career, or had found a role model?

Although Lustig always seemed to emerge intact from his early brushes with the law, his record in those years wasn't quite unblemished. On 2 October 1908, the Provincial Tribunal of Prague sentenced him to two months' imprisonment for what was described merely as 'larceny'. Lustig later wrote of being taken by armoured truck to the city's Correctional Institute – 'a great medieval keep with black stone walls and a moat glowering over the Vltava river' – shackled at the ankles to another inmate. 'Two armed guards sat facing us in our carriage. Another was stationed up front by the driver, holding a cocked rifle. We were dressed out in our own clothes – it was all an ordeal, but not the worst ordeal.'

Once inside, Lustig found that he hated the censorship of his letters more than any other single regulation. 'It inhibits truth, demeans the writer, and tempts him to create small, cheerful lies to please the warden.' Taking prison life as a whole, he was philosophical: 'My intention was always to sit and do *nothing*; do nothing to provoke ill-will or delay my release.'

Lustig served forty-eight days of his sentence, and on his discharge was promptly arrested again for false pretences. A key element of this new charge was that he had failed to disclose his criminal record, as the law required, when attempting to raise a loan from a local bank. In fact he had done more than this, by giving the bank the name 'Von Schlatter' and informing them that he was awaiting payment from a large steel manufacturer in which his family held an interest. It turned out that the title he had put down on the loan form didn't exist and neither did the company in which he claimed to have shares. Lustig was released from police custody the following morning. He'd avoided another trial, but now had a second blemish on his official record. This time he went straight from his cell to the offices of the shipping line to book his passage to America.

On 2 March 1909, just nine days after the Viennese police had called to enquire about his carpentry work, Lustig was picked up by armed representatives of the state Public Security agency in Prague. He had seemingly returned to the Bohemian capital to resume his fledgling career as a writer, because in a letter he sent home to Hostinné he announced that he was 'compos[ing] numerous stories and well-received essays' while living in a spacious city-centre apartment which was already the headquarters of a circle of like-minded 'authors, editors, poets – men of the deepest sort'. The report of the Public Security officials who came for him that March seems to contradict this state of affairs. Lustig's arrest sheet reads, rather unusually: 'Detained for contravention against laws concerning public combustion.' There are few other details, but the complaint notes in passing that the arrested man was 'claiming to act as a trained illusionist and *fakir* under the name "The Inferno"', but had unluckily managed to set himself on fire in the course of a flame-swallowing exhibition. The report also suggests that no lasting damage was done, because after twelve hours 'Suspect was released with a warning as to his future participation in such revues'.

Just a month later, on 8 April, Lustig was arrested again in Vienna. This time the charge sheet reads: 'Larceny and attempted false pretences, general depravity, vagrancy [and] offences against public hygiene.' The specifics are lost, but it seems reasonable to assume that he was temporarily living as a homeless person. Years later Lustig admitted that his life at the time had increasingly been one of isolation:

I slept late and stayed in a café most of the day reading and writing. Sometimes a lady would favour me with a few *krone* … One exquisite such being sat down at a table opposite mine on several days in succession. We did not speak, but communicated by eyes alone … I was hopeful, but then one day she did not come, [and]

I was again reduced to my solitary existence, reading for hours
in the library, wandering the streets at night in search of a patron.

He was given three weeks in the city jail, 'which was quite comfortable by my severe standards'.

More trouble awaited him on 4 August of that year, when
Vienna's Regional Tribunal sentenced him to a further three
weeks' imprisonment without the option for theft. He had tried
to borrow money against a forged Cunard Line share certificate,
possibly a ruse inspired by his first Atlantic crossing. We lose track
of him for some weeks in the autumn, but he spent Christmas of
that year in Paris. When the officials at the US Prisons Bureau later
came to compile a biographical file on Lustig, they included these
details from the winter of 1909–10:

> He had no trade training but was a salesman by occupation. Had
> no military service. Was devoted to slow horses and fast women.
> Smoked, drank liquor occasionally but did not use narcotics.
> Attended church very seldom.

This devotion to women would all too literally leave its mark
on Lustig during his winter's stay in Paris, where he lodged in
a rundown hotel on the Avenue de Flandre. He had been out
one night dancing cheek to cheek with what he called a 'beautiful young filly' in a local bar, and the girl's fiancé had taken
exception. Lustig had remarked that he was at liberty to dance
with whomever he chose, the fiancé demurred, and the two of
them had ended up rolling around on the floor, debating the
matter. Some disparity exists about the outcome. James Johnson
of the US Secret Service wrote that as a result Lustig was 'cut
from the outer tip of the left eye to the lobe of the left ear',
and that the scar never fully healed. Subsequent photographs
seem to verify this account. But Victor himself had a different
memory of events. The young woman in the bar had been 'very

friendly … She took me home later. Her family worked in the fields, and she often helped out at weekends. She was the middle child in a family of four girls and three boys. All the sisters were very friendly.'

In December 1935 the FBI wrote of Lustig: 'Physical examination reveals a white male, 45 years of age, 66¼ inches in height, weighing 139 pounds, and gives his occupation as a salesman.

'He gives no history of any serious illnesses or injuries. There are no outstanding physical defects present.'

The file concludes: 'This is a quiet, responsive man. He expresses no feelings of hostility toward society … Overall, he shows a fair degree of persistence and continuity.'

In fact, Victor's adolescent dream world would sustain him for the rest of his life. Having hit on his ideal role as a creative artist, or at least as a skilful improviser, he stuck at it with little or no variation for the next twenty-five years. On 2 January 1910 he wrote back to his family from his modest hotel in Paris: 'Am greatly enjoying life here. My accommodations are splendid. The French are not very appreciative of foreigners, having heard all the propaganda about their neighbours, but for me they make an exception!'

Lustig was back in Prague again in April 1910, and this time the complaint against him was for breach of contract. A black American woman, named either Breeon or Breonia, had found herself in Bohemia as part of a travelling burlesque troupe, and claimed the dashing 'Baron von Kessler' had promised to marry her. Lustig later tended to discount the story, which remains vague and wholly unsubstantiated. Some months later, while on tour in London, however, the lady gave birth to a daughter. There seems to be no further record of the matter, and neither mother nor child apparently troubled Lustig again. What is certain is that he showed striking sympathy for African Americans when he came to spend extended amounts of time living among them in cities like New York and Chicago. 'It is really my opinion that the whole race would be entirely happy and peaceable if they were not put upon by the whites,' he later wrote. The contemporary note in the Prague police files is less elevated: 'Subject denies offer of matrimony, but admits carnal relations. He tried to get her to steal wigs and clothes from the theatre where she works. Told her he has a professional need of disguises.'

Lustig was pulled in twice more in the spring of 1910, once for imposture and once for the offence of 'selling a bushel of finest Bintje potatoes knowing them to be poor imitations from Poland'. The suspect denied all the allegations against him. He was released without charge on both occasions.

Another carefully preserved newspaper cutting later found among Lustig's possessions was from the London *Daily Mirror* of 14 February 1910. Under the headline 'How the Officers of HMS Dreadnought Were Hoaxed; Photograph of the Eastern "Princes" Who Have Made All England Laugh', the story described how a young Anglo-Irish ex-army officer named Horace de Vere Cole and four friends, including the author Virginia Woolf, dressed in black-face and oriental garb, had presented themselves as the Abyssinian royal family on a tour of Britain, and expressed an interest in inspecting the navy's flagship HMS *Dreadnought* as she lay off Weymouth. Once on board, the visitors were given the full red-carpet treatment: a band played, the crew saluted them and a selection of African flags was hoisted aloft. To show their appreciation, the party communicated in a gibberish of words drawn from Latin and Greek, and conferred fake military honours on some of the ship's crew. One of those in the reception line was Commander Willie Fisher, who happened to be Virginia Woolf's cousin. Even he failed to recognise his relative in her fake beard. When invited to dine in the ship's wardroom, the VIPs politely declined, apparently concerned that the food might not be prepared according to their strict religious customs. They actually feared that their make-up might rub off as they ate. None of the pranksters was ever arrested or officially censured, although the *Mirror* later reported that some of the ship's crew had

The Dreadnought *hoaxers, with Virginia Woolf on the extreme left.*

gone on to take 'informal but none the less vigorous' retribution by thrashing the perpetrators on their bare buttocks, and that Virginia Woolf had been subject to a variation of this practice carried out, it would seem, with at least a degree of sexual sadism.

Whatever its aftermath, the sheer lunatic audacity of the hoax went viral in the press, and one newspaper published an interview with a man who claimed to have witnessed the Abyssinians' visit and alleged that they had used the expression 'Bunga Bunga'. The term quickly became a catchphrase of the era, making its way into song lyrics and theatrical revues. The whole episode has more than a touch of the Edwardian music hall to it. Scrawled across the original report of the incident found among Lustig's possessions is the simple but expressive notation in red crayon: 'Ha! Ha!'

Four months later, on 27 June 1910, Lustig was in front of the Provincial Court of Klagenfurt, Austria, charged with theft. The specifics are lost, but a Herr Bruning, the manager of the town's fashionable Café Dorrer, appeared as a witness. Perhaps there had been some misunderstanding about a bill. Lustig was given a sentence of ten months, but seems to have served only about half that. At Christmas that year he wrote to his brother Emil and sister Gertrude to say that he was enjoying a 'well-earned festive trek' in Zürich, and warmly recommending the area as a winter resort. While there, he found the time to consult with Dr Carl Jung at his clinic in nearby Küsnacht. It was an odd juxtaposition, the one man intent on revealing the inner psyche and the other one equally determined to conceal it. 'I spoke to him about dreams,' Victor noted. He wrote later that he had hoped that analysis might cure his acute sinus problems, but that they appeared to be getting worse.

Lustig celebrated his 21st birthday early in the New Year. He had already honed several professional skills that would serve him as an adult. He had a plausible manner, chiefly with women. He was a fluent storyteller, not hesitant to embellish to make a point or gain an advantage. He preferred to work with his mind instead of his hands, although he wasn't above presenting himself in taxing physical roles like that of a human torch if it served his needs. He generally seemed to have plenty of money to lavish on travel and hotels. He bought a Parisian suit, and periodically grew a moustache to look older. He had already been in jail more than half a dozen times, with a rap sheet as varied as it was long. The FBI later believed that Lustig had 'undergone a "conversion experience" around 1911, becom[ing] an habitual offender from that time', but they were three years late in their assessment.

Impeccably polite and usually (but not always) considerate to women, Lustig was one of those career criminals who prefers the unobtrusive approach to his craft. Of course, it's not unusual for a swindler to know something about human psychology. But Lustig took this a step further. He had read books including Pierre Janet's *Symptoms of Hysteria*, Wilhelm Wundt's *Hypnotism and Suggestion* and Sigmund Freud's *Psychopathology of Everyday Life*. He had personally consulted with Jung. One of Lustig's biographers says of him:

> His great ability was to change tack at a crucial moment. In most con tricks there is a point when the mark's appetite is whetted by a glimpse of the rich rewards just beyond the horizon. Lustig was quite capable of what he called a 'reverser', explaining just how dangerous it would be for the mark to invest money.

While the schoolchild soon masters the simple lie, and the financial lie merely requires a degree of guile easily developed by proximity to other people's money, the truly creative lie demands an instinct for duplicity that must be bred at an early age. When Victor found himself celebrating the Easter holiday of 1911 with a well-heeled young woman in the Grand Hotel, Budapest, he first took the time to shower her with gifts, including an 'antique Ottoman marble inkwell' (it was marked on the reverse 'Made in Canada') before he made his play. He was temporarily embarrassed for funds, he told her. There had been some irritating technical delay in one bank communicating with another. He didn't mind for himself, of course, but there was the matter of the refuge for underprivileged children that it had been his honour to sponsor, and as he proceeded to describe the place and its poor, malnourished inmates with their hungry eyes and simple, trusting smiles the woman had started to cry.

Lustig told her that he was certain it would be all right, and that the necessary wire transfer would surely arrive at any hour. His companion stopped crying for a moment, but seemed unconvinced, and started sobbing loudly again. In between her tears she told him that she would like to help. Victor went to some pains to tell her that she should not do so, but the more he protested the more determined she became. This interplay of the seemingly benevolent and the inwardly mercenary and sociopathic was characteristic of Lustig's approach. He accepted the proffered loan only with the greatest show of reluctance, along with his promise to return to the hotel in an hour or two. That was the last they ever saw of him there.

Naturally it didn't always end quite so well for him. Although one Lustig author describes him as a 'phantom to the law' during this time, he seems instead to have enjoyed a virtual season ticket to the central European court system. The US Justice Department later compiled a partial list that includes a trial in Teschen, Silesia, on 15 November 1911, on charges of embezzlement and vagrancy, with a sentence of two months. On 4 February 1912, Lustig was back in front of magistrates in Vienna, charged with fraud, and given five weeks. On 26 July of that year it was the turn of the Regional Tribunal of Prague to remand him for fourteen days for theft. On 27 November, the assizes at Zürich convicted him of swindling, with another fourteen-day term. He seems to have been released just in time to again go into the dock at Teschen on 8 December, where he was handed five days for larceny. It's the sheer variety and persistence of the offences (as well as the relative leniency of the judges) that is most strik-ing. Even so, this was a 'golden period for me', Lustig later wrote, particularly as one court system was often slow in communicat-ing with another one in a foreign country. Arriving for a 'highly pleasant and productive' first stay in Britain on 11 January 1913, Victor put down on his landing card in the space for criminal convictions: 'None'.

In fact, Lustig was already a world-class grifter. Today, he would probably spend his time devising internet investment scams, or sending emails telling people they had received an unexpected inheritance and needed only to contact the claims agent or award department and answer a few personal questions in order to collect their windfall. But in the climate of pre-Great War London he was a natural addition to the ranks of those who took advantage of the gullibility or credulousness of the city's large transient population, and more particularly as a so-called 'snoozer' of the type who books into a hotel before robbing its guests.

When Lustig walked off Pall Mall and into the sumptuous gold-and-white lobby of London's Carlton Hotel, with its rococo side tables and huge, gilt-framed portrait of King Edward VIII as the Prince of Wales, he announced himself as Count Franz Honiok of Hesse, visiting Britain on some 'small currency-exchange matter' involving the Bank of England. In the days that followed, the Count discreetly let it be known that nine months earlier he had been one of those on board the RMS *Titanic* when she sank in the icy waters of the North Atlantic, and had survived the ordeal only after sliding headlong down the ship's deck into the sea, where, surrounded by the drowned and drowning, he had remained for four hours before the occupants of a passing lifeboat pulled him to safety. He was very modest about it all. The whole concept of premature or violent death was one that was quite familiar to a generation of men and women in the early years of the twentieth century. As well as the individual human tragedies of the era, such as that of the *Titanic*, there were wars or revolutions everywhere from Morocco to Bosnia to Mexico, and few European states were immune from the heady atmosphere of patriotic fervour that would later be characterised as the 'spirit of 1914'.

So Lustig's life story, which also included an account of youthful adventures fleeing from tomahawk-wielding Lakota Indians in Wyoming, and helping suppress the Asir Rebellion on the Arabian Peninsula, perhaps seemed more plausible to his auditors in 1913 than a comparable yarn might do today. Of course, news also travelled more slowly then than it does now, and the press tended to convey the accidents and disasters of the age only in broad detail of the sort a talented fabulist could adapt to his own ends.

It's said that Lustig kept a card index of fellow guests at the Carlton, whom he studied for any possible discrepancies between their public personas and private conduct. The celebrated American light opera composer might have an unhealthy interest in auditioning local choirboys for the chorus of his latest touring production, for instance, or the wealthy City financier with an attractive young lady at a corner table in the restaurant had a wife and six children waiting for him at home in Esher. Once Lustig had successfully applied the data to his own advantage, he tore up the card. He was always extremely generous when it came to tipping chambermaids and waiters. They were among his most trusted informants. After an exceptionally good dinner one night, Lustig went into the Carlton's football field-sized kitchen and distributed bonuses to everyone there for the meal he had just enjoyed. The dishwasher on duty was a bone-thin young man named Nguyen Sinh Cung, although in deference to his chain-smoking habit he was known to his British co-workers simply as Bac. He told Lustig that he was from Indochina. The two men were the same age, and they seem to have struck up a rapport in their short time together, because Bac remembered that he gave him not only a pound note but also a sliver of wood held in a small glass phial that he pulled with some ceremony from a chain around his neck. It was taken from the wreckage of the *Titanic*, he announced. He hoped it would bring him luck. After that Lustig circulated around the room for a few more minutes. We don't know if he also met the Carlton's head chef, Auguste Escoffier, the man who brought us the Bombe Nero among other confections. The manager of the hotel later wrote that Victor 'distributed money freely to the employees, but also demanded their service be perfect to the last detail'. Several of the staff formed up in a receiving line for him, bowing and curtseying, when he finally checked out. He seems to have satisfactorily paid his bill. A few years later 'Bac' became Ho Chi Minh.

It's strange to equate the well-spoken man swanning around the upper echelons of London society with the shiftless petty criminal already so familiar to the European court system. Lustig was back in front of Vienna magistrates in March 1913. Charged rather vaguely with 'uncivil behaviour', he was found guilty and given a token forty-eight-hour sentence. Some years later, sitting in a suite in New York's Plaza Hotel, he reflected: 'As far as I was concerned, it was a completely just verdict. I *was* uncivil. I refused to comply with what was expected of a young man at that time, which was to marry, settle down, attend church and so on. On the basis of the law, I could never complain very much.'

Even stranger than this discrepancy between the respectable Lustig and his degenerate alter ego was the story to come to the attention of the FBI twenty-five years later that one night at around this time Victor had encountered a fellow drifter in a nondescript Vienna cafe. This individual was described as a 'deathly pale, skinny adolescent with a rough voice'. Just eight months older than Lustig, with whom he shared a broadly similar family background and frustrated artistic ambitions, he apparently dominated their conversation, speaking heatedly about society and politics 'not avoiding vulgarisms, in a very impetuous way'. The young man gave his name as Adolf Hitler.

While there are some implausible points of the story – none of Hitler's many biographies mentions it, and the FBI files of the late 1930s often evoke an air of paranoia and sensationalism as much as scholarly research – it conjures up an intriguing picture of two undereducated but persuasively articulate young itinerants, each in his own way imbued with a compelling mixture of fanaticism and calculation. At the age of 23, Lustig already seemed on track to become a sort of real-life Leonard Zelig, interacting with some of the most notorious political figures of the later twentieth century. If he at no time met Joseph Stalin, who also lived in Vienna in 1913, that must have been the one future genocidal dictator he avoided.

Lustig quickly found his footing back in Paris that autumn. He was not a conventionally handsome man – still on the small side, with rather prominent ears – but it was said he could be 'charming in six languages when he wished', and knew how to treat a lady. He served another short sentence that winter for theft, but emerged with a version of the 'pigeon drop' swindle that quickly made him several thousand francs. Lustig, back in the guise of Count Otiok, persuaded a young woman whom he met one Friday evening at the Hôtel de Crillon, and who later identified herself to the police only as 'Nadia', that he happened to have just received a large inheritance and wished to distribute this to various local children's charities. But he was a foreigner – from Berlin, actually – and there were administrative problems with transferring the funds, let alone the misgivings many in the French society of the day had in dealing with Germans. The young woman assured him that she had no such inhibitions. In fact she would be glad to help him. And she did, advancing Lustig what he called a 'token amount' in cash to tide him over until the banks opened for business the following Monday morning. Over her protests, he insisted on leaving the woman an exquisite gold watch as security against the loan. The funds then changed hands, and Otiok, now a distinguished professor of molecular diffusion, told his friend that he would return immediately after delivering a brief Saturday-lunchtime lecture at the nearby Société botanique. She waited for many hours before calling at the society's offices. They had never heard of Otiok, and in time the watch was found to be made of a then little-known material called stainless steel, with a thin veneer of gold paint. The woman told the police that, the central deceit aside, her companion had treated her with 'the utmost courtesy'.

Again displaying his knack for being present at some of the most seminal moments of twentieth-century history, Lustig was back in London during the last weeks of the gathering international storm of late July and early August 1914. Though concerned about the effect a European war might have on general business confidence, he wasn't averse to what he called 'a swift resolution of the questions' that lay between the rival states. Of course, he was speaking of a conflict that he thought might last two or three months. Like almost everyone else, Lustig underestimated the duration and savagery of the warfare ahead, entertaining fantasies of a massive blow that would 'knock out one side or another' – he wasn't fussy – and again make the world safe for free enterprise. It was as if the opposing European rulers were merely the heads of so many hostile business concerns, and that following the takeover of one by the other conditions would again be favourable for a morally flexible operator like him to resume his former activities. Naturally, he wasn't planning to do any of the fighting himself. So far as we know, Victor failed to register with the military authorities of any of the half-dozen states that might legitimately have called on his services, although in later life he liked to produce a certificate supposedly signed by the adjutant-general of the central army recruitment office in Prague. 'Unfit for combatant and auxiliary duties on grounds of severe nasal occlusion,' it read. 'Unable to bear arms.'

It's a striking feature of Lustig's early life that so many apparently worldly women wanted to sponsor him, and frequently more than that, whereas men generally kept their distance. An unmarried Vienna schoolteacher named Sylvia Nenni immediately took a shine to Victor when they met in the spring of 1914, charmed by his 'unspoiled nature' and 'quiet demeanour', as well as by his obvious affinity for the fairer sex. Often, after they had had tea or gone dancing together, she remembered, 'He would make a great fuss of me as he described his hopes and dreams for the future, and how I had brought the first gleam of real light to his life.' Lustig had grown up with no money, not much love, and little in the way of guidance, she believed. As a result, he had the air of a 'lost child whom you wanted to clasp and foster'.

On another level, Victor was quite precocious. He'd seen more of the world than most people, and could turn on an easygoing, cosmopolitan charm when it suited him. Often slovenly as a younger man, in recent years he had smartened up, leaving an image of a 'vigorous and elegant gentleman' in the mind of the manager of the Carlton Hotel and apparently also those of his staff. Like many dishonest people, he had the gift of inspiring confidence. Perhaps all of these circumstances combined to produce what we would now call a high-functioning sociopath. Sylvia Nenni soon tearfully agreed to marry him after Victor had led her to believe he was suffering from a terminal illness. She had immediately given him the funds with which to consult a specialist in Paris, praying that there might yet be hope for their future together. But somehow Lustig failed to keep the appointment. His ruse only became apparent after Nenni grew suspicious and found that the bottle of liquid morphine he had left behind in his modest Vienna lodgings contained only nasal spray.

Lustig was back in London on the day Britain declared war on Germany. Again a witness to history, he reacted with notable sang-froid, as we've seen, merely jotting down the weather statistics and other trivia in his diary. Even so, he can hardly have failed to be impressed by the pace of events all around him. In most parts of Britain military recruiting depots were crammed to overflowing for the rest of the summer. There was a macabre pantomime in many of them, where young men, grinning, stood on tiptoe in order to appear taller and pass muster. Adding to the exhilarating air of drama of the first days of the war, the streets of London were full of Americans ordered out of Germany, many of them standing in open-topped taxis that raced through the capital's streets, waving handkerchiefs and shouting 'Good luck!' Other cars flew round Piccadilly, Lustig wrote, 'with flags fluttering and klaxons sounding. It was all a great circus. As one group ran past me singing and dancing I heard an older man in a dark suit mutter "Bloody fools! If they only knew what they're cheering".'

Lustig did his bit for the war effort by walking to the London Guildhall one morning about three weeks later and enquiring at the front desk to whom he might make a donation 'for our boys in the field'. By then the first shocking reports of the 'delaying action' at Le Cateau and the subsequent full-scale retreat of the Allied armies from Mons had begun to appear in the press. So far from the swift victory they had been led to expect, the British public were now forced to accept the reality that, just across the Channel, their soldiers were even then desperately pushing their shoulders against a front line being battered by the advancing German army on the outskirts of Paris. It truly did seem that, in a ghastly way, the war would be over by Christmas.

When Lustig presented himself at the Guildhall that day, he must have struck Richard Ogden, the 22-year-old clerk on duty, as an odd sort of walk-in contributor to the British cause. For one thing, Victor had dressed down for the occasion, and Ogden would remember being moved by his seedy appearance. 'I was almost ashamed to receive him in that splendid building. I felt very sorry for him – poor fellow.' More pertinently, Lustig also had what must have seemed uncomfortably like a German accent. This was not necessarily something to be flaunted on the streets of Britain in the particular atmosphere of late August 1914. Emotions on the home front were 'understandably inflamed', *The Times* wrote on the same morning it began publishing the lengthy casualty lists from the fighting in France. Just a few nights earlier, a group of patriotic citizens had set fire to a butcher's shop in London's Regent Street, incensed, apparently, by the owner's name Rubenkraut spelled out in bold letters over the door.

But Lustig was seized by a sense of duty as he stood in the sumptuous Guildhall lobby that late-summer morning. In time a more senior official appeared and announced that he was authorised to receive gifts on behalf of the Lord Mayor's War Fund. Lustig reached into the pocket of his shabby jacket and produced a diamond necklace. He had extracted the gems with his own hands from a mine in which he had an interest in German South West Africa, he told the astonished official. It had been a hard struggle to successfully export them when he subsequently emigrated to Europe. Crocodiles were wrestled, terrible thirst endured, battles fought with murderous business rivals. Lustig had finally arrived in Paris, where the jewels were set into a fabulous matinee necklace. Victor had kept the piece locked safely in his Left Bank apartment while he went about town trying to establish himself as a painter. But he had failed to find a patron, and in desperation he had finally hocked the necklace. After several trying weeks he had been lucky enough to win a small commission to design the murals on a government building. The necklace was retrieved, but by then the international situation was no longer to his liking. He had decided to relocate across the Channel and dedicate himself to the British cause. Regrettably, his health was indifferent and thus he would not himself be able to bear arms. But he hoped this small token of his regard for his adopted country might nonetheless be acceptable.

Although neither Ogden nor his colleague raised any objection to Lustig's gift, a note later inserted in the files of the Lord Mayor's Fund would read:

> An individual named Otiok presented himself at the Guildhall. He made a number of antic statements as part of a general avowal of his loyalty to the Crown. Did not leave an address or any other particulars.

Lustig was more than usually active during this hectic period of world affairs. We know, for instance, that on at least one occasion he was a first-class return passenger on the White Star Line's RMS *Olympic*, shortly before the ship suspended commercial operations in late October 1914. The voyages seem to have served both as an enjoyable break in themselves and also an opportunity for him to complete his criminal apprenticeship. According to James Johnson of the US Secret Service:

> Having mastered his basic skills, he looked about for a field in which to apply them … The wealthy international set had taken to transatlantic travel on fleets of glittering new vessels advertised as floating palaces. Where better to find partners for a friendly game of cards than among the jaded and temporarily captive millionaires aboard ship? Victor duly set sail on the Atlantic.

In practice the junkets seem to have involved Lustig in a certain amount of innocent recreation and a good deal more of separating his fellow passengers from their money. Victor's primary forum for doing so was the poker table. Sometimes he worked alone, perfecting his skills as a 'mechanic' who could imperceptibly palm, switch or steal cards from the table. Sometimes he teamed with an older passenger named Julius 'Nicky' Arnstein in a so-called squeeze play, goading an innocent third party to keep calling and raising the stakes until the cash was heaped up on the table, at which point one of the two conspirators would triumphantly sweep up the entire pot. The ability to pull this move off in such a complex game of bluff and deceit owed something to raw skill, but also to the fact that Lustig and Arnstein had worked out a system of signals and codes beforehand.

Born in Berlin in 1879, the tall and aquiline-faced Arnstein had already forged a long if not always illustrious career working the transatlantic liners. Equally known for his skills as a bookmaker, fence and loan shark, in 1915 he was convicted of wiretapping a business rival and sent to New York's Sing Sing prison to serve a four-year sentence. American women adored him. Arnstein was blessed with a mellifluous mid-European accent, crisp, centre-parted hair and bedroom skills said to have brutalised his many partners and had them begging for more. The light actress Fanny Brice (later depicted by Barbra Streisand in *Funny Girl*) visited him every week while he was inside, and in 1918 Arnstein's long-suffering wife Carrie finally sued him for alienation of affection. He then married Brice, although she in turn divorced him when he was sent to jail a second time a few years later.

For Lustig, attaching himself to Arnstein was like adopting a father figure. He was fascinated by the older man's ostentatiously anglicised manner and larger-than-life swagger, qualities he went on to emulate. Victor would, probably, have made a name for himself as a master criminal even had Arnstein not come his way. But the flamboyant German American certainly hastened the process

Nicky Arnstein and his wife, Fanny Brice, later of Funny Girl *fame, with their two children.*

and instilled in his largely self-taught protégé a sense of his own intellectual distinction. 'I owe him a good deal,' Lustig remarked towards the end of his life, a rare tribute coming from one generally so sparing of praise.

In the meantime, the two men paired up to clip the Marquess of Lansdowne, a former British foreign secretary on his way to Washington for talks with President Wilson, for $300 at Texas stud.

3

A MASK TO SHOW THE WORLD

As war settled over Europe in the autumn of 1914, bringing an end to most commercial travel, Victor Lustig, ensconced in London, dug in for a period of relatively petty but lucrative crime, characterised by fraud, subterfuge, imposture and more specifically the fleecing of hotel guests in his familiar role as a 'snoozer'. As a variant, he once successfully sold Tower Bridge to a wealthy Australian tourist for a bargain £2,500 (about £65,000 today), telling the mark that he was the chief treasurer of the London County Council, the competent local government body for the city, and that they needed the funds for emergency civil defence measures 'because the Huns are expected over at any time'.

Writing to his younger brother Emil on 7 September, Victor remarked that he was supporting himself by transacting with the 'surprising surfeit' of those both gullible and well-heeled enough to fall for his scams. It's not known why exactly he went into the phony real estate market, but he may have been inspired by the activities of George C. Parker, an American con man active in the early years of the twentieth century who disposed of Madison Square Garden, the Metropolitan Museum of Art, Grant's Tomb and the Statue of Liberty, among other New York landmarks, by producing documents to suggest that he was the legal owner of the properties. Parker also proved adept at selling the rights to several hit Broadway shows to which he had no legal claim. He was eventually sent down to Sing Sing for life. The press ran similar stories in the immediate pre-war years of other entrepreneurs such as Reed C. Waddell or the brothers Fred and Charlie Gondorf, all of whom successively sold New York's iconic Brooklyn Bridge on a regular basis. The simple but effective ruse: the seller or sellers timed the path of beat cops working the area, and when they knew the officers would be out of sight, they propped up signs reading 'Bridge for Sale', showed the property to their targets, and separated them from their money as quickly as possible. The essence of the deal was to be fast, persuasive and flexible. Once Waddell improvised by selling half the bridge for $250 because the mark had only that amount of cash on him.

Although the war put paid to most recreational ocean travel, Lustig appears to have been on at least one voyage by the new HMHS *Britannic* in the early weeks of 1915. Built as a luxury transatlantic liner, the *Britannic* instead entered service as an Allied hospital ship. But before that she first went out on a number of sea trials, once making it as far as Godthåb in southern Greenland with 400 civilian volunteers on board. That this was dangerous work would be seen in tragic fashion when the *Britannic* subsequently hit a German mine when sailing near the Greek island of Kea and sank fifty-five minutes later, killing thirty people. She was the largest ship lost during the First World War.

But if Lustig was undoubtedly brave to volunteer his services when the *Britannic* put out on trials, he may not have been entirely blind to the commercial opportunities this involved. These were obviously strange and troubled times. By all accounts the bulk of the *Britannic's* (all male) passengers were gamblers. According to Lustig's arrest file, 'truly fabulous' sums of money changed hands each night in the ship's improvised card room. Perhaps the sort of person who merely enjoyed a quiet flutter in peacetime behaved with greater abandon when the prospect of death stalked the scene. An accomplished student of psychology like Lustig not only counted on the gullibility or greed of his targets; he also appealed to their sense of the precariousness of life. Possibly they thought they were living dangerously while they still could.

Lustig wrote back to his brother Emil in April 1915: 'I have worked out a "blueprint" for travel on the boats. Anyone can earn thousands of dollars by doing nothing that is outlawed but only winning over your fellow pilgrim's trust. Once done, you will scoop up his money.' Lustig reported elsewhere that he had taken Nicky Arnstein's advice 'never to push your victim to the [card] table. You always let *him* suggest the game. That way he feels in control. He feels the need to gamble, and you simply give him what he desires.' It seems to have been a winning strategy. 'Cleared another £400,' Victor serenely wrote in his diary the following October, on the day the London press reported the news that 60,000 British soldiers had been killed or wounded at Loos.

At some point later that autumn the 25-year-old Lustig decided to return to Hostinné. Although spared the worst of the fighting, the material cost of the war had begun to tell in the Bohemian republic. Bohemia's governor wrote to the foreign ministry in Vienna about worsening food shortages in the state: 'We receive only small quantities from Hungary, thus far we have got 10,000 wagons of maize from Romania, and so there are at least 30,000 wagons outstanding, without which we must simply be ruined … Without relief our industry, our transport network will come to a standstill, and [we] must collapse.'

When Victor arrived in Hostinné, he discovered that his father was both seriously ill and unemployed, and his infirm mother was working as a washerwoman, living in a small stone house a few streets away from her estranged husband. It must have made a bitter contrast to the world of floating casinos and luxury hotels he had come to inhabit elsewhere. Not long after he arrived, a group of German soldiers clambered out of a truck one morning. They had all been wounded in the fighting and given a week's medical leave to stay in a nearby lodge on the banks of the Elbe. With his eye for the small but telling detail, Lustig wrote in his journal that the men had a 'distant stare' to their eyes, sunken cheeks, seemed 'visibly weakened' both by injury and malnutrition, and 'hobbled off, some in boots still caked in battlefield mud, others [on] bandaged feet leaning on a comrade's arm'. He added: 'It is the more pitiful because they are only boys drafted from nice homes, knowing nothing about the conflict or the great issues at stake in London or Berlin or Paris. They just don't see what it is all about.'

It may have been this close encounter with the reality of war, or the fact that both his parents would be dead only a few months later, but Lustig rarely visited Hostinné again. He was back in London at Christmas of 1915. Amidst all the capital's communal sacrifices, the West End theatre at least survived. Suitably patriotic old plays were revived, and many new ones with evocative titles such as *The Beast of Berlin*, *The Master Hun* or *The Wages of Hell* were commissioned. There was also a somewhat less elevated offering of topical revues with names like *Bubbly Buzz Buzz* and *Shell Out!*, whose chief characteristics were their rows of scantily clad young women. Not everyone approved. General Sir Horace Smith-Dorrien, commander of the Home Army, made a much-publicised complaint about the musical *Pell Mell*'s 'indecent and suggestive unnecessaries', and the apparently damaging effects 'barely dressed girls and songs of doubtful character' were having on 'our chaps on leave'.

It was a 'high time [to be] in London,' Lustig wrote, by contrast. Rival factions jostled together on the home front in a more benign facsimile of the war itself. Moralists such as Smith-Dorrien flourished, taking the opportunity to reform a metropolis 'made soft by luxury, vicious by lust, spineless through liquor, and undisciplined through democracy', as he put it. Provocatively dressed women were seen in pubs and alleys and the back seats of music halls touting their 'luscious wares', the general complained. Gambling, drinking, dancing and even the ownership of cats and dogs accused of consuming precious stocks of rationed food came under attack. On top of all this, the long-feared German Zeppelins first appeared in the night skies on 31 May 1915, dropping their bombs and grenades on the East End. Seven people were killed in their beds, including four children. The silent and sinister airships returned at regular intervals during the next three years. It was a bewildering and frightening time, and a born opportunist like Lustig could hardly fail to take advantage.

Perhaps taking his lead from George Parker in New York, Lustig next posed as a musical producer who sought investment in his latest West End production. Sometimes the property in question was an already-running work like *Buzz Buzz* – an acknowledged hit, which required only a small further injection of capital – and at other times it existed solely in Victor's imagination. The target would be extensively wined and dined, and sooner or later the conversation would turn to the theatre and Victor would mention what very little outlay was required to ensure that the chorus line of fetchingly attired young ladies would continue to entertain the fee-paying public in the times ahead, and how the girls themselves would be personally grateful to their patron, and at that point the mark would acknowledge that he had always been keen on the stage. 'Oh, really?' Lustig replied, with an attention that did not need to be feigned. The exact details are elusive, but we know that he presented himself as 'André Dupre', a displaced Parisian impresario, at a series of meetings in the newly opened Ritz Hotel early in 1916, and that as a result a respectable if not prudent Harley Street specialist named Cyril McLintock was left to conclude ruefully that 'Monsieur Dupre offered me a quarter-share in his new West End enterprise for only £500. It was literally a steal, as no such revue existed.'

According to Dr McLintock, 'It seems easier to pretend to be what you are not than to conceal what you are. The person with whom I enjoyed those splendid dinners could accomplish both. He was a consummate manipulator.'

Not long after that Lustig again relocated across the Atlantic. He travelled on a Barbadian tramp ship returning to port after delivering a cargo of sugar at Liverpool. After 'several leisurely days – and nights' in the Caribbean, he made his way from there to New York.

Victor's parents were now both dead and his siblings remained behind in Europe. In his diary he wrote: 'The old happy days [of family life] are gone. I do not grieve. This is the time and the place for a gay wide smile – or at least for a mask to show the world.'

According to the 1911 census, Manhattan had become the most densely inhabited spot in North America, with a population of 243,728 packed into its 22 square miles. When all five surrounding boroughs were taken into account, the figure rose to a prodigious 3.4 million, and within ten years New York City would overtake London to become the largest metropolitan area in the world. By 1916 New York already boasted a state-of-the-art subway system, a vibrant arts scene and a fast-growing financial sector. More than a third of the nation's 200 largest corporations were headquartered there. Several prominent American literary figures made New York their home, and twenty-one newspapers were published locally each day. According to the census, 86 per cent of adult New Yorkers could read and write fluently (if not always in English), and more library books were borrowed per capita there than in any other world city. In stark contrast, Hostinné made do with a population of just 6,000, and at least half the adults were illiterate.

On another level, New York was a soiled, sad place whose inhabitants routinely murdered, stole, lied and cheated as they slithered around in a sea of immorality. Protests and riots regularly broke out that pitted one immigrant group against another, inviting violent police intervention. There was a series of catastrophic arsons, shootings and explosions, including the 4 July 1914 terrorist bomb, apparently intended to blow up John D. Rockefeller's suburban mansion, that went off prematurely and destroyed a seven-storey downtown apartment building.

Gambling was illegal, but widespread. An Italian syndicate operated the 'Bronze Door' network of unlicensed casinos, and paid off the police and politicians as needed. One English visitor walking around Manhattan's Lower East Side in 1916 described it without irony as a 'war zone … an absolute scene of disrepair, streets tram-pled down to a mass of broken cobbles and filthy straw, huge craters making a miniature lake and mountain district, leprous-looking hovels tilting in as if on the brink of collapse, and everywhere one's nostrils assailed by smells'. There were some 35,000 horses on the streets of Manhattan, producing nearly 500 tons of manure daily. It accumulated in the streets and was swept to the sides like snow.

For at least one New Yorker who could make the comparison, there were reminders on the avenues of Manhattan of the utter desolation of wartime Europe. Lustig wrote that it was the 'best city in the world to live in, but [simultaneously] the worst'. The best because the New Yorker was on his mettle day and night, always alert for the chance to advance himself. The worst because the penalty for failure ranged from starvation to incarceration, or (if your nemesis was not the police, but a rival gang member) a knife in the back. Either way, it was a land of opportunity for the truly unscrupulous swindler or the really proficient con man.

Lustig displayed a prodigious work ethic during his first months in New York. He signed on at a Brooklyn fishmonger at night, took correspondence courses to improve his English during the day, and devoted every free moment to concocting new ways to extract money from Americans. He allowed himself some personal leeway, too. Shortly after he arrived, Victor sent a photo back to his brother and sister in Hostinné, showing him sitting at a well-stocked table across from a striking blonde. It must have seemed like another world to the one he had left behind in the peasant village in war-torn Europe. 'The good life!' he scrawled across the bottom.

But business was still business, and one author has written of Lustig at the time:

One of Victor's minor swindles was of girls in [a favourite] brothel. On leaving the premises, he would show a $50 bill which he would apparently tuck into their stocking tops, telling them that if they looked before the next day it would turn into tissue paper. The girls were naturally unable to stop themselves looking at what, if genuine, would have been a handsome fee.

It says something both for the gullibility of Lustig's young victims, and also for their essential generosity, that he was able to return time and again to this same establishment without the least show of rancour on their part.

Other Lustig scams were more sophisticated, if not morally elevated. There was his role, for instance, in the phony off-track betting caper headquartered above a Chinese restaurant on Manhattan's Orchard Street. The idea was to lure a wealthy mark on to the premises and, once having won his confidence, invite him to wager on the outcome of a nearby horse race. Of course, the entire operation was simply a theatrical set, everyone there was an actor, and the 'broadcasts' from the track were actually being made up by an announcer in the back room. Anyone familiar with the plot of 1973's Oscar-winning film *The Sting* need only think of that same feature, if with a slightly less formal wardrobe, to get some of the flavour. Lustig introduced himself as 'Count von Kessler', a fellow high-stakes gambler, and his role was to lend an air of European class to the proceedings. Since con men are really actors, he generally pulled it off with some success. '$300 flush – dined at Plaza,' he wrote contentedly one day in July 1916.

Following that, Lustig again thought it best to travel out of town, and later in the year he was living as 'Charles Baxter, Wall Street man', in a neatly painted riverside bungalow in suburban Mount Pleasant, about 30 miles north of Manhattan. Since the notorious Sing Sing lay just down the road he may have taken the opportunity to visit his old partner Nicky Arnstein during his enforced four-year residency there. It's been said that Arnstein was a sort of Svengali figure in Lustig's early career, but there seems to have been a falling out later in the 1920s, when Arnstein wrote an article in which a 'Count L' was said to have 'presented himself in the war years as a great international man of affairs [and] the rest of us merely his vassals. This is actual nonsense, and represents a total reversal of fact.' Lustig was too sensible to reply in public, although he sent Arnstein a note requesting that he omit any further references to their experiences together, because he thought it unseemly for members of the same profession to engage in a public feud.

Although relieving high rollers of their money is the best-remembered of the ruses associated with Lustig's early days in America, it's not the only one. Among other things Victor set himself up as a fairground medium, able, for only a modest fee, to reunite the living and the dead; dabbled in blackmail; and found he had a talent as a forger. With little more than some tea-stained paper and a bottle of ink he was able to pass off documents from at least fifty historical figures, including George Washington, Abraham Lincoln, Marie Curie and the flying Wright brothers. Some of these works changed hands for 'hundreds', he noted – 'and for 25 cents I was [once] able to buy a slick magazine with the words "Newly Discovered Tale by Mr. Mark Twain" blazoned on the front'. Eventually Twain's estate wrote enquiring into the story's provenance, and the magazine in turn wrote to Lustig to seek further details on the matter. But their letter was not pointed enough to penetrate his armoured self-confidence. 'Have told them my sources are private, and they must accept this,' he wrote to his brother. 'That hushed them.'

A few days later Lustig went in for a meeting at the magazine's Fifth Avenue offices, where he not only reassured the editors about the Twain affair but also took the opportunity to sell them a handwritten poem he happened to have with him by the late Walt Whitman. It later emerged that Victor himself had composed this by cobbling together a few lines of authentic Whitman along with those of other, lesser-known poets – 'which makes me the true creator of the piece,' he noted, with perhaps not entirely unjustified pride.

Lustig's daughter Betty later wrote of this period:

Victor came to the United States looking around for contacts he could make with rich Americans. He also had rich European friends who were visiting or living in the US. He visited many cities, meeting people, studying [them], plotting a course that he was not sure of himself.

Again, this seems a notably generous version of the events surrounding Lustig's activities at around the time of the First World War. Many of the same contacts Betty mentions would become marks for his money-making schemes following his arrival in America. At least one of them was utterly ruined as a result. Victor was really the ultimate self-made man, working hard to hone his skills as a proficient counterfeiter, bookie, hoaxer, forger, gambler, all-round entrepreneur and budding lothario. At one stage in 1916 he even briefly set up his own small church in a disused seaman's hall on the Manhattan waterfront. Lustig simply hung a notice on the door announcing the date and time of a special service that would 'swell all hearts and souls with joy' and, what was more, guarantee those in attendance an 'eternal place of rest in God's acre'. There was a gratifying turnout on the day. By way of a sermon, Lustig made do with a speech by Adolf Bertram, the Roman Catholic archbishop of Breslau, translating it from the original German, adding one or two words of suitable seafaring vernacular, and pretending that he had originated the ideas. It all went over so well that he collected over $90 ($2,400 today) in the offering plate. Although there would be no further services held at that particular parish, Victor persuaded himself that it was really a victimless crime. 'The people had come to be uplifted, and, by God, they were.'

Lustig wasn't the first confidence man who could be both cold and calculating, but also strikingly kind – even gracious – when the occasion demanded. For him the 'acknowledgement of nobility within simple acts', such as donating his time or money, became a conscious philosophy. 'I earned' – or stole – 'the lucre, and then I gave it away,' he later remarked. Another of Lustig's more positive values was his lifelong optimism. When he first arrived in New York he made do with a rented room in a Brooklyn tenement house that was vermin-ridden, unsanitary and squalid. Six residents shared a bathroom, where the water emerged, if at all, 'like a sort of sticky red cod-oil'. The building's tenants cooked on a wood-burning stove and, in winter, put warmed bricks wrapped in a towel at the foot of their beds. There may have been no village in the Carpathians quite as primitive as the Manhattan that Lustig and many of his fellow immigrants experienced in the early years of the twentieth century. But he was enchanted by it. Merely to walk down the same streets as John Rockefeller or Andrew Carnegie was intoxicating. 'As a newcomer to the land it was the fulfillment of all my boyish dreams,' he wrote in 1943. 'The pride and thrill of being an American has never dimmed.'

Betty Lustig paints a picture of her father at this time as 'an habitué of Paris and the leading European cities, dressed in the latest fashion, with walking stick and Homburg hat, all of which enabled him to invade social circles [in] America'. This may be a child's forgivable bias toward her late parent. Other accounts of Lustig's initiation into New York society suggest that he lived from one scam to another, at least until he achieved the mastery of his chosen path later in the 1920s. But all parties agree that he already possessed two priceless qualities that helped shape his adult career. He was fiercely ambitious, even by the most rabid New York standards, often rising at two in the morning to walk the 3 miles to his first fishmongering job. And he was completely imperturbable in a crisis.

Arriving for work in the dead of one winter's night, Lustig's boss, a second-generation Anglo-American named Carl Repard, encountered his young assistant coming the other way. They paused to speak. Pleasantries were exchanged. Courtesies were extended. The weather was discussed, sport was touched on, and family matters reported, and then the soft-spoken Repard having asked if his employee was setting off on a sales call, Lustig replied evenly: 'No, but if you'll excuse me, sir, I must be on my way. I've had an urgent message to say my building is on fire.'

At some stage a year or two later, during his tenancy in Mount Pleasant, Lustig met a Jewish American racketeer named Arnold Rothstein. Born in New York in 1882, Rothstein was a somewhat unlikely-looking criminal mastermind – small and slightly

Arnold Rothstein, the man who fixed the 1919 baseball World Series,
among other activities.

stooped, muttering in his low, distinctive voice 'like bees around a honeypot', Victor later remembered, and never too busy to remember a child's birthday. Known as 'the Brain', he became a prolific gambler, loan shark, Wall Street swindler and, as if that weren't enough, godfather of the modern American narcotic drug trade. He's perhaps most notorious today as the man who fixed the 1919 baseball World Series between the Chicago White Sox and the Cincinnati Reds. Like all the best gangsters, Rothstein had a sentimental side. He helped to build a number of synagogues in New York, and was known as an easy touch by many local charities. When Rothstein was fatally shot by rival gambler George 'Hump' McManus in November 1928 his father told reporters at the hospital that Arnold had been a model son: 'I could not ask for a better one. He was not the kind who neglects his parents.'

Not long after Lustig made Rothstein's acquaintance, a mysterious series of hijackings took place in and around Wall Street.

Their actual execution was brutally simple. The major New York banks all employed messengers to transfer large bags of cash from one location to another. In several cases, the courier in question never arrived. Sometimes he would be waylaid and relieved of his goods, while on other occasions both he and his cargo inexplicably vanished. The police could never identify a suspect. The few eye-witnesses spoke of the assaults as being carried out by an individual variously disguised as a rabbi, a priest or even a nun. There was a certain amount of mordant humour in the ensuing newspaper reports as a result. Over an eighteen-month period from the spring of 1917 to the autumn of 1918 more than $3 million in cash and securities vanished, the equivalent of some $70 million today.

There is no direct evidence that Lustig himself was personally tied up in this crime wave. He had an alibi for most of the dates, and no known history of personal violence. On the other hand, he moved in the same circles as both Arnold Rothstein and the jailed Nicky Arnstein, who it's widely believed were the masterminds behind the robberies. He had some experience of fencing goods. And in November 1918, just as the spree of Wall Street thefts came to an end, he moved into an eight-room home on Manhattan's Upper East Side – a notable step up the social ladder for someone who'd been employed in a suburban fish market just three years earlier. The striking thing about Lustig at this time is that he really appeared to be several different people. There was the hard-working Bohemian immigrant who, his daughter would insist, was then 'as straight as a die – he didn't know any criminals and was never in trouble with the law'. And by contrast there was the unlicensed bookie, rare document forger and bogus vicar. Lustig could compartmentalise his affairs, and apparently kept the details of his numerous scams in his head. The different accounts of Victor's life are as various and colourful as the character they seek to describe, and the only certainty is that he made short work of successfully assimilating himself in American society.

★★★

One of Lustig's smaller-scale but lucrative swindles following his arrival in America was the 'pocketbook' scam. Like most of the best plays, it involved first winning over an innocent mark's confidence. Victor would ingratiate himself with a suitably prosperous-looking stranger in a bar, on a train, or even while waiting to cross a busy New York street. Looking down, he would suddenly notice a well-stuffed wallet, which he picked up and showed to the other party. Together they would carefully examine it for any identifying name and address, and, once having found these, Lustig would propose that they walk the short distance to the rightful owner's house and return his property. The two good Samaritans would politely decline the grateful man's subsequent offer of a cash reward. But then the wallet's owner – Lustig's confederate – would suggest an alternative formula. He would bet all the money in his wallet on the outcome of a horse race and, were he to win, as he was confident he would, share his good fortune equally with his two benefactors. It seemed almost too good to be true, and of course it was. At that point the mark was asked if he might wish to invest some of his own cash in the wager, thus increasing the expected jackpot, and more often than not he found that he would. The poor dupe never saw either man, or his money, again.

The specifics and the scale of the sting varied over time, but the pocketbook scam was characteristic of Lustig's basic approach to his craft during these early New York days. The essence of it was to lull his mark into a woefully false sense of security. Victor himself would generously offer to hold the cash until they met again to divide the profits. For some reason, Americans have always been susceptible to the seemingly obvious charlatan, the imposter who wins their trust before removing their money. Lustig was a natural in the role. He later wrote: 'The successful [con] hinges on desire – what can the [perpetrator] offer the victim that will make him abandon rational thought for the promise of a fantasy? It's very easy. All you really have to do is to probe and be patient. Sooner or later, the sap will tell you their innermost dreams, [and] then you pull the trigger. Victims don't ask a lot of questions. They answer a lot of questions.'

There were significant developments for Lustig during 1917 in not only personal affairs but geopolitical ones.

On 1 February of that year the German Kaiser announced that he had 'come round to the idea that total submarine warfare was now called for', a decision leading in short order to the sinking of the US steamer *Algonquin* as she lay 60 miles off the coast of south-west England, and President Wilson's consequent summoning of a special session of Congress to hear 'a communication concerning grave matters of national policy'. Four days later, Wilson announced that a state of war existed between the United States and Germany.

There were soon repercussions for Lustig, whose original Bureau of Naturalization landing card listed him as a 'citizen of Bohemia, Monarchy of Austria-Hungary', and thus on the wrong side of the conflict. As a legal alien he was at least spared the immediate consequences of the 1917 Immigration Act, which published a list of undesirables barred from entering the country, including 'alcoholics, anarchists, contract laborers, epileptics, idiots, illiterates, imbeciles, paupers, persons afflicted with contagious disease, radicals, polygamists, prostitutes and vagrants'. But along with some 2 million other individuals similarly classified as 'enemy allegiants' he was now obliged to register at his local post office, to carry his identity papers at all times, and to report any change of address or employment. In the space left for 'current occupation' in the card issued to him on 19 April 1917, Victor wrote in 'Businessman'.

In time many Americans took their duty further than the strict letter of the law and engaged in ad hoc vigilantism. German-language newspaper offices were attacked, Lutheran church services were disrupted, and foreign-born nationals dragged out of their homes at night and interrogated, while the patriotic citizenry of Collinsville, Illinois, removed a 30-year-old German immigrant from his bed, wrapped him in an American flag and lynched him by tying a rope around his neck, throwing the other end over the branch of a tree, and slowly pulling him off the ground.

Whether motivated by a salutary sense of self-survival, or a genuine love of his adopted home, Lustig went out of his way to demonstrate his loyalty to the American cause. He made it known that he had been an early and enthusiastic subscriber to government-issued Liberty Bonds, as it was 'the right thing to do', and, what was more, 'these will show a nice profit to the [bearer] when redeemed in twenty years' time'.* Soon he hoisted a large Stars and Stripes flag outside his home and took to calling himself Robert Duval, a name he apparently chose because it sounded unexceptional. On 22 October 1917 Victor told a US Selective Service Board, with some exaggeration, 'I am presently responsible for providing [the] sole upkeep of my large dependent family in a nonbelligerent state,' and was once again excused military service as a result.

The Board members were evidently impressed by the 27-year-old man with the lightly rumbling accent and the American flag pin prominently displayed in the lapel of his smart blue suit. 'Anyone who spends time with this individual,' they wrote, 'cannot come away with any other impression than that he has been in the presence of an educated, thoughtful personality' with 'a broad and comprehensive mind, and a fine command of English'. Even so, the board's chief psychological examiner admitted that some might be put off by 'a certain demonstrative manner in the subject, and his verbosity'.

Lustig could also be disarmingly courteous, even chivalrous, if the situation demanded. He was a vocal champion of women's rights, including the right to vote, and in 1919 put his name (albeit an assumed one) to a nationwide petition calling for a more equitable divorce law. A Manhattan doctor's secretary named Ruth Spivack later wrote that she had been on terms of some intimacy with Lustig

---

★　Lustig never enjoyed the anticipated fruits of his twenty-year bonds, because in 1937 he found himself in the custody of the US Prison Bureau.

at this time, and that he had been a perfect gentleman. Forty years later she still spoke affectionately of a 'handsome young man with a mischievous smile … He was a suave and sophisticated New York in a straw hat with a courtly European manner. We were enchanted by his looks and charm. All of the girls were mad about him at once.'

Some disparity exists between the immaculately clad Bohemian man of affairs and the shameless hustler who had so cruelly exploited Sylvia Nenni and several other women like her. Spivack also knew Lustig when he later made one of his frequent moves and settled in the American Midwest. It was an unlikely home for an Old World patrician like him. Lustig's persona took on a newly childlike quality of wonder and gratitude that 'he found himself in this vast and untapped land of endless opportunity', she wrote. He insisted that he wanted nothing more from life than to settle down and become a farmer.

But it might be a stretch to portray Lustig's incursion into the American heartland as marking a record of unblemished good citizenship on his part. He was arrested under the name Robert Duval in December 1917 while passing through Denver, after complaints that he had hawked a number of boxlike 'electro-magnetic curative machines' around town, said to be effective at relieving the effects of gout. One of the devices had been dismantled and found to contain only a household light bulb, some coloured string, and the buzzer from a kitchen egg-timer. Lustig jumped bail and made his way to Chicago, where he was in turn arrested on 27 December, and duly returned under escort to Denver. At the subsequent hearing on 7 January 1918 he was ordered to forfeit his bond of $1,500 ($40,000 today) but avoided jail time. A later FBI memo about Lustig's activities at the time displays a mixture of official censure and grudging respect characteristic of the way he was habitually treated in law-enforcement circles:

DUVAL, alias Miller, alias Lustig, etc, has always possessed a very poor reputation. He is well known in the underworld as a top notch confidence man. He has been arrested many times in the USA without once having served a sentence, and the criminal record indicates he also ran afoul innumerable times of the law in Europe, but with the same result that he never was forced to serve a sentence of any reasonable duration.

Lustig's extended tour of the American hinterland highlighted a number of contradictions in his character. There's no reason to doubt that he was happy enough there, and his remarks on the subject to Ruth Spivack appear sincere. Yet he was if anything even more brazen in his scams than before. Young, old, male, female, native-born or immigrant: all were equal to him as the necessary marks to keep a grifter of his quality in business. And he worked hard to maintain his competitive edge. There may have been one or two professional players who could match Lustig's skills at poker or on the billiard table, but nobody has ever brought to the con man's art the austere self-discipline or meticulous planning he did. Before he lured an unwary victim into a fake off-track betting shop, he had already had dozens of getting-acquainted meals or soul-searching personal conversations to win the other party's confidence. Similarly, when he said he could flick all fifty-two cards of a pack into a hat at 30ft he had behind him hours of practice in lonely, rented rooms. If he bet that he could bring off a rare 'butterfly' shot at pool, sinking six balls with a single stroke, he could stake big because he had gone to the trouble not only of endlessly practising the move, but also because he had carefully rigged the table the night before.

As the war in Europe continued, Lustig constantly reinvented himself for an American audience. There was never going to be any shortage of suckers to keep an artist of his undoubted ability in business, but over and above that, as he wrote back to his brother Emil, 'the great thing here [is] that you can be whatever you want to be'. After initially calling himself Duval or Miller or Lamar, Victor increasingly put it around that he was a political exile from what he loosely called 'the Balkans', a duke or baron of some sort summarily evicted from his ancestral seat. Since most American Midwesterners knew as much about central European society as they did about the dark side of the moon, he was generally on safe ground, even if one Lustig victim when later coming to write about his experiences of him saw fit to abridge the title 'Count' by omitting a critical vowel.

It was the sheer scale of Lustig's operations that most impressed, particularly at a time when it could take a week of arduous train and horse travel to move between towns accessible today within a few hours. The speakeasies of New York, Al Capone's Chicago, the gold mines of Colorado, the farmsteads of Missouri and Iowa, Lustig would play them all. In February 1918 he was back working the riverboats around New Orleans, stinging the legendary gambler and boxing promoter George 'Tex' Rickard for $500 at poker after having first taken the trouble both to bribe the game's dealer, and to spend hours practising a straight face in front of his rooming house mirror.

Shortly before dawn on 21 March 1918, a 7,000 gun-strong German artillery bombardment opened up over a 150-square-mile area of the Western Front, the signal for the start of the *Kaiserschlacht*, or spring offensive, that produced the most significant territorial gains since 1914. By the end of the first day, the British had suffered some 47,000 casualties, of whom as many as half were captured, and the Germans had broken through at several key points around the Somme. Although there was no final collapse, the situation was still grave enough three weeks later for the Allied commander Douglas Haig to exhort his troops to fight to the end and to add: 'The safety of our homes and the freedom of mankind alike depend on the conduct of each one of us at this critical moment.'

This same perilous hour in mankind's destiny found Victor Lustig some 5,000 miles away, working his pocketbook scam on the streets of Omaha, Nebraska. He was arrested there, under the name Lamar, on the very day that Haig issued his rallying order to the troops. The charge sheet read simply: 'Con game.' Lustig was booked and released on a $1,250 bond. He soon forfeited this by again failing to appear in court, but the authorities seem not to have pursued the matter. Victor recalled with some animus that he had been seized in his New York home later that summer and thrust behind bars as a suspected enemy agent. 'I was jailed through some mistake, probably a confusion of names,' he wrote, perhaps overlooking the role he himself might have played in the muddle, and barely escaped deportation. The guns in France fell silent that November. He had, for now, staved off disaster.

Christmas that year saw Lustig hustling around the pool halls of Toronto, Ontario, where he joined thousands of other recent European refugees in the city. To welcome the new year, a disaffected German exile threw a bomb into the club where Victor was in the process of relieving some other players of their money. Three people died in the blast, and more than a dozen were injured. 'We were scared to death,' a witness named Paul Maze later told the *Toronto Star*. 'When the smoke cleared there were terrible scenes … the [room] was nothing less than a vision of hell, with the tables blown to splinters and the ground strewn with burned and hideously charred bodies.' Amidst the chaos, a bruised and bloodied Lustig helped to pull survivors to safety, 'and acted as calmly and quietly as the way one might sweep up after a summer storm'. When the worst was over and the victims had been removed, Lustig proposed that they repair to a nearby hotel where, despite the official prohibition of alcohol, he was able to buy everyone a round of drinks. 'He may have been putting on a show [for] our benefit,' Maze thought, but he couldn't help but feel a sense of admiration for Victor's grace under pressure. Asked what they should do about their damaged club, Lustig answered with a quip: 'We'll fix it. Sometimes it's endurance alone that makes a man famous.'

They were words he would make into a career.

Along with the perseverance, Lustig's great talent was for rein-vention. He was back in Paris in the spring of 1919, strolling around in his neatly tailored overcoat with the specially deep pockets and again introducing himself as Baron von Kessler. On 2 June, a brief ceremony took place in the old royal chateau at Saint-Germain-en-Laye, about 10 miles west of the city centre. Delegates from the Allied powers told representatives from Habsburg Austria that their satellite territories were being assigned elsewhere. Bohemia became the core of the newly formed state of Czechoslovakia. Again managing to be present to see history in the making, Lustig wrote in his journal of the 'Viennese bigwigs strutting around in [their] long hunting coats and little green hats, so calm about losing their whole world'. He wondered if he himself might have some small administrative role to play in the new European order, and asked in the privacy of his journal if he should seek an interview with Tomas Masaryk, the Czech nationalist and de facto first state president who was then living in exile in Chicago. 'He will require men around him who are [able] to assign tasks and think about our nation's future.'

In the end, Lustig's services as a Czech political strategist would not be required. He wasn't entirely idle, however. Victor's US Department of Justice file shows another sorry lapse from grace early that summer: 'June 1919: Arrested in Paris for the counter-feiting of bank deeds.'

Lustig again avoided jail time for the offence, and in due course made his way from Paris to Brussels and then Amsterdam. In each town where he settled he would quickly establish himself with a new circle of friends, charm them with his wit, intimidate them with his brilliance, flatter them with his confidences, and then separate them from their money. He was back in London on 19 July in time to join one of the victory parades celebrat-ing the official end of the war, wearing a uniform he had bought for the occasion from a Piccadilly theatrical outfitter's, and in New York again by the end of August. From there it would take him a further twelve days of train and buggy travel to reach Kansas City, which was then undergoing a municipal growth spurt with the construction of a new downtown railway station, as well as a network of Parisian-style boulevards and parks, and a thriving bootleg liquor industry.

Not since the fictional Phileas Fogg had circumnavigated the globe in eighty days had a private individual travelled quite as tirelessly as Lustig did now. He had already crossed the Atlantic at least five times, and paid extensive visits everywhere from Vienna to rural Nebraska. He radiated nervous energy. Too driven and already too notorious to simply settle down in one place, he appeared to have found just the right balance of financial chicanery, transient female companionship and constant mobility to keep his adrenaline at the pitch he required.

At least some of this regimen would be temporarily modified by Lustig's marriage on 3 November 1919 to an attractive young Ukrainian American woman named Roberta Noret, whom he affectionately called Bertie or Buckle. Robust, flame-haired and occasionally capable of tremendous flashes of indignation and jealousy, Roberta was nonetheless remembered as a 'quiet and demure midwestern girl who spoke softly and with effort, as if trying to remember her grammar lessons'. The couple met at a tea party in Kansas City, where she had worked successively as a laundress and a shop assistant, and eloped to New York just a few days later. Roberta had left school at the age of 12, and seems to have had little social life up until the night she met Lustig. 'The world suddenly became larger,' she later wrote of their first days together. 'Somehow, things glowed … He never seemed to have enough of life, never seemed to tire.'

The newlyweds were soon spotted around Manhattan, often arm-in-arm, clothes shopping or dining at smart Italian restaurants. Since the marriage was unannounced, the exact nature of their relationship remained unclear, even to many of Lustig's closest circle. Muddying the waters further, Roberta was a churchgoing

Catholic, devout and scrupulously honest, making her Lustig's moral antithesis and, perhaps, an unlikely partner. Of course, he may simply have welcomed the chance to set up home with a good woman after the years of constant upheaval, let alone the professional advantages it afforded. More so than today, marriage conferred a public respectability denied the single man, and for a while Lustig seemed to embrace his new role, hosting dinners with his attractive new bride, promenading around with her, even learning to play golf together. Victor was 'very sociable, curious, fond of a large number of people', Roberta later wrote. His business activities were often dark and mysterious, she acknowledged, but as a person 'he wasn't so at all'.

As a wife, Roberta seems to have tended to the possessive – 'I'll throw myself in the ocean and let the fish eat me [if you] look at another woman,' she informed her husband on their honeymoon cruise – and with good cause. Perhaps it was the normal hormonal eruption he had never fully been able to indulge as an adolescent. Or perhaps it was because he'd always been fascinated with glamorous and preferably wealthy women. More likely, it was simply part of his restless nature. Whatever the reason, Lustig lived from con to con, from city to city, and from partner to partner. He continued to see his friend Ruth Spivack well into the first years of his marriage. A little later in the 1920s he met an aspiring actress and dancer named Lucy LeSueur, whose 'wide, hurt eyes' and – striking a less-refined note – 'great maternal orbs' he particularly lingered over in his journal. She became Joan Crawford. One way or another, Lustig would continue to explore the limits of his wedding vows throughout the 1920s. He loved Roberta, she was sweet and loyal; yet when he met Billie Mae Scheible – the buxom blonde proprietor of a Philadelphia prostitution ring, and later prosecuted by federal authorities under the White Slave Act – he loved her, too.

Any lingering doubts Roberta might have had about her new husband's business were soon dispelled on that same honeymoon cruise to Europe. There was the fact that he booked the tickets under the names of Mr and Mrs Eric von Kessler, for instance. Not long into the voyage, Roberta noticed that her husband had sewn $25,000 into secret pockets in his overcoat. He bought her a fabulous emerald-green velvet gown with a fur cape as soon as they reached Paris. One night when he disappeared for several hours she discovered a scrapbook tucked inside his suitcase lining. In it Lustig had pasted press cuttings describing his crimes. When Victor came back in the early hours and she challenged him about it, he told her without the least show of embarrassment that he had just been out to 'work' at a nearby casino, and had extracted over 5,000 francs from the pockets of his fellow gamblers. Roberta seems to have quickly recovered from any shock she may have felt about the true nature of her husband's calling in life. Besides, as she later wrote to the couple's daughter, there was another side to this inveterate confidence trickster. He was a superb judge of character and situation; he stole only from those who could afford it; and whatever his other moral lapses, 'he always treated me like a lady'.

While in Paris, Lustig interested himself in the case of a 47-year-old decorated American army veteran named Frederick Stuart Greene. The two men's paths had first crossed in 1917, when Lustig had been rapidly traversing Europe in the role of André Dupre, a theatrical impresario, and despite the fact of the war they had enjoyed some convivial nights together. Greene had quickly decided that deep down Lustig was a good man. 'He is stridently anti-Hun and wants the Allies to win the day.' On the other hand, he was morally flexible. 'It seems that he is prepared to do whatever it takes to bail out a friend. But if you're his enemy, God alone will help you,' Greene wrote. 'I feel that I shall be hearing more of him in the future, because he is not a man to slip quietly into the shadows.'

Now Greene himself was back in New York, and had attached himself as an adviser to the state's charismatic new Democratic governor, Al Smith. Smith, who happened to be a Catholic, had attracted a number of particularly vehement critics, as well as powerful allies, on the way up. One of the former, identified only as 'the judge', had dedicated himself to sabotaging Greene's career as a preliminary step to destroying Smith. Lustig in turn resolved to undermine the judge, which he did with the help of some forged French police files he brought back with him from Paris. It was a typically labyrinthine plot he put in motion. Lustig first approached the judge, claiming that he had irrefutable evidence of Greene's moral turpitude while stationed in France during the war. The judge quickly agreed to buy the incriminating dossier for the prodigious sum of $15,000. But in short order the apparently official French papers were revealed as a complete forgery. Greene was vindicated, and the judge retired into private life. Somehow he was never able to locate the 'Baron Kessler' who had sold him the salacious material in the first place.

Frederick Greene went on to be appointed New York State Superintendent of Public Works, and to become an important early figure in the design and construction of the United States highway system. Smith later consulted him about again adopting what he called 'unorthodox tactics' at the time of his 1922 gubernatorial re-election campaign. But Greene advised against any such covert activity without Lustig himself, arguing that any attempt to emulate his 'European friend's' methods would pose a 'considerable risk, because [Lustig] has a singular genius for this sort of operation'.

Lustig was then unavailable, Greene reported, because his wife had given birth to their daughter Betty the previous February, 'and at present he is utterly devoted to the role of the family man'. She would be Lustig's only acknowledged child. It was a remarkable thing to see the love and attention Victor showered on her. 'In fact,' Greene added, 'he is becoming so respectable that I understand he himself may yet run for office on our side.'

Not entirely convinced of the soundness of this plan, Smith grunted.

4

THE PRIVATE MINT

In the sweltering early afternoon heat of 18 August 1920, Harry Burn, a 24-year-old Republican member of the Tennessee General Assembly, mumbled the word 'Aye' from his seat on the back benches of the wooden-framed state legislature building in Nashville. Though monosyllabic, Burn's remark had momentous consequences. The chamber was then deadlocked 48–48 in its protracted debate on the resolution before it that torrid Wednesday, which read: 'The rights of citizens of the United States shall not be denied or abridged by any authority on account of sex.' Burn's tie-breaking vote swung the day. Tennessee was the thirty-sixth of the then forty-eight state assemblies to ratify the motion, which became the law of the land as a result. The United States would be the twenty-seventh country in the world to give women the right to vote.

Though important, this was by no means the only factor destined to alter the daily status or habits of Americans in the 1920s.

The first national radio broadcasting station – operating out of a tent pitched on the roof of a Pittsburgh office building – opened on 2 November 1920, for instance, and just six months later a San Francisco newspaper described the miracle of the new medium that millions were already enjoying: 'There is music in the air, every night, everywhere. Anybody can hear it at home on a receiving set, which any child can put up in an hour.' Further diversions were on the way. Scott Fitzgerald's debut novel *This Side of Paradise*, published in March 1920, revealed to suitably shocked American parents what their sons and daughters were up to, and how long it had been going on. Apparently the 'petting party' had been in vogue as early as 1916, and was now widely established as an indoor sport. 'None of the Victorian mothers – and most of the mothers were Victorian – had any idea how casually their daughters were accustomed to be kissed,' Fitzgerald wrote. In July, a fashion writer reported in the *New York Times* that 'the American female … has lifted her skirts far beyond any modest limitation', which was to say that the hem was now only 6in or so below the knee. It was predicted that hemlines would come down again in the winter of 1920–21, but instead they rose higher still. Before long, legislatures in several states introduced bills to regulate feminine dress once and for all. In Ohio, a law was passed to prohibit the sale of any 'garment which unduly displays or accentuates the lines of the female figure', and to forbid any 'female over fourteen years of age' from wearing 'a skirt which does not reach to that part of the foot known as the instep'.

The nationwide ban of alcohol, meanwhile, had the unintended consequence of making drinking a popular act of rebellion. The results were the bootlegger, the speakeasy, and the promotion of the idea that both sexes could equally enjoy a bracing cocktail, rather than it being a largely male prerogative. This was also the era when column after column of the front pages of the daily American press shouted the news of pro- and anti-Bolshevik riots; of violent labour strikes; and of a widespread fixation with the threat and reality of terrorism that would be eclipsed only after the events of 9/11 eighty years later. In January 1921 the 26-year-old J. Edgar Hoover, head of the FBI's new General Intelligence Division, sent a memo to the bureau's field agents. He was concerned that 'Communistic free-thinkers and subversives' ('as red in their politics as their unmentionables', he rather curiously added) were at work in the US, that school textbooks should promote only 'heroes of American history', and that individual lecturers or teachers deviating from this ideal 'be brought to the attention of my office immediately'.

In time Hoover's escalating obsession with Communist influence in the United States itself became a sort of national epidemic. But at least at this stage it may not have been an entirely idle preoccupation on his part. A series of booby-trap bombs exploded at the homes or offices of prominent Americans in a wave of terror that lasted at intervals from May 1919 to March 1922. One such attack narrowly failed to kill Mitchell Palmer, the US Attorney General, but managed to destroy his home. All of the explosive devices came wrapped in a pink slip of paper, which read: 'We will kill to rid the world of your tyrannical institutions.'

J. Edgar Hoover.

When you add in a generally bullish stock market – and seven fat years of conspicuous consumer consumption beginning in 1922 – the sudden and widespread popularity of true confession magazines and novels, and 'yellow' films with titles such as *Sodom and Gomorrah, What's Wrong with the Women?* and *Smouldering Fires* (promising audiences 'neckers, petters, white kisses, red kisses, pleasure-mad daughters, sensation-craving mothers … the truth – bold, naked, sensational'), not to mention an obsession with spiritualism and even more exotic rites on the one hand and the arguments of religious fundamentalists that the country was morally adrift on the other, you again had the ingredients for one of those turbulent, rackety, often chaotic periods when Americans were kicking up their heels and generally taking things to extremes in a way they seem to do better and more often than anybody else. It was a situation in which a past master of psychology and a deft manipulator of human foibles and vanities like Victor Lustig could hardly fail to clean up.

Lustig's latest money-making device was in fact literally just that: an impressive-looking heavy oak chest with brass trim that could supposedly reproduce any banknote that was fed into it. The idea was to ply a mark with a well-oiled meal in a luxury hotel, and then to invite him into a private room upstairs to inspect the wonder machine. Lustig would produce a genuine $100 bill from his wallet, insert it into one of the box's two end slots, and turn a lever that sucked the bill into the interior. Into the other slot he fed a sheet of banknote-sized white linen paper. After twirling a few knobs, Victor would tell the expectant customer that they needed to wait a further six hours in order for the miracle of alchemy to take effect. The delay served only to heighten the air of anticipation. When the two men returned, possibly fortified by more drinks, the demonstration would swiftly reach a climax. After Lustig again carefully adjusted all the knobs and turned the crank, the box obligingly issued two crisp $100 bills, the original and its duplicate. Both were quite genuine. Lustig had concealed the second bill in the device before his victim ever set foot in the room. The results were uniformly gratifying from Victor's point of view. Sometimes he sold one of the boxes, which typically took him a couple of hours to knock up in his workshop, for as much as $30,000 ($800,000 today). The device's new owner would eagerly repeat the procedure he had just witnessed with his own eyes, but somehow no more money would ever emerge. The six-hour waiting period was generally more than enough for Lustig to put a couple of hundred miles between himself and the scene of the crime. Besides, he reasoned, the party buying the box was dishonest himself. He would be unlikely to welcome the attention of the police.

Soon Lustig owned apartments in New York, Chicago and Detroit. He kept three Rolls-Royces, a tan one, a black one and a white one, and had Tony, his chauffeur, dress in a uniform coloured accordingly. There was also a full-time German valet and a young French maid. Lustig brought his younger brother Emil, currently a deserter from the Austrian army, to the United States on a forged passport and soon had him running errands for him, such as lifting a potential mark's wallet or opening an account in a bank where Victor himself preferred not to linger. Sometimes Lustig lost money almost as fast as he made it, dropping $5,000 in a single night at roulette or playing *klaberjass*, a trick-taking card game popular in the old country. Win or lose, he was almost always upbeat, a human holiday who often sat down with twelve or fifteen guests for dinner in his New York home, and motored off to Florida in his white trousers and slightly overdone Henley Regatta-style blazer whenever he felt the need for some winter sun. Lustig's daughter recalls that Rudolph Valentino had once urged her father to try his hand as an actor in Hollywood – 'he loved the thrill of fooling the public, [and] was a brilliant mimic' – but Victor thought that being a mere movie star would mean a step down for him financially.

Perhaps due to his limited formal education, Lustig was a confirmed bibliophile who frequently subscribed to mail-order offers from Time Corporation with titles such as *The 100 All-Time Classics (Abridged) of Literature* or *The Twelve Ages of Man*, among other such anthologies. In deference to the intellect, he soon added a pen to the original sword-and-plough design he had commissioned as his family coat of arms. 'He knew a lot of basic world history, and a smattering of undergraduate-level philosophy,' said a US Prison Bureau psychologist who later examined him. Lustig's daughter insisted that her parents' marriage had been both 'conventional' and a 'true mental and emotional union', at least in its early years, but there's some evidence that Victor even then strayed from the traditional monogamous ideal. In later compiling his patient's medical history, Dr Romney M. Ritchey of the US Public Health Service wrote: 'Physical examination done was essentially negative except for a history of Syphilis in 1920.'

One spring day, Lustig had his chauffeur drive him and his family some 200 miles upstate to New York's Saratoga racecourse. There he bet the significant sum of $350 ($10,000 today) on the outcome of the first race, announcing to Roberta that he was 'very sure' of the result. Lustig had good grounds for his confidence, because he had previously paid off all five competing jockeys to finish in a certain order designed to maximise his winnings. He had been officially warned about this practice in the past, but the police had found no reason to prosecute him.

Unfortunately, one of the horses at Saratoga had promptly tripped and fallen, bringing down the horse behind it, and in the ensuing confusion the other riders had failed to keep to the agreed sequence. Commendably calm in the face of this calamity, Lustig had quickly improvised a plan to cut his losses. Standing on a wooden soapbox set up just inside the course's rear gate, under a professionally printed banner reading '"KOSHER" VON KESSLER – NO WAGER REFUSED' (he kept a variety of such promotional material in the boot of his Rolls, ready for any contingency), and offering notably attractive odds, he took a large number of cash bets on the next race on the day's card, handing each punter a neatly embossed receipt as he did so. Victor later claimed that he had cleared over $700 in this way.

When the race itself began, Lustig took the opportunity to swiftly load the banner and the soapbox into the back of the Rolls, before collecting Roberta and their infant daughter and instructing Tony to head out of town without further delay. The family prudently relocated to Florida for several weeks after that. In jail many years later, Lustig told a government investigator that the secret of a successful touch was to keep your head at all times, thus often turning an initial loss into an eventual profit.

In his early thirties, Lustig was clearly both good at his job and more than comfortably off as a result. Yet even during these days of Florida vacations and chauffeured Rolls-Royces, his critics dismissed him as a second-rate con artist and a vain, pompous, arrogant petty hood. Then, and later, they could point to his regular and often undignified run-ins with the law as proof that he was far from the elusive Professor Moriarty-type he liked to portray to the world. Lustig's wife Roberta later compared him to a Greek hero, ultimately brought down from the heights of power by his own hubris – or even, some have argued, his incompetence.

In early March 1921, the US Department of Justice received a note from Sgt Clayton of the St Louis, Missouri, police department:

This man [Lustig] was arrested at St. Louis on Feb 22 1921, when he had in his possession $29,000.00 worth of Liberty Bonds, which had been tampered with and with which he attempted to swindle two citizens.

He was booked with attempted Grand Larceny, but later discharged. Mr. James Haley, US Secret Service agent, wired Federal authorities at New York, and the suspect [Lustig] was ordered held for the NY officials … He was again discharged … Case closed.

Or later in June 1921:

As ROBERT DUVAL, arrested for attempted grand larceny: Discharged.

And in September of that year:

Arrested on bunco charge – loaded dice game. Held overnight. Not wanted.

Set against this, Lustig's supporters and apologists could point to his combination of high intelligence and unflagging energy, as well as to the dazzling powers of improvisation that allowed him to escape the attention of the police far more often than he was caught.

Once, later that same year, a New York FBI agent happened to notice Emil Lustig enjoying what was officially advertised as a cup of coffee in a midtown hotel lobby. In time the agent followed Emil out on to the street. He was keen to speak to the elder Lustig brother about an outstanding warrant for his arrest and wondered if this might be his chance to do so. Sure enough, Emil unwittingly led the officer to a nearby cigar stand, where Victor was waiting for him. Betty Lustig later described what happened next:

My father, spotting [the agent] looked around to see what to do. He spied a blind man, with a tin cup and pencils, not far from him and his ingenuity, always working overtime, was ready. Before the blind man realized what was happening, he was hustled into the Rolls-Royce Vic was using, with Tony at the wheel. The touch of a $100 bill in his hand assured the man that whatever was happening was good for him, although he had to take Vic's word for the denomination. Soon they had changed clothes, and the blind man was riding away smiling from ear to ear in the chauffeured Rolls. And on the street, he left behind a new character, with dark glasses covering his eyes, in ragged clothes and with a hat pulled down over a seemingly weary face.

He clutched a tin cup filled with pencils and cried out weakly as shoes passed him by, saying, 'Help a poor blind man, sir. Buy a pencil'.

The FBI man obligingly dropped a coin into the cup.

After that, Lustig again decided to spend an extended period out of New York, this time in a comfortable but secluded waterfront estate near Naples, Florida, with only the occasional alligator or snake for a neighbour. The one local reference to him was a brief item in the *Sun-Tattler* newspaper that quoted a police report about a 'Shoobie', as out-of-towners were euphemistically docketed when they appeared in court for some reason, who had been detained following a 'tussle' over a cash transaction at the local market. The case was dismissed.

Lustig did not deliberately choose to withdraw from the world. He was by nature a gregarious man who enjoyed meeting new people, particularly those of them who might be future victims of one of his scams. But he increasingly recognised the merits of keeping a low public profile. The nature of his work had become ever more delicate, and he accepted that a degree of subterfuge might be the price it demanded for fulfillment. Betty Lustig came to think of it as a tragedy: the warm, loving father who dressed up as a clown at children's parties and ran laughing along the beach outside their Florida home, forced to live much of his life 'hiding away behind locked doors and answering only to an alias'. Even in those days, Lustig often spoke of retiring from the whole racket to raise his family. Yet nowhere was there any real indication that he was seriously willing to alter the path he was travelling. To the outside world, and above all to most law-enforcement officials, it was proof that Lustig had entered into a Faustian pact like the one legendarily undertaken by Robert Johnson. But to Victor's family, he was simply a smart businessman who was forced to take certain precautions to protect his loved ones. Betty Lustig remembers that the first words her father ever taught her were not 'Mommy' or 'Daddy', but 'Never speak to the police.'

After the blind man incident, Lustig apparently decided that from now on he would have to communicate with Emil by more indirect means. He did so in almost comic fashion. Employing an elaborate system of couriers, Victor arranged for a friend named Robert Holles, who worked in the insurance trade, to deliver private letters to a business contact at the Wall Street branch of Mellon Bank, Walter Reeve, who would in turn pass them to Emil when he came in each Friday morning ostensibly to discuss his financial portfolio. Lustig also invented his own code for sending messages to his brother that didn't require logbooks or any other decrypting device. Victor was so pleased with the system that he once proudly showed it to a contact in the US Secret Service – the same agency that would later feature his name on its Most Wanted list – and came away convinced that nobody could break it.

Sometimes Lustig asked that Emil's messages to him be embedded in the personal columns of the *New York Globe*, which his chauffeur picked up for him each weekday morning for two cents a copy at a newsstand in Herald Square. Such a message might read: 'Saw your note in yesterday's paper. It came too late. You must try to forget. Brown Eyes.' Or alternatively: 'Wish to communicate with a young lady matrimonially inclined. Must be a blonde and willing to accompany me to Dagestan.' Victor would know what to do with this information, which was generally either a warning that the police were watching for him in a particular neighbourhood or, conversely, that the coast was clear for a rendezvous in a more remote New York locale such as 'Dagestan'.

The stolid but willing Emil seemed happy to play along, knowing how much his elder brother enjoyed this sort of cat-and-mouse game. Occasionally their correspondence took a more direct form. To thank Victor for a birthday gift, Emil mailed a postcard with a beach scene and a postmark from the New Jersey resort of Asbury

Park. The card noted that the writer had been on the pier's 'merry-go-round, [and] seen all the sights as I spun every which way. The weather is fine.' The message, as understood by Lustig, was that Emil had taken the opportunity to reconnoitre the area, that law enforcement seemed not to be in attendance, and that it was a propitious place for them to meet.

Lustig wasn't one to overlook a lucrative new mass obsession when he saw it, and as a result he soon boarded the great spiritualist bandwagon of the early 1920s. The movement had first gained traction in late-Victorian Britain, where it often came with a feminist subtext. Women were thought to be uniquely qualified to communicate with spirits of the dead, and in the séance room, at least, a medium could enjoy a degree of independence and authority not readily available to her elsewhere. There are no reliable figures on actual attendance at séances or services, but in one census the Society for Psychical Research asked 17,000 British adults whether they had ever experienced a 'spiritual hallucination' while fully awake and in good health. Of the 1,684 who said they had, there were several who insisted that they had been bodily 'embraced' or 'kissed' by an unseen force, among what the society called 'more intimate' liaisons.

The whole affair took on a furious new momentum following the First World War, and nowhere more so than the United States. 'A memorial to the dead had appeared in every town, and many people naturally sought some divine solace for their grief,' the magician Harry Houdini, a cynic in these matters, remarked. By January 1921 there were reported to be more than 14 million 'occasionally or frequently' practising occultists in North America, served by a network of 6,200 individual churches. Barely a week passed without some sensational paranormal claim appearing in the newspapers or over the radio. 'MY FRIENDLY CONTACT WITH DEPARTED SOULS: MESSAGE RECEIVED FROM MURDERED CZAR, by Grand Duke Alexander of Russia' ran one such headline in the *New York Tribune*. Lustig may not have been that drawn to either orthodox or occult religion per se, describing the latter to Emil as 'the world's most dangerous clan'. But it seems fair to say that the entrepreneur in him was fully alive to its commercial potential.

In August 1922, while trading under the *nom-de-séance* Count Kokum, Lustig set up shop for a late-summer season in Cape May, New Jersey, a popular vacation resort about 150 miles down the coast from Manhattan. Clad in a flowing oriental robe and turban, his skin darkened by boot polish, Kokum announced that for only a small admission charge, members of the public could see him produce 'supernormal' writings on ordinary playing cards when these were pressed against the forehead of a 'receptive' sitter. One such message, he insisted, bore spirit tidings from the late President Lincoln. Later in the demonstration Kokum went on to flourish a small slate blackboard and place this on the ground hidden from view by the patterned lace cloth covering his table. When he retrieved it a few moments later, the board displayed a message – generally some Delphic phrase along the lines of 'Love of money will ruin a man' – allegedly brought from the beyond. Kokum's audiences seem not to have countenanced the possibility either that the cards might have been pre-prepared, or that the slate writing owed more to the clever manipulation of tiny pieces of chalk gripped between the medium's toes than to any divine agency. The *New York Times* reported on 4 September 1922 that Kokum's last performance of the season had ended in some disarray, when rival groups of sceptics and believers had begun to pelt one another with 'assorted light refreshments', the scene 'fast becoming a bedlam'. In the ensuing confusion, 'the splendidly garbed master of ceremonies had himself taken on a wraithlike aspect, and simply vanished into the ether'.

Despite Frederick Greene's prediction, Lustig modestly insisted that after giving the matter due consideration he was not inclined to run for political office. Even so, in October 1922 the progressive-minded *Brooklyn Times-Union* dispatched a writer to interview the man described as 'Charles Gruber, proud émigré to these shores from his native Austria', who had recently made a stirring Columbus Day speech in Scandinavian Hall on the 'restoration of our nation's post-war health and vigor'.[*]

Receiving the press in an 'elegant frock coat and a black skull-cap, giving him the solemn aspect of a French Renaissance prelate' (while simultaneously distancing him from his recent role as an end-of-the-pier New Jersey mystic), Lustig announced gravely that 'nothing could be further from my thoughts than the possibility or the desirability of campaigning for high elected status'. This was probably true, because just three weeks later, as Robert Duval, he was moving briskly around the Kansas City area serving as a broker for what the indictment called 'crooked whiskey' by marshalling the efforts of 'distillers, rectifiers, and gaugers, plus corrupt men in the Treasury Department and Bureau of Internal Revenue'. Again compelled to hurriedly leave town, Lustig relocated some 200 miles south to the small farm community of Springfield, Missouri, temporarily leaving his wife and young daughter behind in New York. For an immigrant who already had half a dozen criminal charges to his name in his adopted country, it must have been a relief to find refuge from his own reputation in the sleepy Midwest hamlet nestled among the lush green forests and clear, fast-moving streams of the Ozark foothills.

Lustig lost no time in exploiting his anonymity and presumed respectability among his new neighbours. On the crisp Monday morning of 30 October 1922 a neatly dressed man describing himself as 'T. Robert Roebel', president of United Chemists, Inc., of New York walked into the sparsely furnished one-room office of Springfield's American Savings Bank. Aside from his appearance and apparent business credentials, the visitor had several other traits

---

[*] Despite his various shows of patriotism over the years, Lustig felt no compulsion to ever formally apply for full US citizenship. He remained what the immigration authorities called a 'landed alien'.

that would have inspired confidence in the typical semi-rural bank official of the day. He was – or at least seemed to be – a stickler for the truth, remarking to Mr Marchand, the branch manager, that he was in town to purchase land for a new chemical works, having been disappointed by the terms offered to him for a similar venture in nearby St Louis. 'Roebel' went on to add that he had already spent many years travelling the country from coast to coast in order to establish a chain of more than a dozen such plants, and that in all his long experience in the field the present location seemed to him to be the most ideal – 'both for its natural setting, and the presence of ready capital and sound business judgement' as represented by the institution in which he now found himself. From listening to this eulogy, one would have thought the speaker was a grey, reverend businessman with decades of real estate experience behind him, whereas Lustig, the late fugitive seaside clairvoyant, had just turned 32.

Before long Lustig, the trusting Mr Marchand and an equally credulous Springfield city official were strolling through an ill-smelling expanse of neglected swampland on the edge of town, which the distinguished party from New York declared would be perfect for his new business premises. After some cursory nego-tiations, the three men agreed on a cash price of $10,000. Lustig said that he would return to the bank in the morning to sign the papers, and in the meantime he agreed to host a hurriedly convened meeting of Springfield residents held in Casper's Chili Joint downtown to give them the good news that up to 400 new jobs would be coming their way, a significant boon in a town of only 18,000.

Lustig further endeared himself to his audience by providing them with a hot meal fortified by cups of what the reporter from the local *News-Leader* described as 'explosive-grade coffee'. Asked by one sceptic about his long-term plans for the factory, Lustig said: 'I state unqualifiedly that reports circulated in the press and elsewhere that the hard-working male citizenry of this burgh, or any member of it, might in any way be incommoded or upset by this enterprise, are false.' On this last count Lustig was probably sincere, for what he envisioned was less a scam directed against individual Springfield residents than against their town's premier savings bank, although it could be argued that his scheme ultimately affected all parties impartially.

When Lustig returned to the offices of the American Savings Bank in the morning, he brought with him a $20,000 Liberty Bond, roughly the size of a broadsheet newspaper, which he unfurled with some ceremony on the desk in front of a suitably impressed Mr Marchand and his head cashier. Lustig explained that he had nothing smaller on hand, and that perhaps the bank could oblige him by letting him have his $10,000 change in cash. Not unreasonably, Mr Marchand first examined the instrument carefully, finding it to be 'completely in order'. At that point, the bank manager placed the bond in an unlocked drawer of his desk, and walked across the room with his cashier in order to retrieve the necessary paperwork for the land transaction they were there to conclude, as well as their client's $10,000. Lustig then pocketed the cash and was on the point of signing the papers when what was described as a 'terrible alteration' suddenly came over him. As Mr Marchand later put it, in an instant his face became 'flushed' and 'bloated', his whole body 'violently convulsed', and he seemed to grow alternately 'lucid and delirious', calling out hoarsely for a glass of water. The bank manager later insisted that he had then left his guest unattended for only 'ten or twelve seconds' while he walked quickly to and from a sink situated behind a wooden partition in a corner of the room. When he returned, '[Lustig] drank the proffered glass of water at a gulp, and then thanked me, saying that, while greatly improved thanks to the restorative, he would nonetheless prefer to rest a while in his hotel before returning to conclude our business later in the afternoon'.

But Lustig did not go to his hotel. Instead he walked swiftly around the corner to a waiting cab and instructed the driver to take him to Springfield station. A short time later he was on the fast train east to St Louis, wearing a nondescript workman's cap and overalls and further disguised by a rather grubby walrus moustache. He looked nothing like the smooth Wall Street operator who had circulated among the public of Springfield during the previous twenty-four hours. It was later discovered that he had used the few seconds that he was left alone at the bank, while apparently in extremis, to lift his original $20,000 Liberty Bond (which was genuine enough) from the manager's desk drawer. There never was any such organisation as United Chemists, nor a 'T. Robert Roebel' known anywhere in New York financial circles. Lustig had shown a handsome $10,000 profit for his day's work.

Another man might have taken the money and disappeared with his family to some faraway part of the world. But most men lacked Lustig's cavalier approach to life. He was arrested while hiding in plain sight in New York on 13 November 1922 and returned to Springfield on a charge of defrauding the American Savings Bank, 'in so do[ing] both depleting that institution [and] placing its public under the shadow of communal financial ruin'.

Although the prosecution seemed to have an airtight case, it may have underestimated the stubbornness and tenacity of the defendant. The same mind that had created United Chemists and dozens of other such entities over the years was soon actively engaged in raising a torrent of procedural objections and tactical delays as the criminal proceedings against him dragged on at intervals through the winter. A virtuoso of evasive testimony, Victor turned the spotlight on his accusers. It later emerged that the bank's Mr Marchand had entertained many previous investors to his area, and had been in the habit of pocketing a small cash commission from each of them for his troubles. With the moral waters muddied in this way, Lustig was eventually able to propose that he return $2,800 of the pilfered $10,000 – all that remained, he told the court – and in April 1923 the government accepted this formula as resolution of the matter.

In his implacable quest to separate people from their money, Lustig soon returned to his currency printing device, or 'Rumanian Box' as some American law enforcement officials dubbed it in homage to its creator's central European roots. The new, more ambitious version of the machine was an elegant, mahogany affair with an enhanced series of highly polished brass knobs and dials. As James Johnson of the US Secret Service said, 'It was so beautifully and painstakingly crafted that its very appearance promised something remarkable.' In time Lustig upped the scale of the basic con by withdrawing a thick pile of sequentially numbered $100 bills from one of the several New York-area banks where he kept an account. His daughter Betty remembers:

> At home or in a locked hotel room, equipped with a razor blade, a bright light, a special ink and pen, egg white, white gloves and a green visor, he would set to work changing the serial numbers on each bill, [so] that all of them would have the same number. This was the come-on to point out to his customer the perfection of his machine's copies. Because all the numbers on the bills were the same after Victor's doctoring had taken place, the buyers thought that they were duplicate notes which the money box had made and which my father assured them they could redeem at any bank; for bank tellers never took time to look at individual numbers. But he would caution the buyer not to cash more than one bill at the same window just to be safe.

As a small child, Betty would recall sitting up late at night with her father, patiently helping him to get just the right consistency to his egg-white solution, sometimes holding his engraving pen or razor blade for him while he sat hunched at his desk like a medieval scholar poring over his scrolls and manuscripts. It was an unusual form of parental bonding, but Betty took it all in her stride. As a young girl she had the finest clothes, a pet Chihuahua named Togo and a chauffeured car to take her to school. When a suitably awed classmate once asked her, 'Whatever does your father do for a living?' she answered innocently, 'Why, he is in money.'

Lustig soon took his portable cash machine on the road, selling it to two businessmen in Chicago for $10,000 each, to a Kansas City banker for $22,000, and to a pool hall owner in copper-rich Butte, Montana, for the truly fabulous sum of $46,000. Victor's lengthy police file shows that he was arrested later that year in San Francisco under his alias of Charles Gruber 'for possession of money-making outfit [and] as a suspected pickpocket', though once again his courtroom skills rose to the occasion. 'Writ Habeas Corpus granted and prisoner discharged', the file adds.

Although Lustig took genuine pride in the essential evenhandedness of his crimes – Midwestern bankers or Viennese drifters, the marks were all as one to him – he did sometimes act out of personal pique. In early 1923, Victor's chauffeur Tony fell foul of a notorious Chicago hoodlum named Olin Starkey. According to Betty Lustig, this individual was the 'produce king of the city … His wagons combed the streets, selling tomatoes and other goods which farmers brought him every morning. Buying at a pittance and selling at a 100 per cent profit made him the king of hucksters. Loud mouthed, crude and boastful [if conversely well-educated] he personally oversaw the departure of his produce trucks each day and exacted a complete accounting when they came back.'

One snowy January night, Starkey had been engaged in a street brawl with a business competitor, and, seeing this, Lustig's chauffeur had somewhat impetuously leapt out of his car to intervene. The two warring fruiters had promptly fled the scene, leaving the police to arrest Tony, who was found to be in possession of a knife. In time Lustig was able to bribe the presiding magistrate in the case, and the charges were dropped. But that wasn't the end of the matter. A day or two later Victor was back in his current suite at Chicago's Drake Hotel, where he complained to his wife that his chronic sinus infection had returned and that he wanted his nose cauterised again, no matter how dire the procedure. 'I don't feel any more pain,' he said, adding as an afterthought, 'Pain is meant to make a man *hard.*' He proved it a minute later when he turned to read an article in the morning *Chicago Tribune* touching on Olin Starkey's business activities. 'This man is nothing but a *schurke* [bully],' Victor said, tossing the paper aside. He vowed to 'tear out this cancer by the roots', then reviled Starkey for his cowardice. 'He at least should have stood his ground when our friend met him. He ran away screaming like a little girl.'

Twenty-four hours later, Lustig was ensconced in another hotel room across town, demonstrating to Starkey and some of his associates the latest model of the Rumanian Box. He had used his brother Emil to lure the grocery mogul to a meeting. Posing as a potential wholesale customer, the younger Lustig had happened to remark that he was comparatively flush with cash just then, before adding conspirationally: 'There is a machine of the most wonderful sort – a bank, really, financing those lucky enough to possess it, continuously pouring out large sums of money for a modest one-time investment.'

It was a simple but effective pitch, and Starkey duly rose to the bait. Emil's revelation that the machine had recently been modified to produce 'literally dozens' of high-denomination bills at regular intervals, rather than just one at a time, did not dampen the mark's enthusiasm. 'I never knew anyone to swallow a line as quickly as Starkey,' Emil later wrote. 'He seemed almost to fly with me to our rendezvous.'

Clearly, by 1923 Lustig was not merely an accomplished con man. He was a master puppeteer, adroitly manipulating his marionettes, with the strings artfully concealed. When Starkey appeared at the hotel to inspect the miraculous cash-making device, Lustig at first feigned reluctance to sell it to him. He was not in the business of randomly circulating crude counterfeit bills, he remarked with some emphasis. Instead, statesmanlike, he treated Starkey to a scholarly *tour d'horizon* of matters such as the newly created Federal Reserve's concept of the nation's money supply, and how this was currently marred by the recent rise in key interest rates and the concomitant fall in investment, with lowered stock prices and disinflation the inevitable result. Seated behind a large mahogany desk and wearing a neatly tailored black suit, Lustig must have seemed less like an itinerant huckster and more like a sober-minded Wall Street financier who modestly advanced his cash box as a legitimate aid to the nation's economic wellbeing.

Despite Lustig's 'occasional European vulgarity', Starkey later wrote of his host that 'he had that sublime self-confidence that speaks in a quiet voice. He produced [the box] most guardedly, and assured me that he was determined to strictly control the number of such devices in circulation, the better to calibrate the combined total of cash and demand deposits then in currency, but that after giving the matter careful thought he was prepared to sell me one for a nominal sum.'

The result was that, a machine having been produced and in due course dispensing a series of $100 bills to Starkey's satisfaction, the supposedly hard-nosed Chicago wise guy paid $50,000 ($1.3 million today) for a small wooden crate that was in reality worth a dollar or two as scrap. When asked for specific operating instructions, Lustig again mentioned the all-important point about the operator needing to wait a minimum of six hours in between each individual transaction, stressing that anything less than that would be to jeopardise the machine's delicate inner mechanism. Other than that, he again restricted himself to general economic platitudes and replied in brief, opaque terms only to urge Starkey to be a conscientious guardian of his truly miraculous new prize. At that the mysterious alchemist was gone. Henceforth Starkey's wealth would be limited, so he believed, only by such tactical self-restraint as he might wish to apply.

Lustig meanwhile quickly collected his wife and daughter from their suite at the Drake Hotel, summoned his Rolls-Royce and relocated back to Kansas City. In time Starkey hired a hitman and paid him $2,500 to whack the individual who had introduced himself merely as 'D.R. Crissinger' of Ohio. This latest fee only added to his already steep losses in the matter, because no one of that name ever came to light. Starkey soon claimed to have forgotten about the whole affair, perhaps preferring not to dwell on an incident from which he himself seemed to emerge with so little credit, although he might have been reminded of it when President Warren Harding later tapped a political donor hitherto known chiefly in Midwestern banking circles to serve as the chairman of the Federal Reserve Board, with direct responsibility for regulating the nation's money supply. The new appointee's name, Starkey may have noted, was Daniel R. Crissinger.

Lustig must soon have tired of Kansas, because later that spring he was arrested under the name 'George Shobo, secretary' in downtown Los Angeles. It was yet another mask from within his capacious internal wardrobe. The police blotter read: 'Charged bunco – Reduced to vagrancy same day; bail forfeited. NOT WANTED.'

In the autumn of 1923, as Lustig took his miracle money box with him on another extended tour of the American west, he met a 43-year-old displaced southerner, of French descent, impeccably clad in a frock coat and top hat, named Robert Arthur Tourbillon. Tourbillon, who went under the sobriquet of 'Dapper' Dan Collins, seems to have polarised the opinion of those who knew him. A blackmailer and shakedown artist, as well as a lover on the Valentino scale, he had an extensive business resumé, ranging from selling soap to running bootleg liquor on to remote Florida beaches at night by way of a fast cabin cruiser that he piloted while wearing his customary nautical uniform of white flannels, a blue blazer and yachting cap. A distinctly foppish gangster with a head of peroxide blond hair and a wide smile like that of a model in a toothpaste advertisement, Collins could repel as well as attract. James Johnson of the Secret Service, for one, saw him as the prince of darkness, evil incarnate. A few years later, while dictating a passage that he called 'The Men Without Morals' for his memoirs, Johnson had this to say of Dapper Dan:

> He was bright enough, but not too bright … At 15 he ran away from home and joined a circus, where he was given the job of lion tamer. He achieved such a sadistic pleasure from tormenting the animals that the rest of the troupe grew to despise him and gave him the nickname 'Rats' … Later he became a front man for a counterfeiting ring, ran a white slave racket, and played the transatlantic boats as a gambler. But there was a flaw that prevented him from ever getting to the very top – he was a double-crosser. Since he was so attractive and cosmopolitan many wealthy women fell in love with him and he did not hesitate to blackmail even them. He'd take them to a hotel room, then have a flunkey break in and pose as a detective … The mortified women, usually married, would of course pay up to avoid a scandal. Dapper Dan played both ends against the middle.

Set against this poor opinion, Lustig thought Collins a 'very capable, clever fellow' who, like him, had emerged from his numerous brushes with the law virtually unscathed. He was also unusually versatile in the sheer range of his crookedness. By 1923, Collins had been investigated, but not charged, in at least three murder cases and had recently pulled off an audacious scam that had netted him some $8,000 ($200,000 today) for an hour's work. One sultry July afternoon he'd been relaxing with a lady friend on a yacht moored in the harbour at Hueneme, between Los Angeles and San Francisco, when a squad of convincing-looking policemen burst in on them. The lead officer had gone on to mention the Mann Act, a law that then made it a felony for even a consenting couple to cross a state line for the purpose of having sex, and the woman, who happened to be both married and domiciled in New York, had quickly decided to hand over her cash and valuables rather than face arrest. The 'police' were, of course, Collins's confederates, and later that evening they divided up the spoils between them, half for him, half for his accomplices.

Lustig was far too shrewd an operator to ignore the obvious advantages of an associate who was plausible, experienced and completely unscrupulous. 'A wonderful character … a gentleman of romance, cool and smooth as ice,' he wrote appreciatively in his journal, before going on to suggest that they pool their resources. He seems to have been further impressed that Dapper Dan had retained the services of New York's William J. Fallon, the 'great mouthpiece', as his personal attorney. Collins once scammed even Fallon. He stole a sheet of the lawyer's headed stationery and used it to extort $4,000 from a vulnerable client.

By way of a warm-up exercise, Lustig engaged Dapper Dan to bilk a banker in Topeka of $15,000, or some $400,000 in today's money. The two grifters mirrored each other in their moral contempt for most such predatory American businessmen. At that time the official supervision of funds lent by banks was not very stringent. Lustig and Collins had only to present themselves as local investors seeking a loan in order to open a competitively priced family restaurant in the area. They went to some lengths to stress the very tangible benefits their operation would bring to the cash-strapped public. The banker appeared to care little about providing a community service such as they described, but agreed to the deal once an off-the-books $5,000 cash sweetener was thrown in. As he later complained, 'the absolute charm and apparent propriety of the two merchants' and their 'unfailing courtesy' to him personally were among the reasons that he swallowed their hook so readily. It would be several days until he discovered that whereas his own disbursement of $15,000 was painfully real, the $5,000 bribe consisted of a neat pile of $50 and $100 bills, all of which bore the same serial number. Lustig and Collins had promptly taken the loot back to their nearby hotel room, stuffed it into two laundry bags, dropped them into the arms of Lustig's chauffeur waiting in the alley below, then briskly packed up their remaining belongings, paid their bill at the front desk, got in the car and drove off into the night.

What was it about banks? Aside from the fact that that was where the money was, Lustig had several other reasons for making them a special target. He seems to have taken a marked dislike to the sort of men who, as he later put it, 'sat around a desk, smoking fat cigars and discussing earnestly how to foreclose on a poor working family's home' and felt himself morally justified, if not compelled, when it came to fleecing them. Of course, it could be, and was, argued that Lustig's actions ultimately hurt not only the banks themselves but, these being the days before federal insurance policies, also the communities they purported to serve. 'The Count took the pose of Robin Hood and assumed all the credit for avenging the indigent masses,' the government's James Johnson wrote. 'Such was not his true intent.' More than one individual who lost his life savings in this way later accused Lustig of having ruined him.

On a cloudless Monday morning in June 1924, a man calling himself Baron von Lustig, later described in court papers as 'a dignified, neatly-shod European gentleman, pleasant faced, soft spoken, entirely without ostentation', walked into the modest offices of the Citizens Trust Bank of Salina, Kansas, a community of about 25,000 souls deep in the heart of wheat country. What followed was a close variant of the property-buying scam he had pulled nearly two years earlier in Springfield, with certain new and improved rhetorical flourishes thrown in. Lustig told the suitably dazzled manager who greeted him, one Tormut Green, that he was a displaced Austrian nobleman who had recently been expelled from his ancestral castle by a Bolshevik-inspired mob. He spoke at some length of the terrible upheavals ripping the old European order apart, and how America in its bounty had provided a haven and a sanctuary for tens or hundreds of thousands of unhappy refugees like himself. He quoted the words inscribed on the Statue of Liberty. His voice quavering, Lustig told the banker that all he now desired in life was to purchase a simple farm where he and his dear family might settle, and that he had brought with him a small cache of $70,000 worth of Liberty Bonds – supposedly the pittance he had been able to smuggle out from under the gaze of the barbaric Reds in the old country, but which he had in fact printed himself – to expedite the purchase. Lustig then handed over a single bond for $5,000, which looked sufficiently convincing to fool the professional banker. But the set-up didn't end quite yet. In an act of moving self-mortification, Lustig admitted that he was temporarily embarrassed for ready cash, and perhaps Mr Green could advance him, say, $2,000 against the bond now in his hands? The financier readily obliged, and on that note they made an appointment for the following day to tour several nearby properties lately foreclosed by the bank.

What followed will perhaps fail to shock the reader of a Lustig biography. But it came as a rude surprise to Mr Tormut Green. The two parties quickly agreed terms for the sale of a freshly vacated tract of land. On the face of it, it was a notable coup on the banker's part. Lustig would pay $25,000 in addition to the $2,000 already advanced him and a further $3,000 that now changed hands in the same fashion for a semi-derelict property probably worth only half as much. Mr Green later remarked that it had all seemed almost too good to be true, and so it was. Lustig went on to propose that they finalise their deal not in the bank but in his nearby hotel suite. It was an unusual request, but Green seems to have raised no insuperable objection to it. He and his colleague John Rose quickly consented to do as their eccentric but undeniably patrician European client asked, and to meet him to conclude their business.

When they reconvened at the hotel the following morning, Lustig signed the property deed the bankers brought with them and then unlocked a desk drawer, extracted a bulky envelope, opened it, and fanned out an impressive number of Liberty Bonds. 'Thirty thousand dollars, gentlemen,' Lustig specified, lest there be any doubt in the matter. Then he dropped the envelope back in the desk and closed it. 'In Austria we have a small ceremony that accompanies the purchase of land,' Lustig continued. From a different drawer he produced a bottle of officially prohibited Canadian Club whiskey and three glasses.

According to Agent Johnson of the Secret Service, who later investigated the matter:

> The bankers were more than ready to participate in the old Austrian ceremony. In fact, they participated several times, and since they were already heady with success, the liquor soon befuddled them. At last Lustig indicated the ceremony was completed. He handed them the package of bonds [and] received the deed and repeated handshakes.

By the time Green and Rose had made their somewhat circuitous way back to the bank, sat down at the conference table and begun the pleasant task of counting their money, a further hour may have passed. When they finally shook open the enticingly fat package they had brought with them, Green said nothing, merely stared open-mouthed at the appalling sight that greeted him. Rose was similarly at a loss, for the envelope Lustig had handed them, though apparently identical in every respect to the one they had seen invitingly stuffed full of government bonds, now contained only ripped up strips of old newspaper.

Curiously, Lustig, when tracked down in New York, made no particular efforts to deny his guilt in the affair. But before agreeing to accompany the two privately hired detectives who came for him, he suggested that they should perhaps check back with their employers in Salina. A public trial could raise troubling questions about the soundness of the Citizens Trust Bank and its principal officers, he added. These matters might compromise the institution at a vulnerable moment in the nation's economy and undermine shareholder confidence.

Lustig's alternative formula was that he simply return the bank's $5,000, minus $500 for his own trouble in the matter, and that he never again venture within 50 miles of their premises. Tormut Green quickly agreed to these terms, but then Lustig seemed to have a change of heart and requested another twenty-four hours to think it over. The next day, he wired the bank to say that he believed he was entitled to a full $1,000 compensation, but that he would extend the exclusion zone to a radius of 100 miles in any direction from their front door. Again the bank consented. By stalling, Lustig believed, he pinned down the deal on the most favourable terms.

In general Lustig considered himself a lucky man, and with good reason. Among other properties he had a large New York family home, a fleet of cars, and plenty of time and money with which to travel. He clearly doted on his daughter, whom he nicknamed Skeezix, after a winsome young girl in the popular *Gasoline Alley* comic strip. After five years his marriage to Roberta may have had its ups and downs, but he still had little of which to complain. The one surviving photograph of the couple shows him as wiry and jug eared, with a schoolboyish leer, and his seated wife staring adoringly up at him. Of the two Lustigs, Victor had the dominant hand.

In every scam he pulled, Lustig nonetheless later told a policeman, 'my wife was in all senses my partner'. In time he came to consider her even more than that – 'simply my inspiration and muse'. 'I am madly in love with you,' he wrote at a particularly effusive moment on Valentine's Day 1924. 'I live upon your love – and take pride that you bloom in mind as well as in soul.' These last words are perhaps the most significant. She may have been his muse, but it's clear that Lustig's priority with Roberta was to mentor her, to mould her character into the kind of woman he thought was ideal. He also wanted to protect her from the consequences of his crimes. James Johnson, the government man who had a low opinion of Lustig's morals to begin with, thought that

Roberta was 'really a child' in the marriage, one whom Victor indulged so long as she served the needs of his orderly domestic life and singular professional activities. 'I doubt that real companionship much entered into it,' Johnson wrote.

Finding time between his hectic round of Midwest bank scams, Lustig took his wife and daughter with him on an extended European tour, treating them to a stateroom on the luxurious SS *Paris* on the crossing from New York to Le Havre. Victor seems to have comparatively restrained himself while on board the liner, merely clipping an obnoxious Texas oilman for a casual few hundred dollars one night at the poker table. Betty Lustig would remember that her father had taken her one morning later in the month to stare up at the Eiffel Tower – 'he thought it a monstrosity, and, he believed, so did many other people'. While in Paris the family and their maid took three adjoining rooms in the elegant Hôtel de Crillon, the scene of Lustig's pre-war role as 'Count Otiok'. Although still just 2½ years old, Betty would apparently remember that Victor:

charmed his three female companions one night by reading us beautiful poems he himself had composed … He turned down the lamps till the room was almost dark, then settling in a beautiful red damask armchair he began to recite those wonderful lines in the most melodious of voices … Even as a small child you hardly dared to draw breath lest the magic spell be broken.

The only cloud on the horizon seems to have been Roberta's continuing sense of unease about her husband's relations with other women. There was some validity to her suspicions, and she often reacted to these real or supposed infidelities in dramatic fashion. Once, while walking down New York's Fifth Avenue, Roberta became distraught over the number of 'young hussies' whom her husband acknowledged by courteously raising his hat and had to hurry back home with a sudden migraine. On another occasion, when Victor mentioned in passing an attractive woman he happened to have noticed on the SS *Paris*, she flew into a fit of jealousy so intense that it led to a full-scale epileptic seizure.

There were more serious moral transgressions than this on Lustig's part. In fact, he once remarked to a trusted friend that 'Venus has been kind to me', and that as a rule he preferred '*balcon* [busty] ladies with rosy cheeks' who were cheerful, willing and not too intellectually exacting. The list of his partners came to include both his Philadelphia brothel keeper friend Billie Mae Scheible and more than one of her employees. Roberta was understandably horrified to once find a book full of nude photographs – evidently a sort of menu of Scheible's available staff – tucked away in a drawer of her husband's desk. Lustig justified the matter to his wife as being no more than a professional resource. 'There is nowhere better to find a mark than at a madam's,' he explained. 'The girls are the best people in the world to point out such a man to you. They know them all.'

Even so, there was no such ready explanation for Lustig's infatuation with the popular American singing star Ruth Etting. Blonde and pert, Etting would hit the big time with her role in Flo Ziegfeld's *Follies of 1927* on Broadway, for which she was paid just $6 for each of her 147 consecutive performances. Whatever else could be said of his behaviour, it took courage for Victor to step out with this particular character. In fact, the affair might be said to represent an almost suicidal risk on his part. Born in Nebraska in 1896, Etting had migrated to the comparatively bright lights of Chicago, where she found work as a chorus girl in an artistically undemanding revue at the Marigold nightclub. While employed there, she met the notorious gangster Martin 'Moe the Gimp' Snyder, who came to take a close interest in her future career. Etting married Snyder on 17 July 1922 in Crown Point, Indiana, where coincidentally Lustig was hauled off to the cooler a few years later. She wrote that she had taken this step 'nine-tenths out of fear and one-tenth out of pity'. Etting told friends, 'If I leave

Ruth Etting in her Ziegfeld *days.*

him, he'll kill me.' Her fears were not entirely unfounded, because
some years later Snyder forced his way into his then-former wife's
Los Angeles home and put a bullet in his successor. He was found
guilty of attempted murder but served only a year in jail, living
long enough to see himself depicted by James Cagney in the 1955
film *Love Me or Leave Me*. Snyder was dissatisfied with his screen
portrayal and promised to 'whack' Cagney accordingly, although in
the event the latter died in his bed at the age of 86.

One way or another, then, the Lustigs' marriage became an
increasingly stormy affair. Victor was out walking in New York one
morning at the height of his friendship with Ruth Etting when he
saw Roberta approaching him behind the steering wheel of the
new Model T he had just bought her. When they were a few feet
apart, Roberta twisted the wheel so violently to one side that her

husband had to jump back into a doorway to avoid being knocked over. As Roberta drove off she shouted over her shoulder that on their next meeting she would slit his throat, and perhaps wisely Victor found it best to spend several weeks after that attending to his business affairs out of town.

One of Lustig's haunts in the autumn of 1924 was the newly opened Mount Royal Hotel in downtown Montreal. While there he was laid low either with a severe case of flu or possibly a recurrence of his lifelong sinus troubles. A local doctor, informed that his patient was a Wall Street broker, advised him to rest, eat simply, avoid alcohol and shun all but the most urgent business matters. These traditional remedies worked like a charm, and by the end of his month-long stay Victor felt well enough for a little light criminal activity. Discovering that one of his fellow guests at the Mount Royal was a Vermont bank president named Linus Merton, Lustig first relieved Merton of his wallet and then returned it to him intact the following day, claiming to have found it lying in the hallway. It was not difficult for him to win over the man's confidence from that point, and only a day or two later Merton found himself in another one of those phony off-track betting establishments, listening to an apparently live race broadcast actually being made up by one of Lustig's lieutenants in the back room. He lost $40,000 and left town a broken man. Lustig seems to have regarded it all as a relatively innocuous bit of mischief on his part. It's possible he even saw himself as a moral avenger in the matter, having learned from the Mount Royal's bell captain that Merton was in the habit of visiting the hotel three or four times a year, accompanied by a different wife on each occasion. Perhaps wary of the reception waiting for him from his own spouse, Lustig did not hurry back to New York. His police file shows that on 19 December 1924 he was picked up as 'Victor Gross' in Chicago, for what was described only as a 'con game'. The file notes simply: 'Released'.

In general, Lustig did an excellent job at avoiding the personal consequences of his crimes. In the five years beginning on

1 January 1920 he'd been arrested at least eight times, and had spent only a handful of days behind bars. After enjoying a family Christmas in New York, he was pulled in once more by the police in suburban Chicago in January 1925. Charged under the name of Albert Grauman for kiting $10,175 in homemade Liberty Bonds, the file again tersely ends: 'Freed'. In later years Lustig liked to claim that he had sawn through the bars of his Crown Point jail cell while in custody, and that the authorities had been too embarrassed to pursue the matter any further. More than one subsequent newspaper report recycled this tale, endowing what it called the 'elusive count' with superhuman powers. It's more likely that Lustig simply paid off a prison guard to let him out. He always carried a large stash of high-denomination bills sewn into the lining of his coat for just such an eventuality. For an FBI agent evocatively named Edgar Poe, a confirmed Lustig hater, 'the so-called Count was nothing but a walking bank … He liked to fix, entice, corrupt the course of justice with a view to enabling him to walk away from any responsibility for his actions … This is the whole story of Mr. Lustig.' In fairness to Lustig, Poe later tried in vain to extort money from him, asking an outrageous $45,000 ($1 million today) in order to 'lose' certain incriminating files in the FBI's possession.

Young Betty Lustig always spoke touchingly of her father, even when she later came to understand the true nature of his work. 'He was in many ways a tender man,' she wrote, describing an individual almost comically unlike the one Agent Poe and others saw as posing such a dire threat to public safety. Lustig spent his mornings at home writing more of his 'divine poems', Betty insisted, and his afternoons playing golf or driving the family out to enjoy the seaside attractions at Coney Island. As an older woman, she remembered Victor chiefly for his Rumanian Box, his exquisite manners and his heroic urge later in the 1930s to bring peace to the world.

Betty's devotion was enduring, but it told at best half the story. Lustig's claim that he had swindled only those who deserved it was an inadequate picture of the whole man. It would be hard to wreak quite as much havoc as he did without a certain amount of collateral damage. According to James Johnson, after the banker Linus Merton left Montreal $40,000 worse off than when he arrived, 'He had to go home to his wife, a gentle elderly woman with a heart condition … When she heard the full story of her husband's unfaithfulness, she left him. And two days later she died.'

Lustig always professed that he bore little or no personal malice toward his victims, and rarely if ever ruined anyone just for the thrill of it. As his domestic life and kindness to most strangers attest, he was not by nature a cruel man, and clearly made a distinction in his own mind between scientifically extracting people's money and sadistically persecuting them. In order to do this, he often made it a habit to first find a character flaw in his victims, whether they be a chronically promiscuous Vermont banker like Linus Merton or a big-city racketeer like Olin Starkey. Once having stigmatised the men as morally faulty, Victor then proceeded with a clear conscience.

In March 1925, Lustig told his wife and daughter that he was thinking of taking them with him across the Atlantic to spend a few weeks back at their old *pied-à-terre* at the Hôtel de Crillon. Roberta and Betty raised no objection to the prospect of abandoning a snowbound New York for the charms of Paris in springtime, and the family duly set sail on the RMS *Mauretania*, bound first for Southampton, on 2 April. Their on-board suite was a virtual 'home on the water', Betty wrote, with a drawing room adorned by daily fresh roses; meals brought in to them by a white-liveried steward, and featuring the finest in silver, linens, china and stemware; and a master bedroom with a marble-tiled bathtub. Roberta, as always, looked forward to the stimulation of travel, and to the opportunity to replenish her wardrobe from among the couture houses of the Champs-Elysées. In her excitement, she seems to have barely noticed that among the family's travelling entourage of six, including a maid, a chauffeur and a nurse, was a neatly groomed and dynamic little spark plug of a man whom Victor introduced as his valued associate and native Frenchman Monsieur Tourbillon, but whom the police back home knew better as 'Dapper' Dan Collins. It turned out that Lustig had in mind a trip that combined pleasure with a little business.

5

FRENCH CONNECTION

A dove-grey Hispano-Suiza H6 saloon drove the Lustigs from Paris's Gare du Nord to their old quarters at the Hôtel de Crillon. Intending to stay for three weeks, the family checked into a quiet suite – a large drawing room lit by Baccarat chandeliers, two bedrooms and two gold-tapped baths, a balcony directly overlooking the Place de la Concorde, and even a secret door concealed behind a sideboard opening on to a private staircase that in turn led down to the jewel box décor of the Salon des Batailles, where hotel guests could sip a reported eighty-six kinds of champagne under a gilded ceiling. 'It [was] all a long way from Pratt, Kansas,' Roberta was forced to admit.

The Lustigs were delighted with the food and drink, impressed by the meticulous service, and probably flattered by the staff reverently addressing them as 'Monsieur le comte' and 'Madame la baronne'. In comparison to New York, there were one or two minor drawbacks as well. Victor grumbled that the French were always gouging him for his accommodation and other services. In the midst of an unusual April heatwave, Roberta would come to regret the hotel's lack of any American-style air conditioning, and commented tartly in her diary that the water emerged from her bathroom taps 'warm and cherry like, smelling of old wine'. Both Lustigs were 'half amused, half incensed' by the Crillon's nineteenth-century

PARIS. - HOTEL CRILLON, Place de la Concorde, 10. - Le Restaurant   Gorce, édit., Paris

The restaurant of the Hôtel de Crillon.

hydraulic lifts, which sometimes stranded passengers in between floors until enough water had trickled from one reservoir tank to another. But aside from these relics of the hotel's *ancien régime* past, the returning guests had little of which to complain. To again quote Roberta: 'Our accommodations provided most of our needs in the way of comfort, if not all the other malarkey.'

Reunited in Paris, Lustig and his brother Emil took long road trips out through the forests of Chantilly and Compiègne, some-times leaving their car to stroll along country lanes where 'the chestnuts [were] in full bloom, the mountain streams running by clear and fast and ice-cold to the touch'. Roberta, Betty and the maid preferred to explore the high-end shops on the Rue Saint-Honoré near the hotel. In general terms it would be hard to think of more agreeable family circumstances. 'We are having a heavenly time here,' Roberta wrote. 'The hotel baked a pink cake for Betty, [and] have supplied a nice little office downstairs for Vic and his friends to gather.'

The friends included both 'Dapper' Dan Collins and a local connection by the name of Maurice Rosseau. A stern-looking ex-cavalryman with a square face featuring penetrating grey eyes and a well-waxed moustache, Rosseau brought a military snap to any meeting he attended. In some ways he seemed an unlikely companion for Lustig and the rest. So far as anyone knew, Rosseau, a decorated former officer and veteran of the Somme, was now a legitimate Paris businessman. Apparently honest, conscientious and a bit stolid, he did not immediately fit the pattern of Lustig's male friends. He had never been in trouble with the law, nor ever committed a crime. But he soon overcame these defects, falling, like many others before him, into the habit of giving in to or agreeing with Lustig's views and wishes. Rosseau also brought two specific assets with him to the meetings held in the small, soundproofed office discreetly tucked away in the Crillon's basement. The first of these was the fact of his long years of experience working as a Paris commodity broker, with a special interest in the lucrative scrap metal market.

The second of Rosseau's unique qualities so far as they pertained to Lustig was that, while just thirty-nine years old, he was now dying of cancer. He had a wife and two young children, and was prepared to do whatever it took to provide for their future.

Although Rosseau had been reluctant to consider 'anything intemperate, [such as] trusting all to the spin of a wheel in a casino' to raise the necessary funds for his family, he was immediately receptive to the note he read from his old pre-war business associate Robert Tourbillon inviting him to meet with a 'remarkable gentleman' in a private room at the Crillon. On 13 April 1925, Rosseau wrote in his diary: 'Resolved – I shall hear out M. Lustig. We have a reasonable parity of interests.' Looking back on the whole affair some weeks later, he added: 'Everything that happened afterward was simply a continuation of that first encounter.'

On the evening of the 17th, Lustig and his crew duly met with Rosseau at the Crillon, and then went on to dinner at the equally sumptuous Maxim's restaurant. It had been a momentous day in the French capital. Édouard Herriot's centre-right government had fallen because of opposition to his financial policies, ushering in a protracted period of political instability, with the next morning's *L'Humanité* newspaper promising 'The Future Belongs to the Socialists, not the Capitalists'. This particular development would likely not have been to Lustig's taste. Like most con men he was a firm supporter of the upper classes. Apart from the fact that they made the best marks, there was something about their overall attitude he admired. 'The real gentry have this approach to life,' he once wrote to Emil, 'and it's not only to do with where they went to school … It's a sort of *laissez-faire*. They just don't care. The real nobility are almost as hard as the best gangsters.'

Lustig seems to have been pleased enough with the outcome of his first meeting with Rosseau and the others, because nearly twenty years later he still fondly remembered that he and Emil had 'relaxed' later that night at an establishment in Pigalle. 'It was a splendid place,' Victor recalled. 'The main salon resembled the majestic lounge of some great ocean liner, although there was one important difference. Most of the *jeune dames* there wore nothing but their high-heeled shoes. They were, in fact, a commodity to be purchased … It was strictly a temporary diversion, and the gentlemen were assured that they could at all times rely upon the ladies' discretion. I know that I did.'

Even so, Lustig's marriage increasingly seemed to be on shaky ground that spring. Roberta may have been comparatively uneducated, but she was nobody's fool. In January 1925, in New York, she wrote to a Kansas friend named Josepha Gore, '[Victor] has companions whose "spirits" he says are "congenial", though he denys [*sic*] any more warmth than that … I have seen these same creatures mooning over his fine speeches, and realize there is nothing I can do about it, at least for a while, and maybe never, but I sometimes think I shall die of the pain of it all.'

Although there may have been a characteristic touch of hyper-bole to Roberta's note, she was clearly not happy about the situation. As Betty later wrote of her mother:

> She never wanted for anything. Victor kept sums of money in lock boxes in every major city of the United States and Roberta kept the keys. But money did not suffice, she was beginning to realize. She wondered what a normal life would be like.

After their night out together in Pigalle, the Lustig brothers met at least twice more that week with Maurice Rosseau and their other colleagues. On 19 April, a group of six of them sat down for lunch at the Crillon. They were 'formulating the preliminary progres-sion of a proposal,' Lustig wrote alliteratively, and a bit pompously. Rosseau's role was to exploit his local business connections to the syndicate's advantage. 'He knows all there is to know about the waste-metal market,' Lustig wrote approvingly. Clearly some sort of major new caper was in the making. Later that same evening the phone rang in the Lustigs' hotel suite. Picking up the receiver, Victor mumbled a few words in French that seemed to be part of a code. Betty later claimed to have heard her father say '*Le soleil brille*', which struck her as odd given the time of day. Later on she listened as her parents loudly debated the matter in the next room. Lustig had apparently announced that he had to go out to work, and his wife had not unreasonably enquired who, exactly, he proposed to meet at that time of the night. Roberta had become enraged, picking up a heavy antique writing slope and throwing it on the floor. One or other of the Lustigs had then seemingly thrown a glass of red wine at the other one, hitting the white wall of the family's living room.

On 23 April, Lustig met Rosseau and another business associate for lunch at the popular Dingo American Bar and Restaurant on rue Delambre, a mile or so south of the Crillon. It was another example of his Zelig-like ability of managing to appear at some of the most seminal moments of twentieth-century social or political history. 'Very interesting tribe of artistic persons present,' Victor wrote to his sister Gertrude, who had now also settled in America. 'Bought them all champagne.'

Although Lustig didn't name the artists in question, we know from Ernest Hemingway's memoir *A Moveable Feast* that he first met F. Scott Fitzgerald in the Dingo one day in late April 1925. Hemingway's recreation of the historic event manages to be both comic and perhaps a little sadistic, portraying the alcoholic Fitzgerald as having passed rapidly from the euphoric to the maudlin and finally to the catatonic stage, at which point *The Great Gatsby* author's eyes had rolled up in his head, his face taking on a death mask expression. A mutual friend reassured Hemingway that Fitzgerald did not need medical help. 'That's the way it takes him,' he said. While we can't know for sure, it's somehow tempting to think that Lustig was present to witness this first encounter of arguably the century's two greatest American writers, the chronicler of the Jazz Age and the hard-boiled creator of the Lost Generation.

On 24 April, Lustig wrote in his ledger, 'We now move on *E*.' Roberta, having picked the lock in order to read this, at first assumed that the 'E' in question was a woman of her husband's acquaintance. But after another bottle of wine she somehow convinced herself that it referred to Émile Loubet, the former president of France. Although retired from public life, Loubet, she had heard, was the force behind a major new commission set up to coordinate the efforts of the Western powers against currency counterfeiting. Delving further into her husband's diary, she came across the same two letters repeated on consecutive pages: TE. Roberta gave it some thought, and then a phrase materialised that matched the initials: *Tuez Emile*.

If the elderly Third Republic president was really so intent on making life difficult for the world's freelance money-makers, Roberta reasoned, was it possible that Vic and his mysterious new friends might take some sort of direct action to stop the old man in his tracks and thus protect their own livelihoods? Her imagination racing, she couldn't shake the fear that Loubet might be hunted down and murdered right there in her living room. After Lustig returned to the Crillon that night there was another distressing scene that ended with an expensive room service dinner strewn across the floor. When Victor tried to placate her, she became even more irate, pounding her fists against his chest. Roberta wasn't buying it. When Lustig made the traditional male appeal – 'You're pretty when you're angry' – she ushered him to the French window, handed him his coat and hat, and told him he could spend the rest of the night sleeping on the balcony.

Three days later, on the morning of 28 April, the French press was full of the news of the opening of the International Exposition of Modern Decorative Expression and Contemporary Industrial Design in Paris, and, by the time it closed six months later, Expo 25 (as the general public understandably preferred to call it) was judged a major artistic and financial success. The opening ceremony was blessed by a clear blue sky. A fleet of distinctively angular open-top, cream-and-black Avions Voisin saloons – a fashion statement in themselves – carrying Herriot's short-lived successor in office, Paul Painlevé, and members of his government led the way to the main entrance by the Grand Palais on the banks of the Seine. There were pavilions representing twenty-one different nations. The Polish exhibit was one of the more arresting, consisting of a flamboyant glass-and-iron silo-like tower with geometric swirls, perched on a base of wooden cubes and filled with deco statuary and tapestries. The Dutch opted for a huge oriental structure with a gaudy pagoda roof that soared up over the site like a fussily iced wedding cake. The host country, by comparison, restricted herself to a severely utilitarian building made of concrete and steel, with no ornament at all: the interiors had plain white walls with a few cubist sketches and some pneumatic rubber furniture. The British contribution was a stylistic pile-up that combined a traditional twentieth-century red-brick cathedral decorated on the outside with colourful flags and on the inside with expressionist murals and a porcelain ceiling. The Soviet Union produced a suitably austere wood-and-glass box with a vertiginous exterior staircase, while the United States, having 'regretfully misunderstood the true purpose of the event', in the words of the subsequent presidential report, sent only a few privately funded designers, journalists and department store buyers rather than an official delegation. Taken as a whole, the exhibition grounds teemed with towering glass pillars, pyramidical roofs and domes, and rooms filled by a variety of electric-controlled aluminium blinds and radically stylised paintings of jagged heads or elongated torsos bathed by multi-faceted Lalique glass installations that could be made to turn slowly, showering the walls and boxlike, synthetic furniture in specks and splashes of eerie, wriggling light. Although the exposition was somewhat floridly advertised as 'implanting a new heart in all mankind's body', Germany was not invited to participate.

As a result of all this, Lustig again found himself in the right place at the right time to exploit a general atmosphere of social, artistic and cultural dynamism of the sort we now retrospectively know as the 'Roaring Twenties'. There were 15,000 separate exhibitors on hand at the Paris fair, and more than 16 million visitors during its six-month run. They were gazing into the future. A journalist assessing the whole spectacle noted that 'almost everywhere the will to modernism dominates the craftsman [in] an almost total suppression of traditional ornament'.

Although the world's most iconic image of the modern age stood outside the main site, it was not immune to the Expo's festivities. Beginning on 26 April, the car manufacturer Citroën paid for its name to be vertically displayed each night in shimmering blue and white lights that descended some 400ft down the latticework of the Eiffel Tower. Visible over 20 miles away, it was the world's largest billboard. Just before dawn on the fair's opening day, Lustig took his wife and daughter up to the heights of Montmartre to survey the city that stretched below. Victor was very moved. After

The Eiffel Tower in 1925, with its distinctive Citroën display.

a lengthy silence he turned to his family and said, 'It is the most beautiful sight in the world.' At that he lapsed into pensive silence again. In due course the sun came up and the illuminated Citroën sign faded to black. The moment came as an apparent epiphany to Roberta. It was then that she suddenly realised that the curious initials TE might not refer to the 86-year-old Émile Loubet after all, but to the comparatively modern Tour Eiffel, first opened to the public just thirty-six years earlier.

In the few brief, cryptic references Lustig later made to the police who enquired about it, he always said that the decision to sell the Eiffel Tower was just one of those sudden improvisations that came to him from time to time. 'There was no preexisting scheme for this outrage,' the FBI was left to conclude, adding that it seemed to have simply come about spontaneously as Lustig strolled among the bustling crowds at the Paris Expo that spring. It was no more than a straightforward target of opportunity, they believed. There was even a note of grudging respect of the sort often seen in official accounts of Lustig's criminal deceptions. 'This individual's mind is abnormally fertile … [and] he combines assiduousness with an originality and vivacity, no-care-madcap-devil-of-a-temperament that distinguishes him from the common thief.'

On the other hand, Lustig rarely if ever undertook a major criminal venture like this one without first carefully studying the odds. However inspired he was when gazing down from the heights of Montmartre that spring morning, he already had weeks of research behind him. As we've seen, he'd used the opportunity of an earlier family visit to Paris to take his young daughter to inspect the Tower, declaring it 'a monstrosity'. Back in Kansas the following month, Betty writes, 'Victor had a clipping with him that a friend had sent from Paris. It was regarding the Eiffel Tower. It was getting quite rusted, the clipping said, and city officials wondered if it was worth the cost of repairing it … "I doubt if the people of Paris are that fond of the thing",' Betty's father had added after reading the story. The presence in the Lustigs' entourage that spring of the fluently French-speaking Robert Tourbillon – 'Dapper' Dan – also suggests there was more than mere whim or casual opportunism involved on Victor's part.

In fact Lustig was vividly alive to the commercial possibilities of the rogue real estate transaction, having long studied the prior disposal of bridges and other public landmarks in this fashion. When the police finally took him into custody in New York they were naturally curious to search the nearby rooming house that had served as the latter-day headquarters of one of the world's acknowledged criminal masterminds. When they did so they found a scene more redolent of some meticulously well-organised banker's office than any chaotic underground hideout. There was a roll-top desk, and inside it were two neatly stacked piles of paper. One pile consisted of newspaper cuttings about the trials of various individuals apprehended for just the sort of furtive estate agent practices Lustig himself was known to dabble in. And the other one was a list of public buildings for possible future sale. Reviewing the material as a whole, the police were left to conclude that Lustig had been in the habit of carefully examining the first pile in order to avoid any errors made by his criminal peers, before methodically sifting his way through the second pile to select his next enterprise. In the same way, one or two of the investigators came to believe, it was as though Lustig divided his life into compartments and kept two separate sets of moral account books: one governing his generally decorous private life, another detailing his iniquitous criminal behaviour. 'We found false papers, forged documents and the counterfeit currency of six nations,' one investigator later wrote. 'And looking down on all this on the Count's desk stood a framed picture of his kid on top of her report card from convent school.'

Of course, the first real requirement of the confidence man is self-belief. And no one was better equipped in this area than Lustig in April 1925. The stuff almost palpably wafted from him like potent cologne, presumably one marketed under the name of Elan or Zest. He was sufficiently sure of himself and his status that he could even afford to take a lofty view of the numerous imitators who had emerged in his wake, men with tailored European suits and vaguely aristocratic pretensions who, like him, largely went about relieving gullible Americans of their money. 'Count' Boris Dobrzynski, for one, had now been nipping at Lustig's heels for a decade. Like his role model, Dobrzynski, who described himself as a former officer of the Russian Imperial Army, presented his victims with a Rumanian Box, but one with an explosive variant on the standard model. 'He sprinkled the device with a chemical … there was a flash and a boom, followed by fire,' the New York *Herald Tribune* reported. 'By a sleight-of-hand the count transferred all the cash to his pockets in the confusion.' Lustig initially viewed Dobrzynski as both a blatant knock-off and a sign of flattery, although when he heard about him offering discounted Liberty Bonds for sale he wrote indignantly to his daughter Betty, calling it 'indecent, lewd, criminal, filthy, disgusting' – making it sound almost as if it was a perverse sex act that was involved – and adding that it was shameful that another man should filch the fruit of his own labours in this way.

If Lustig later tried to portray his career-defining score in that spring of 1925 as just a sudden flash of inspiration on his part he seems to have conveniently forgotten some of his own prior experience in the field. As we've seen, he'd successfully disposed of London's Tower Bridge for a bargain £2,500 as long ago as 1914, explaining that he was authorised to do so on behalf of the local authority. He would have read of the activities in the same general area of men like George Parker, who sold off much of New York's best-known scenery at the turn of the twentieth century. It's also said that in a five-week period in the early 1920s a Scotsman named Arthur Furguson managed to peddle Nelson's Column to an American tourist before hawking Big Ben to a second visitor and finally taking a deposit from a third for the sale of Buckingham Palace. After that, Furguson apparently emigrated to the United States, where in short order he went on to offer the White House to a Texas rancher on the instalment plan, before trying to sell the Statue of Liberty to an Australian businessman, who promptly had him arrested. Some historians now believe that Arthur Furguson (who shares his initials with April Fool) may himself just be a figment of someone's imagination. The confidence game can sometimes be a wilderness of mirrors. But real or not, the whole idea of the spurious real estate deal tallied so perfectly with Lustig's instincts that it ended up defining him.

Today the Eiffel Tower has about 7 million paying visitors a year. Many more go simply to stand and gaze up in awe at the *Dame de*

Fer, by common consent one of the most recognisable symbols in the world and widely acknowledged as an object of engineering beauty. A century ago the edifice still provoked a lively aesthetic debate. It may have been a 'magnificent, shimmering nocturnal vision', as President Woodrow Wilson had declared on his first post-war night in Paris, with its 'four statuesque legs taper[ing] up into a slender neck where a beacon sent out delicate rays of red, white and blue, illuminating the lawned bridge and babbling fountains below', but in the cold light of day it struck the same visitor as a 'hollow carcass' with its 'strangely unfinished' look that did 'everything to remind us of the folly of human taste' and all in all stood as a 'stark shell that suggests the ugliest parts of a raised suspension bridge, with the added deformity of permanent scaffolding attached'. Other contemporary reviews of the Eiffel Tower were not as good as this one. Even the state president had called it a 'loathsome tin ogre, brutal in its desire to shock and offensive in its ugliness'.

Lustig was well aware of the controversy about whether the Tower was in fact a monument for the ages or a slab of ferrous vulgarity that soared up over the Paris skyline like a gigantic factory chimney. He could hardly have avoided the question, since it appeared with such regularity in the city's daily press at the time of the 1925 Expo. One of Lustig's goals that April was to persuade a small but influential group of Paris businessmen that the Tower was sufficiently unloved to encourage the civic authorities in their belief that they should sell it off. He and his confederates drip fed to their listeners the sort of prevailing criticism – 'physically grotesque', a 'matchstick prank', 'impossible to maintain', and above all with 'no redeeming military or scientific potential, as once claimed' – that suggested the city government would be only too glad to see it consigned to the scrapheap. Like any fable, it could only succeed by inducing its audience to suspend its disbelief. But by this stage of his career, Lustig's powers of persuasion and his ability to put over not only a line, but himself, were beyond dispute. When he informed a room full of hardened Paris industrialists that he was an accredited member of the new administration (it helped his cause that these changed on such a regular basis) on a clandestine mission of state, as opposed to an itinerant Czech American bunco artist, they immediately swallowed the bait.

On the first morning of the play, Lustig sat behind an antique desk in his subterranean office in the Crillon telling his invited guests that the information he was about to give them was of the utmost delicacy. In fact, each one of them would be required to sign a formal secrecy agreement sealed with wax before they proceeded. He was going to talk to them about the high cost of maintaining the Eiffel Tower, Lustig continued, and to reveal in the strictest confidence that the government now proposed to demolish it. He was bringing in an independent financial expert to examine the Tower's books, he added, and to propose a fair evaluation.

Lustig introduced this strictly disinterested assessor as Robert Tourbillon, a supreme French patriot who had fought for his country at Verdun. Tourbillon 'radiates integrity', he assured the room. When Dapper Dan then joined the meeting, he presented each of the potential bidders with an impressively detailed ledger listing the Tower's assets and liabilities. The bottom line was that the monument was attracting around a million paid admissions a year, but was still operating far in the red. Although the government had now reluctantly renewed its lease, he reported, 'it will be a day of intense satisfaction to see the monster's raw components [repurposed] for bridge or railway construction'.

Lustig then opened the negotiations in earnest. Over the next two days he sat down in private session with eleven individual scrap dealers ushered in by Maurice Rosseau. Each meeting lasted for just one hour. Lustig explained to his visitors not only about the Tower's financial plight, with an annual operating deficit of 3 million francs, but also threw in what one half-admiring mark later called a 'generous and amusing history lesson on the subject as well'. As Victor himself recalled, 'The buyers were entranced by what they heard … They knew they were getting not only a good deal, but also the chance to possess a piece of history.'

The Tower was first envisioned as a suitable centrepiece for that earlier Parisian municipal extravaganza, the 1889 Exposition Universelle, Lustig reminded his guests. According to the contract signed on 8 January 1887, the engineer Gustave Eiffel's company would build the 300m pylon – making it the tallest man-made structure in the world – and retain all the income from its commercial exploitation for the next twenty years, at which point it was widely assumed that it would be torn down. The financial challenges implicit in a civil engineering project of that magnitude began at once. President Sadi Carnot's Republican government, which had initially talked about underwriting the entire 5-million-franc construction cost, back-pedalled, offering only 1.5 million francs. In the end the project cost 7.8 million francs. Gustave Eiffel put up half the necessary capital himself.

Eiffel's tower may have been both a struggle to finance and then to sell to the French public, but it also made a striking theatrical prop for some of the first truly global celebrities at the turn of the twentieth century. The luxuriantly bearded old Indian War fighter 'Buffalo' Bill Cody used the structure as a backdrop to his travelling 'Wild West Show' no fewer than seven times between 1889 and 1906. It was somehow all a bit incongruous, but still fabulously successful with the French public. The Paris *Herald* wrote of one performance:

Colonel Cody's circus entertained us most brilliantly on and around M. Eiffel's iron erection. The crowds turned out in force to cheer the colonel and his galloping cowboys, as well as Miss Annie Oakley, 'Marm' Whittaker, good old Rocky Bear, and the other Indians, Chiefs, braves, squaws, and papooses … The applause became a veritable ovation when, after his downhill shooting on horseback act, Col. Cody and his troupe were presented with a superb wreath of flowers. Miss Oakley unfastened a button of her bejeweled shirt in the commotion, and the colonel was seen in an expression of rapture.

By contrast, the Paris authorities expressed no great excitement when, in 1907, they extended what they called 'the thing's' original twenty-year lease, remarking only that, 'If it did not exist, we would probably not contemplate building it there, or perhaps anywhere else; but it does exist.' It took the outbreak of war in 1914 to prove the higher strategic value that Eiffel himself had long argued for his Tower. The somewhat precarious but powerful radio mast guyed to the summit became an early-warning system for pinpointing nearby German troop movements. At a critical moment late that August, to quote the official French war history, 'this aerial captured a signal from the enemy, whose cavalry was bearing down on Paris, except that [they] had been forced to pause and reprovision their horses – intelligence that helped convince the General Staff that the time had come for a decisive counterattack on the Marne'. Perhaps the Tower enjoyed a more positive reputation as a result, because in 1919, 700,000 visitors paid to ascend to the summit, more than double the pre-war number.

For all that, there were those who never quite took to the prototype skyscraper in their midst, seeing it much like a high-maintenance new family member whom they had struggled long and hard to come to terms with, let alone to love. The former prime minister Pierre Tirard, himself a civil engineer, publicly called it a 'brutish lump'. A few years earlier, the author Guy de Maupassant was said to take lunch each day in the Tower's base restaurant, because 'inside that room was one of the few places where I could sit and not see the hulk itself above me'. Nor was the whole project untainted by scandal by the time Lustig came to take up residence at the Hôtel de Crillon. In the 1890s a long and involved financial storm had blown up over the bankrupt Panama Canal Company in which Gustave Eiffel had an interest. Like the

Schleswig-Holstein Question, it defied easy explication, but the result was that close to half a billion francs of French public money vanished into a tropical quagmire and Eiffel himself was sentenced to two years in prison. Speculation about his finances relegated violent anti-immigrant riots raging throughout France from the front pages.

The Tower itself had soon attracted the attention of various entrepreneurs of equivocal repute, who regularly informed gullible marks that they were authorised to lease them the structure for only a small cash down-payment. From time to time, the gendarmes would have to intervene to break up the ensuing demarcation disputes between these innocent purchasers and those officials actually licensed to collect the Tower's entrance fees from the public. In August 1921 a cashiered former soldier named only Granet was given a police escort out of La Santé Prison, where he had just served eighteen months for fraud. *Le Temps* reported that 'more than forty officers had to hold back a furious crowd composed of investors who had each paid M. Granet around 20,000 francs for apparent proprietary rights to the Eiffel Tower', including, the paper added, 'the authority to rechristen the structure whatever the buyer chose'.

The press could not help but notice, since they themselves had contributed to the fact, that more than thirty years after its construction the Eiffel Tower still failed to enjoy anything approaching its modern popularity. Even those who came to accept and ultimately to grow fond of it often tempered their approval by deploring the coarseness of the post-war culture it seemed to represent. According to the popular gossip columnist 'Rastignac' of the widely read *L'Illustration* – the '3AM' or 'Bizarre' figure of his day – the French people embraced the Tower, in so far as they did at all, only because they were 'wild about the giddy, the unexpected, the gigantic and fanciful'. To him, the edifice looming nearly 1,000ft over the city's rooftops was just a regrettable if unavoidable sign of the times. By April 1925, when Lustig came to interest himself in the Tower, it was still widely regarded as an undeniably bold but at the same time absurd novelty item destined for the scrapheap, and which in the meantime acted as a magnet for many of the city's more outré characters. Among other such entrepreneurs of the 1920s, the Paris historian John Baxter writes, 'The city had no more permanent fixture than the shabby guide who flashed an envelope of pornographic postcards which, once you handed over your money, proved to have been switched for views of the Eiffel Tower.'

Back in his suite at the Crillon, Lustig kept a steadily growing file on the Tower, adding in any newspaper comment he could find on its various scandals and squabbles. Victor may not have been the first party ever to take advantage of such an unmistakable target of opportunity. But he was the only one who now went on to lay plans for such a literally monumental score beyond the resources or imagination of any mere confidence trickster. It was truly his crowning hour, and it's striking to see how calmly he went about his business as he approached his date with destiny. On 28 April, for example, he wrote: 'Escorted Skeezix [Betty] to the Lafayette and other department stores. Bought her a scarf patterned with dainty horses' heads … Proceeded in the sunshine amidst the fair pavilions. Two frosted lemon ices, 4f.' Again, it was as though he really inhabited two worlds: a real but unspoken one of criminal intrigue and a make-believe one of innocent family life that saw him stroll lazily around the Paris fairgrounds hand-in-hand with his 3-year-old little girl. It is hard not to find it poignant.

In general Roberta was not as happy, writing to her Kansas friend Josepha Gore, 'I pray for an end to this position … It agitates my heart for V to be so enchained … It is a daily worry.' Years later, Roberta insisted that her husband had never said a word to her about the specific reason they were in Paris, far less taken her into his confidence about the mechanics of the crime. She admitted to being increasingly bothered by this tight-lipped approach.

Like God, Lustig's ways were mysterious, if, she rightly assumed, not quite as benevolent. It wasn't that Victor fought with his wife so much as he now simply ignored her. As Robert Tourbillon later observed of their Paris visit: 'The Count remained unmoved when a woman's shrill speech was roaring in his ears.'

Lustig did pay attention when on the morning of 29 April two representatives of the police came to the Crillon to question him about some stolen money. There had been an armed robbery on the nearby Rue Saint-Florentin, they announced, and they were interviewing all foreign hotel guests in the vicinity. Lustig disguised any concern he may have felt at this confrontation with the local servants of the law by smoothly producing a restaurant bill that placed his family and him several miles away at the time in question. Roberta and young Betty corroborated the story, and the two gendarmes departed the suite, impressed, perhaps, by its opulence, leaving behind only a brief note for the file:

> We found the gentleman in a large room. He was with his family and a secretary. They treated [us] with courtesy. After lengthy questioning, we withdrew with their [alibi] document in hand … Monsieur saw us to the door with the same cordial gait.

Nonetheless, something about Lustig's demeanour was not altogether convincing, because the officers added: 'It was not considered that he was culpable of the robbery, but we could not have complete certainty of this. There was a sensation to [Lustig's] handshake that emanated evil.'

On 30 April, the Eiffel Tower job got under way in earnest.

Dapper Dan Collins had not been idle during his own extended stay in Paris. After producing his closely detailed appraisal document laying out the Tower's current assets and liabilities, he had quickly gone on to befriend a young woman who worked as a file clerk at the Ministry of Commerce. This was the office that bore primary responsibility for the upkeep of several buildings deemed to be of outstanding national significance, and ensuring they were kept safe and properly maintained for public use. Collins took his new friend out on the town, lavishing her with gifts and attention. She was 'most amenable' to his advances, he wrote in a report to Lustig later that night. The lady's name was Fleur, he added, a slight, thin spinster in her early thirties whose former fiancé had died in the fighting at Amiens in August 1918.

Collins modestly told his new friend that although he happened to own a large estate back home in New York thanks to his good fortune on Wall Street, his real calling in life was as a poet. In time, he shyly recited a few lines of one of his recent compositions to Fleur, and she told him that she was very moved by them and that were they to be published they would surely be enjoyed by many thousands of people around the world. She was right on this last point, because what Collins read to her was his own free translation of one or two of the lesser-known but richly sensual verses by the Greek poet Constantine Cavafy. Soon Collins was gazing deep into Fleur's eyes over their candlelit dinner table and informing her that the face was his experience and the hands were his soul; 'anything to get those *culottes* down,' as he rather ungallantly told Lustig. Things evidently went as planned because on the morning of 30 April, Tourbillon – or Dante, as he now called himself – sent a note by hand upstairs to Lustig's suite at the Crillon: 'Mademoiselle F has strong psychological need for congress,' he wrote. 'This has now been achieved.'

A day or two later Collins and Fleur were having lunch at a pavement cafe on the Left Bank, and after they finished he made a rather unusual suggestion to her. He said that as it was a Sunday, and the place would therefore be empty, he would love to take a private tour of her office at the ministry. Fleur apparently thought it mildly odd, but then he told her that he wanted to know all about her life and how she spent her time each day, so that he could imagine her better when they were apart. When he put it that way Fleur found that she actually quite liked the idea, and soon they were strolling arm-in-arm in the spring sunshine to the rear entrance of a tall, granite-faced building on the Boulevard Saint-Germain, only a mile or so east of the Eiffel Tower. She let them in with a pass key, and as they went up in the caged lift Collins said that he didn't really want to waste their precious time together looking at government office fixtures after all, but perhaps they could find somewhere upstairs to express their great mutual devotion, and she agreed to the proposal. In due course Fleur briefly left him to powder her nose, and in the few minutes she was gone Collins took a sheet of headed stationery from someone's desk and wrote out a few suitable lines of an endearing new poem for her. Fleur was duly impressed. She had no way of knowing that he had half a dozen other sheets of headed notepaper folded carefully under his jacket.

Meanwhile, Lustig himself had not been idle while at the Crillon. With the help of two hotel employees in his pay he had converted another little-used utility room in the basement to resemble something that a state agency might plausibly use in the event it needed to arrange a discreet commercial rendezvous away from its official premises. The walls of the room were draped with special blackout curtains, and two green baize-topped tables, each with a simple carafe of water and a tray of glasses, lined the sides. A plain wooden desk was set up on a low platform at the far end of the room so that the individual seated there could look down on his audience to the left or right of him. There were no flowers or other decorations, although a framed photograph of Gaston Doumergue, the state president, silently observed the proceedings from a lectern in the corner. In due course six sober-suited men entered the room and sat down at the two tables. Lustig addressed them from his dais. The men represented the shortlist of the eleven candidates whom Victor had interviewed a few days earlier. He told them that his esteemed colleague Maurice Rosseau had identified each one there as representing the best of the capital's scrap metal fraternity.

What was more, Rosseau had personally vouched for their discretion and honesty. Each man had now had a chance to examine the accounts of the property in question, Lustig noted, and in addition to this he now handed them in turn a brief statement typed on a sheet of official Ministry of Commerce notepaper:

> I hereby authorise the bearer of this letter to represent the ministry in all matters concerning the civil project hitherto stated.
>
> HENRY CHÉRON
> Acting Director

According to Betty Lustig, all six men were 'driven to the hotel in special automobiles that were sent to bring them', and each was 'hardly able to contain his mounting excitement' as he took his seat. The place cards set out on the green baize tabletops identified them as Messrs Reynaud, Maritan, Castaneri, Gourault, Blanquer and Poisson. At the head table Betty's father looked as a French government functionary ought, with a lacquered centre-part in his hair, a dark three-piece suit and a neat blue, white and red tricolour ribbon in his lapel. He was thoroughly convincing. From time to time Emil Lustig entered the room, bowed to the guests and deferentially placed a slip of paper at his brother's elbow. With his pale, expressionless face, hooded eyes and tight lips, he was the picture of a dutiful civil servant. A bit of an enigma, except to those who knew him intimately, Emil was the ideal disciple. Too bashful and stolid to strive for real power, he was prepared to follow Vic wherever he led him.

Of the six men in the room, Lustig soon narrowed the field to two. Roger Blanquer was a well-established but somewhat temperamental Paris scrap dealer – 'a dormant volcano', one business acquaintance said of him. With his long experience in the industry, Blanquer thought himself the best qualified of the six applicants. He therefore bristled when Lustig instead offered the tender to his sometime rival André Poisson, a quiet-spoken family man in his mid-thirties who had moved to Paris only a year earlier after helping supervise post-war clearance and reconstruction work around his home town of Merville, near Ypres. Bespectacled and balding, Poisson's response to this latter condition had been to adopt a rotating stable of wigs of variable lengths that he believed made him look more dignified, a view not entirely shared elsewhere. We know little of Poisson's inner life, beyond the fact that his wife Mette was thought socially ambitious, particularly when it came to establishing the couple in the higher echelons of Parisian nightlife, and that he was only too happy to now find himself seated in a private room at the Hôtel de Crillon with so eminent a host as Victor Lustig. 'He looked at you and he owned you,' Poisson later mused.

Part of Lustig's appeal to the hapless Monsieur Poisson surely lay in the mask of becoming modesty he adopted in their meetings together. In every way he was the antithesis of the fast-talking hustler with the line in slippery salesmanship. When Lustig oiled his way up and down the stairs between assignations in the Crillon, the staff invariably found his movements as wraithlike as his adversaries in the law did. 'You never saw him for more than an instant,' an employee known only as Theo recalled. 'He was never there, and yet he was always there,' echoed a colleague. To André Poisson, Lustig was a sort of phantom of vast, indeterminate resources who operated largely through surrogates. He was the genial but remote principal who shook your hand and enquired after your journey before turning you over to his associates for the detailed discussions.

It was the well-briefed Monsieur Dante, therefore, who at first assumed the primary responsibility for describing the many attractive features the Eiffel Tower had to offer the interested scrap dealer. Aside from the core 8,000 tons of high-grade wrought iron, there were of course scores of removable fixtures and fittings: 2,500,000 rivets, 22,000 light bulbs, 1,710 metal steps, five hydraulic lifts and all the hardwood floors and porcelain associated with its warren of public cafes and lavatories. He had all the figures. It was only after the various subsidiary numbers were set before the suitably intrigued André Poisson, who seems to have initially believed he was being asked to bid only on taking over the Tower's short-term operating licence, that Lustig himself materialised in the room to make his clarifying announcement: the state was instead offering it outright as scrap. It was a bold solution to the problem, Lustig acknowledged, but something about the serene, level-voiced way he put it – and perhaps also the letter of authority he slipped Monsieur Poisson from the Ministry of Commerce – convinced the relative newcomer to Paris with the parvenu wife that all was well.

It was only at this delicate turn of events that Lustig favoured Poisson with the full force of his dazzling if synthetic charm. He did not linger over the sordid mechanics of the actual transaction. Instead he treated Poisson as a valued business partner who quickly became a friend. It was the little things he now came to do, such as standing at the Crillon's front door, precisely dressed as always, waiting to vigorously shake his visitor's hand. But then that hand wasn't released. Still holding it, Lustig would look into Poisson's eyes and remark what a pleasure it was to welcome his distinguished guest, as if only just now encountering him for the first time. After that he would make some unfailingly optimistic remark about the weather, even should it happen to have been pouring with rain. 'He'd say, "Don't worry. It's going to clear up any time. You see that little light in the east over there? It's going to dry up",' Poisson recalled. 'He never dealt in negative terms. He entertained only sanguine thoughts, and you found yourself being swept along with him as a result.'

Lustig's charm offensive really kicked into gear when, following their latest morning conference at the Crillon, he insisted on taking Poisson out to an extended lunch before finishing up at a discreet place of entertainment he knew in the rue Pigalle. Afterwards, he favoured his guest with gaudy certitudes on the paramount importance of family, and moralistic platitudes about 'always going home to the one you love' that he delivered with the same earnestness he had displayed when sweeping a woman like Sylvia Nenni off her feet, or clipping the manager of the American Savings Bank in Springfield, Missouri.

Robert Tourbillon, who now operated under the double alias of Dapper Dan Collins and the somehow fitting Monsieur Dante, described the friendship that blossomed between his partner in crime and the henpecked young scrap merchant. 'Leaving them together the second or third time [Poisson] came to the hotel, I went outside to see to the cabman and ask him to wait. When I returned to the lobby I found the Count not so much sitting in a chair as reclining in it almost full-length, legs crossed, laughing and joking, the picture of self-contentment, with the hitherto muted M. Poisson also nearly convulsed with mirth. Not for the first time, I could only marvel at my esteemed friend's powers of entice-ment.' There seems to have been what amounted to a moment of epiphany in Poisson's life when, fortified by several glasses of Lustig's champagne, the two men had driven out late one even-ing to stand at the Trocadero and gaze across the tulip fields at the illuminated Eiffel Tower. 'It was early May, and unseasonably cool,' Lustig remembered, 'but our friend [Poisson] was perspir-ing heavily, stamping his foot up and down in delight, dancing almost, celebrating his decision to seize the day. It was really a great expression of joy, the *cri de coeur* from this meek little soul who had now reached his moment of destiny as he looked up at that great structure shimmering with thousands of lights.'

He almost made it seem like it was a kind of privilege to be dunned by him.

This was not Lustig's only act of seduction with the also well-named Poisson, whose watery, rapidly blinking eyes and oddly jerky gait seem to have given him the air of a large fish wriggling into a mysterious but potentially exciting new aquarium. In fact it was all a *tour de force* on his benefactor's part. Over the next few days, Lustig took him on long walks through Paris, showing him the sights. 'This is our secret meeting-room' or 'our bomb refuge' he told Poisson, pointing to some nondescript building apparently in classified government service. There were other little flourishes, too. Poisson noticed how several pedestrians they passed in the street courteously doffed their hats to Lustig, one or two of them then greeting him as 'Monsieur le Ministre'. He invariably replied with a gracious sweep of his hand. Sometimes they had a black Grand Luxe Renault limousine with a small tricolour flag fluttering from a front mount at their disposal. Lustig himself always wore a dark suit, and boasting his own patriotic lapel pin, as well as, once or twice, Poisson noticed, the green and red ribbon of the Croix de Guerre (awarded for 'some small service in the Ardennes', he coyly allowed), he looked the complete French government official of the 1920s.

When Lustig announced one morning that he had been called away to Bordeaux on state business, Poisson went too. They travelled down together in the chauffeured Renault. The 300-mile journey afforded another bonding opportunity, and an official deputation announcing itself as from the local mayor's office met them on arrival. Lustig apparently spent most of the next twenty-four hours tied up in high-level meetings, but before they left town he treated his guest to a sumptuous meal served to them in the private room of a restaurant overlooking the sparkling River Garonne. Back in Paris, they were joined by some other purported colleagues from the Ministry of Commerce for what Poisson later described to an old Merville school friend as a 'wonderfully varied evening' of dining, drinking and the most rarefied discussion, 'interrupt[ed] only by a knock at the door to admit a young lady playing an unexpected accordion serenade'. Her clothing showed an unusual touch. 'It was of the most sparse cut,' he reported in the privacy of a letter to his Merville friend.

By this stage, even some of Lustig's colleagues themselves well versed in the art of the swindle looked on him with unfeigned awe. After their latest dinner together, Tourbillon-alias-Dante, who had initially preferred the candidacy of Roger Blanquer as their victim, was effusive. 'You had him eating out of your hand, Victor. My God, it was masterly … You were right about everything.'

The most gracious of winners, and occasionally also of losers, Lustig modestly deflected his friend's accolade.

'It's still not over,' he reminded him. 'He hasn't been taken yet.'

'You don't think he'll get suspicious, do you? I mean, if he decides to go to the government and investigate …'

'My dear fellow,' said Lustig, recovering his former poise, 'to André Poisson we *are* the government.'

It seems almost absurd today, when a typical 'end-user license agreement' for a basic phone service can run to an eye-glazing 10,000 words, but the contract eventually set before André Poisson in the private downstairs conference room of the Hôtel de Crillon on 13 May 1925 covered just two double-spaced sheets of paper. The essence of it was that he would pay 1,200,000 francs, or around £170,000 (roughly £4.2 million today) by certified cheque, and the Eiffel Tower would then be his to dispose of as he saw fit. There were one or two subsidiary clauses concerning matters such as confidentiality and the timetable for the tower's demolition, but nothing that gave him any cause for alarm. This was a Wednesday morning, and Poisson requested forty-eight hours in which to raise the cash. There was some question of him needing to put his family home on Avenue Montaigne up for collateral against a bank loan, he explained. That was all perfectly acceptable, Lustig smoothly replied. Poisson later remarked that the seller's utmost courtesy throughout the transaction served only to aggravate the final horror of the scene.

There was just one further technical point, Lustig added. The cheque should be made out not to the Commerce bureau itself but to a Monsieur Banchard. It was all to do with the department's byzantine inner workings, Victor explained, adding that in this way the transaction would be immune to any tiresome interference from his ministerial colleague Anatole de Monzie, the Secretary of Finance. He was always careful to couch even the fine print of his deceits as mere expediencies. Poisson again readily swallowed the hook.

Highly impressive as all this was, it was only now that Lustig took the whole affair from the realm of a first-rate scam into one of true genius. Waiting until they were alone, he favoured Poisson with a wry smile and said, 'André, we have one final bit of business that is outstanding.'

In closing their historic deal, Lustig continued, now adopting a more subdued, almost apologetic tone, there was one party who was sadly excluded from the general air of celebration. That individual was himself. Lustig proceeded to make an affecting presentation to his new friend of his professional and personal circumstances. It was not easy serving as a mere functionary of the state, he confessed. Although there were occasional occupational benefits such as the hotel and the car, these were of course strictly dictated by the needs of official business. The life of a humble public servant such as himself was more typically characterised by both penury and the permanent spectre of unemployment. Each time a premier fell, as happened on roughly an annual basis, such loyal assistants as him trembled for their jobs. Even at the best of times they were paid pitifully small wages. Their wives and loved ones lived lives of the utmost frugality. It was a constant struggle merely to put food on the table, Lustig confided. His own small children attended a paupers' school where up to eighty or ninety students were crammed into a malodorous basement room formerly used as a pig slaughterhouse. Sitting on planks suspended between old cradles used for skinning carcasses, and shuffling their feet across an indelibly bloodstained stone floor, the young pupils were confronted by a hellish overhead vista of spiked hooks and an ill-repaired roof that frequently admitted a drenching rain or an icy sleet on winter days. But for the presence of a few electric lightbulbs (and even these were so fitful that the children couldn't read on overcast afternoons), Lustig added, it could all have been a scene out of the most primitive pre-colonial African village rather than a modern place of learning in the heart of Paris.

This poignant recital would have wrung tears from a rock, and André Poisson was suitably moved. It was now that Lustig made his crowning play. In an echo of his deft extraction of a $1,000 convenience fee in the Tormut Green affair, he went on to sheepishly inform Poisson that it was customary on an occasion such as this for a government official to receive a small cash commission. It was a regrettable state of affairs, he agreed, but there it was.

It was a masterstroke. Lustig had judged his man to perfection. Not only did Poisson instantly buy this wrenching tale, it had the further effect of removing whatever lingering doubts he may have had about the whole Eiffel Tower matter. Although a relative newcomer to Paris, he was well aware of the culture of graft and influence peddling that typically surrounded the French state contract system of the day. He had encountered it too often while engaged in the rebuilding operations around Ypres not to realise that it was simply an implicit part of the cost of doing business. 'It was not really corruption,' he later rationalised the matter in an unpublished manuscript. 'These [were] mere routine issues of commerce … One made a small disbursement of cash and matters were resolved the more easily as a result.' It appeared that Poisson had not only expected a suggestion such as the one Lustig made. He regarded it as *usage du monde*.

This is how James Johnson of the US Secret Service, perhaps a shade histrionically, recreated the scene:

> An expression of relief crossed Monsieur Poisson's face and then he threw back his head and brayed with laughter. He pulled out a handkerchief and wiped his face and his neck, and then he said, 'Monsieur, you think I have not heard how one does business with the government? You think you must explain it to me?'

He reached inside his jacket and removed a wallet bulging with bank notes. 'You see?' he smiled. 'I have come prepared … I have been around and I know how things are done'.

Smiling in turn, Lustig duly relieved Poisson of another 70,000 francs, or some £8,000 (£200,000 today) for his poor, woebegone wife and their five shoeless children back in their squalid basement schoolroom.

A day or two later, André Poisson presented himself as instructed for a meeting with the permanent undersecretary of state at the Department of Commerce in the latter's well-appointed office on Rue Bayard. He was there to discuss some of the practical details that would be involved in dismantling a 1,000ft, 8,000-ton wrought-iron structure in the centre of Paris. Expecting only the pleasant prospect of being greeted as a principal partner in an important public and private sector joint initiative, this was not quite what happened. Upon learning that there was no note of his appointment, nor anyone there familiar with his name, Poisson may have had a first queasy intimation of foul play. Eventually an elderly government retainer consented to shuffle out to meet him. Poisson told the man that he was now the rightful owner of the Eiffel Tower, and that he would like to discuss matters such as street closures and other public safety issues before his work crew dynamited the structure. After the laughter had died down, the official told him that the city of Paris and its sub-agents in fact enjoyed a licence to operate the tower at their pleasure until 1 January 1967. He had never heard of a Monsieur Dante, nor a Victor Lustig. A subsequent telephone call revealed that the Maurice Rosseau of whom Poisson also spoke had since moved to a sanitarium in the countryside. He was considered gravely ill, and incommunicado as a result. Perhaps the whole affair had been some sort of pleasantry or misunderstanding, the civil servant suggested, as Poisson reeled back out into the spring sunshine. It seemed the unthinkable had happened: the hardened businessman had dropped over a million francs – close to £5 million today – in an outright scam. He immediately knew that the situation was irreparable. Beyond acknowledging that a Monsieur Laval who fitted the general description he gave them had recently checked out, leaving no forwarding address, nobody at the Crillon could help him. The hotel's downstairs utility room was never used for any guest functions, Poisson learned. When he inspected the area for himself he found it filled only with a janitor's cleaning supplies. Too mortified to go to the police, Poisson swallowed his loss.

By the time André Poisson made his shattering discovery, Lustig had retreated 700 miles east to Vienna. He spent the latter part of May 1925 in the royal suite at the historic Hotel Imperial, where he registered as Robert Duval, a financier of Chicago. He was accompanied by his crew of three, as well as his infant daughter and a maid, but not by his wife Roberta. She had come to the end of her patience with life as a grifter's moll, and now booked a berth on the first available ship back to New York. In due course a new woman entered Lustig's orbit: Irene Kreusch, who had left her home in Munich following the Great War, and embarked on a restless search for material wealth if not social status that after seven years had led her as far as a reasonably lucrative career as a Viennese hotel prostitute. She later wrote that she had immediately fallen in love with the debonair and generous Herr Duval after she went out on a paid assignation with him.

Obsessed with making money and relieving his marks of their own valuables, Lustig remained in some areas of his life relatively normal. He was active sexually: apart from his acknowledged child with Roberta there were thought to be at least two terminated pregnancies among the staff of Billie Mae Scheible's establishment in Philadelphia, not to mention the distressing case of venereal disease later noted by the doctors at the US Prison Bureau. By all accounts, Victor was polite and even rather courtly in his relations with women, at least up to the point of the bedroom door; there is no psychosexual explanation of the lifelong moral turpitude he allowed himself elsewhere. But Roberta, the Kansas girl who had never quite reconciled to her husband's lifestyle as a globetrotting confidence trickster, had had enough. As the couple's daughter Betty would write:

> My mother filed for divorce and, in her pique, she married a Charles Gibson. She regretted it as soon as the ring was placed upon her finger.

The events of April and May 1925 demonstrated the guile and ruthlessness of Lustig as a high-stakes swindler of the first order. He had honed his technique not only for extracting a victim's cash but also for ensuring that no repercussions would ensue. He still had one more trick to play out: the encore, a notion so brazen that even Dapper Dan Collins quailed when he first heard of it.

'We can't sell the Tower again,' Collins told Lustig in genuine alarm. 'We don't own it any more. We've already sold it once,' he reminded him.

Lustig dismissed such petty cavils with an imperious sweep of his arm.

'That may be true,' he conceded. 'But on the other hand, if André Poisson hasn't taken possession of his prize, I think we can safely consider it still ours. Pack your things.'

The result was that Lustig, along with Emil, Collins and Maurice Rosseau once again boarded the evening Orient Express at Vienna's Westbahnhof and alighted early the next morning at the Gare de l'Est in Paris. For once, the 3-year-old Betty stayed behind in the care of a nanny, who in due course accompanied the child on the SS *Mauretania* back to New York. Irene Kreusch was reduced first to speechless apoplexy, and then to inconsolable tears, on learning that her presence in Victor's entourage would be more sparingly required.

On arrival in the French capital, the four men checked in to adjoining rooms at the Hotel Peninsula on the Avenue Kleber, about 2 miles from their old headquarters at the Crillon. Lustig later claimed to have been heartbroken by his separation from his young daughter, although, if so, he put a brave face on it. Later that evening the four colleagues went up to their hotel's rooftop terrace and sipped champagne as they gazed out across the city skyline to the Eiffel Tower, still with its vertical Citroën sign shimmering in lights. To Lustig, it must have seemed almost criminal *not* to attempt a repeat performance. As usual, he paid for everyone's food and drink, tipping generously, and then took his brother off to unwind for several hours at the nearby École de Billard. Victor was an excellent pool player who could have turned professional, but he preferred the adrenaline rush of gambling. He was known to hustle an opponent by playing an entire match left-handed, which he insisted was his natural style. He would lose narrowly, cheerfully pay up, and then bet heavily on himself to win a return game under the handicap of playing with his right hand. One night in New York he made $300 in this fashion, having first taken the precaution of stationing Emil in a car with its engine running outside the club's back door. Although Lustig seems to have restricted himself on this particular occasion at the École de Billard to merely a few friendly frames with his brother, he later wrote to Arnold Rothstein in a curious mixture of the prurient and anthropological that the young lady he had gone on to meet later that night in a local bordel had had 'unusually dark-hued mammilla', and that in his experience this attractive feature was characteristic of women of Shawnee Indian origin.

In the end, Lustig did not quite manage a full repeat performance of his Eiffel Tower spectacular. Although he swiftly identified a mark and followed the Poisson playbook by lavishly entertaining the man and securing his signature on a contract, this time the disappointed buyer went post-haste to the police. As a result Lustig, although successfully banking a further down payment of 90,000 francs, or roughly £250,000 today, was forced to leave Paris more hurriedly than ideal, only rarely to return, thus precluding a possible third sale of the city's iconic monument.

Back in Vienna, Lustig divided up the spoils of the syndicate's Paris spring adventure. After expenses, the four men had about 1,200,000 francs between them. Lustig took half and his three confederates split the other half. With that Maurice Rosseau passed from the scene, although Dapper Dan and Emil would both resurface in future Lustig business ventures. Emil went on to remark with some pride that his brother's current six-figure annual earnings would have 'made his competitors' heads swim'. At the time, the president of the United States, Calvin Coolidge, was paid about $55,000 ($1.3 million today), an impressive salary, but still only just over a third of Victor's tax-free income.

The Lustig brothers' own return ship arrived in New York in the early hours of 4 July 1925, passing directly under the Statue of Liberty as it loomed up in the dawn light while they steamed towards lower Manhattan. The brothers spent that night in the penthouse of a midtown hotel, and applauded as the sky lit up red and green in the traditional Independence Day fireworks display. The Lustigs never lost their professed love of their adopted country, even as they gouged its individuals and undermined its institutions.

Three days later, Victor set off by chauffeured Rolls-Royce for an 800-mile journey over increasingly rustic highways to the small, strawberry-producing town of Dayton, Tennessee. He was there on account of the so-called Scopes Monkey Trial, in which a local high school teacher stood accused of expressing limited classroom sympathy for the principles behind the theory of human evolution, in defiance of state law. It was a major news story, and also one of the first such events to attract the decadent voyeurism of later high-profile criminal trials, with 'oranges and cakes sold as at a seaside fair, and the raucous voices of vendors heard on every side', according to the *Memphis News-Scimitar*. When he got to Dayton, Lustig bluffed his way through a police cordon by posing as an old friend of the presiding judge, John Raulston, and soon set up shop in a small room in the courthouse basement, where he advertised himself as the state's official agent for the sale of souvenir merchandise, which he retailed with the aid of a trained chimpanzee dressed in a straw hat and cutaway jacket. After only a day's trading, Victor had turned a profit of $600, or $15,000 in modern money. He gave the chimp's handler $50, and spent the rest treating himself and his chauffeur Tony to a fortnight's stay at the glamorous new Casa Marina resort in Key West.

There was only one brief interruption to the otherwise idyllic tropical getaway, and that came when two black-suited FBI agents arrived on the premises one afternoon and announced that they were looking for a Count Victor Lustig, who they wanted to question about the matter of some spurious Liberty Bonds that had been changing hands in New York. Lustig wriggled out of an arrest by insisting that he had been travelling abroad for several weeks, and that someone had obviously been impersonating him. The feds bought his story, and to prove there were no hard feelings all three men then went out to Senor Pepe's bar on Caroline Street that night and drank 'Painkiller' rum punches until the early hours.

As Lustig was later to remark back in New York, 'I can't understand honest men. They lead such desperate lives full of utter boredom.'

6

CONNING CAPONE

It didn't take Lustig long to once again fall foul of the law back in mainland America. Evidently he soon felt the old urge to travel, because in mid-August 1925 he made the five-day train journey from New York to San Francisco. Early one warm Monday morning Victor sat on the balcony of his twelfth-floor suite at the opulent St Francis Hotel, watching the first sliver of sun rise above the bay, the only sound the steady rattle of streetcars and the muffled shouts and grumbles from the dawn shift reporting for work at the nearby fruit market. It was an idyllic scene, but it was soon rudely interrupted by the arrival at the hotel's front door of a black Ford Model T with ominous white serial numbers painted on the roof. Lustig watched calmly as four men in dark, knee-length tunics and rounded 'custodian' helmets alighted from the car and filed into the lobby. He immediately knew they were there for him.

While there is no detailed account of Lustig's arrest that day, or of the immediate proceedings that followed, a note in his bulky criminal file reads:

Arr. in S.F., posing as CHAS. GRUBER … Charged as vagrant and figitive [sic] – had money-making outfit in possession, and suspected of pickpocketing. Writ of Habeas Corpus – prisoner discharged.

Lustig, surely one of the few men ever to be arrested for vagrancy while occupying a penthouse suite at the St Francis, was soon back in circulation in New York. We know this because his daughter Betty speaks of him resuming his life there in distressing terms. 'His wife was gone, taking their child [with her],' she writes. 'Life was hard on Vic when he didn't have Roberta to constantly warn him, to tell him when to go ahead and when to hold back. He grew careless and was arrested three times in succession. There were no convictions, for he always managed to pay his way out …'

One way Lustig passed his time was by entering into a joint business venture later that autumn with a still comparatively obscure one-time Chicago nightclub bouncer and boxing promoter named Al Capone. Then aged 26, the bullet-headed Neapolitan roughneck had thus far restricted himself to building up a small municipal empire based on illegal alcohol distribution, loansharking, gambling, prostitution and extortion, with a couple of strictly expedient murders thrown in. Sharply dressed in a variety of tight-fitting pinstripe suits and wide-brimmed hats, with a taste for Cuban cigars and gourmet food, Capone, as he once serenely informed a press interviewer, believed that 'well-directed force is the shortest route between two points'. A psychologist might say that he shored up his precarious sense of self through intimidation, coercion and violence. As a general rule, entering into a business arrangement with Capone – let alone one with the ultimate goal of clipping him – was the equivalent of pulling the pin from a particularly high-powered hand-grenade and then awaiting the inevitable result.

Using their mutual friend Arnold Rothstein as an intermediary, Lustig made a date to meet Capone one snowy late October morning in his office at the Hawthorne Hotel in Cicero, a railroad town located just west of downtown Chicago. This was perhaps not quite the standard professional interview as we would understand it today. For one thing, Capone made the appointment a fortnight ahead of time, but then, apparently in a bid to forestall any monkey business his guest might be planning, brought it forward by a week. When Lustig arrived he was met not by a secretary but by two thick-necked individuals who thoroughly frisked him for any concealed weapons. Their search did not, however, extend to Victor's elegant brass-topped walking stick, which he promptly unscrewed once in Capone's presence to reveal a thin hip flask full of whiskey. This was well received. Capone brought out two glasses and they toasted each other. The psychopathic gangster was justifiably proud of his permanently reserved suite in the hotel. A colonnade of four faux Grecian pillars and elaborately framed portraits of George Washington and Abraham Lincoln flanked a satin-upholstered throne behind Capone's desk, and special bulletproof shutters could be made to leap up and down at the windows. 'Ya never know,' Capone laughed mirthlessly, as he demonstrated this last feature.

He was right. Less than a year later, a rival gang under the control of Earl 'Hymie' Weiss shot into Capone and his entourage as he was eating lunch in the Hawthorne's downstairs restaurant. No one died in the attack, although several innocent civilians were badly wounded. Within a month, Weiss himself would be cut down by a hail of bullets as he walked in the front door of his Chicago office building. He was just 28 at the time of his death.

The details of what transpired that cold October morning in Capone's hotel suite are unclear, due to deficient record-keeping, but whatever Lustig said it was enough to persuade the notoriously hard-headed mobster to invest $50,000 ($1.2 million today) in a double your money scheme. Not surprisingly, he attached certain conditions to his participation. The essence of the deal was that Lustig would return in exactly sixty days and hand Capone his full $100,000 dividend in cash. Although there was no tedious paperwork involved in the whole transaction, both parties were clear about what was expected. 'I don't throw money away,' Capone announced, perhaps unnecessarily. 'When I go into a deal I'm serious about it.'

Al Capone, who actually gave Lustig money.

To illustrate the point, Capone felt under his desk to push a button. When he did so a panel between the presidential portraits on the wall behind him slid open. It revealed a man sitting on a campstool at the controls of a Thompson Type 'C' machine gun mounted on a tripod. The barrel of the gun was aimed directly at the visitor's head. 'I'm that serious,' Capone added.

It's not known if Lustig seriously considered absconding with Capone's money, or if instead he thought he could really double it in the time stated. During the next few weeks he was on his best behaviour. He remained vigilant and sober, lest lips loosened by alcohol provide any pretext for Capone to prematurely put an end to their venture. Lustig spent most of that autumn in a suite at Chicago's exclusive Edgewater Beach Hotel with a young show-girl from Cleveland named Mandy Katz, whom he introduced as his wife. They made a striking couple, strolling arm-in-arm around the hotel's public areas exchanging pleasantries with their fellow guests and distributing gratuities to the staff. The putative Mrs Lustig was pleased with her reception. 'The help are swell to me and are very complimentary,' she wrote. Lustig frequently dispensed envelopes full of cash to particularly favoured employees, and also – so his income tax return insisted – made an impressive gift of $3,500 ($80,000, or £110,000, today) to a relief programme operated by the city's St Patrick's Roman Catholic Church. He was on hand in that same building to celebrate Thanksgiving on 26 November 1925, because the parish register notes that 'Lord and Lady Lustig, temporarily resident in Chicago from Vienna' had graciously hosted a reception following the 11 o'clock morning service.

Perhaps Lustig now had a genuine twinge of conscience, or, perhaps just as likely, he merely drew a blank when it came to thinking up a suitably lucrative short-term new con. Either way, he was back in Capone's suite at the Hawthorne more than a week before the sixty-day deadline expired. The mood in the room was less convivial than before. Capone remained seated throughout the interview, and no one drank any toasts to anyone else. Keeping a level voice, Lustig explained that he had been unable to make good on their investment as he had hoped. He chose the words of his mea culpa with care. He knew that a man was pointing a machine gun directly at him from only a few feet away behind his host's head. No one spoke for some moments after that. Reaching slowly inside his jacket, Lustig then extracted an envelope and laid out fifty thousand-dollar bills on Capone's desk. 'I'm sorry I couldn't turn a profit for you, but here's your stake money back,' he said.

Apparently something about this gesture stirred Capone, because he restrained any urge he may have had to again push the button at his knee. Lustig later remembered the meeting in implausibly hearty terms ('Al offered me a cigar'), but whatever the truth about the encounter, it reflected Capone's personality. In safe hindsight, his malevolence has sometimes been praised as picturesque scrappiness – almost endearing in the way he targeted only fellow hoods, and never picked on the little people – but it often exhibited itself as mere defensiveness wrapped in hostility and tucked inside a tantrum. He was both villain and victim. In any event, Capone wilted in the face of Lustig's apparent candour. After a few moments, he asked him, 'You broke?'

'I find myself temporarily reduced,' Lustig admitted with dignity.

At that, Capone scooped up some of the bills just laid out before him and returned them to his guest. 'Here's five grand,' he grunted.

Lustig left the room at a measured pace, nodding affably to the armed bodyguards who escorted him downstairs to the front door. Although he seems to have decided then and there never to try to repeat the experience, he may have allowed himself a quiet celebration with Mrs Lustig back at the Edgewater hotel that night. Whether acting with premeditation or not, he had just made a patsy of Al Capone and lived to tell of it.

Later in 1925, Lustig brought off another variant of his role as the visiting chemicals tycoon T. Robert Roebel when he clipped the manager of a small savings bank in Manhattan, Kansas. This individual stood accused of widespread duplicity, systematic chicanery, financial gouging, profiteering, exploitation, and in some cases outright robbery of his hard-pressed rural customers. Betty Lustig again portrays her father as a sort of avenging angel when she writes of the Manhattan affair:

> The banker had sent innocent friends to prison for crimes they had never committed, altered records, and misplaced files. He foreclosed on poor farmers ... Victor found him to be an easy mark, ready to listen to any scheme that would make money for himself.

The key to the scam lay in persuading this party to stake $150,000 of his own money in a new start-up bank that, Lustig insisted, would soon be raking it in from local depositors. In fact, he promised, the man would recoup his $150,000 and much more besides in as little as five days. Lacking even his victim's qualms, Victor quickly produced detailed financial projections as well as meticulous architect's plans for the venture. It says something both for the banker's greed and Lustig's powers of persuasion that the former never had the latter's background checked. When the moment came, Victor simply relieved the mark of his cash and left town. Considerations of moral vengeance aside, there's no evidence that Lustig distributed any of the proceeds of his scam to the distressed farmers of east Kansas. Betty would write admiringly that her father possessed a 'deep philosophical knowledge of human nature, and could deceive even those who considered themselves sharp in business'.

Another Lustig characteristic, particularly notable in those days before mass commercial air travel, was how ready he was to move rapidly from one city to another. Perhaps he needed to be. Late December 1925 found him in an old Cherokee settlement that had recently been incorporated as the one-stoplight town of Grove, Oklahoma. Lustig was primarily there to interest the area's leading banker in his Rumanian Box. For once Victor's sales pitch had fallen flat, however, and instead of walking away with a handsome profit he found himself detained in the rather makeshift county lock-up while awaiting the outcome of further enquiries into his local activities. Lesser men might have left it at that, but Lustig got talking to his jailer, one Sheriff Richards, and discovered over a shared hip flask of whiskey that he was not only short of money but had been dipping into public funds to tide him over. After that it wasn't long before the miraculous cash-making device was again under discussion, and the end result was that for only $7,000 Sheriff Richards became the latest proud owner of his private mint while Lustig himself walked free. It seemed like a win for all parties. Six months later, however, Richards burst into Lustig's California hotel room carrying a loaded revolver and demanding a refund. He was now ruined and out of a job, and thus not in a mood to discuss the matter. Even so, Lustig kept his head. He explained that the lawman must have made an error when operating the device, and that he would be glad to correct the problem when he returned to Oklahoma in the near future. Pending that, he handed over $7,000 in crisp new bills, plus a further $3,000 for his trouble, and the two men parted without further acrimony. Some days later, Lustig read that the ex-sheriff had been arrested for passing dud currency, and as a result faced a sentence of between eighteen and thirty years' imprisonment.

This incident may have spurred Lustig to consider yet another change of scenery, because he was back in southern Florida early in 1926. It was a time of delirious real estate speculation in the area. The warm winter air echoed with the clatter of drills and hammers, as, in the words of one historian, 'steel skeletons of skyscrapers rose everywhere to give Miami and the state's other boom cities a skyline appropriate to their metropolitan destinies'. Never one to pass by a golden retail opportunity when it presented itself, Lustig was soon on hand with his Rumanian Box. His latest mark was a voluble New Jersey auto mechanic-turned-engineering magnate named Herman Loller, a man entirely innocent of scruples or honesty. Loller had done well out of wartime government contracts for shell casings, but recent years had proved a struggle for him. In a single day in November 1924 his company's stock price dove perpendicularly from 85 to 19, dragging with it to ruin a number of his small investors. Loller himself was down to his last $40,000 in cash and assets.

While in Florida, Lustig dressed up in a white linen suit and straw hat, screwed a monocle into his right eye, and spent his afternoons sitting in an ornate wicker chair carried down to the beach for him by a uniformed Japanese manservant, who then stood discreetly behind his employer ready to fan him with a large palm or pour out fresh-brewed tea into a monogrammed china cup. Occasionally, the attendant would trot back to the hotel and then reappear bearing a telegram on a silver tray. Each time he did so, Lustig received the message with a bored sigh, glanced at it, and told the flunkey there would be no reply.

It took Herman Loller five days to find the nerve to approach the enigmatic stranger on the beach, and just two more for Lustig to fatally interest him in the Rumanian Box. Some technical exchange ensued over cocktails that the butler poured discreetly into two teacups. It was not the same thing at all as mere counterfeiting, Lustig assured his mark, as the box was really reproducing genuine bills. 'In fact,' he added on a note of unaffected if not entirely merited patriotic fervour, 'I'm doing the country some good, because I am increasing the amount of available currency in the system.'

The nuances of the nation's money supply and such considerations as inflation levels or interest rates temporarily escaped Loller as he eagerly negotiated the purchase of his own mini-treasury. Another $25,000 soon changed hands. Lustig knew he had around six hours' leeway before Loller discovered his error, and he used the time to put as much distance between south Florida and himself as possible. It turned out that he needn't have rushed, because Loller proved a very stubborn fellow. When the money machine at first failed to work, he persisted with it for weeks more to come. Eventually his wife, in a rage of frustration, smashed the box with a hammer. Even then Loller refused to accept the awful truth. 'It must be something to do with the paper or the ink,' he said. 'When I see the Count again I'll ask him about it and then we'll be rich.'

In the meantime, Lustig had parted from his Cleveland showgirl friend Mandy Katz and temporarily reconciled with his ex-wife, Roberta, who had herself hurriedly divorced Charles Gibson. Their daughter Betty insists that her parents had then married for a second time, although there are no records to confirm this. Victor used his recent Florida windfall to take his family back with him to Europe for the rest of the winter. They took in London, Amsterdam, Budapest, Munich, Naples and Vienna, but found it expedient to skip Paris. Later in February, Roberta and Betty went skiing in Switzerland while Lustig stayed behind to visit some relatives in Czechoslovakia. Or so he said. Putting his wife and daughter on the train for Zürich, Victor was touched when he noticed through the window that 'Bertie was trying to hide the tears running down her cheeks'. Whether Roberta's grief was caused by her genuine distress at leaving her husband, or her misgivings at what he might get up to in her absence, is a moot point.

Roberta's worst fears would seem to have been justified when, having sailed back to America ahead of his family, Lustig soon found himself in trouble with the law in the remote logging town of Spokane, Washington. The warrant for his arrest there in March 1926 states, 'Under the alias R.C. Brown [he] did unlawfully, feloniously, and willfully, with intent to defraud and deprive the owner thereof, then and there steal, take, and carry away money and currency of the United States in the amount of $43,500, the said sum being the property of and belonging to one Col. P.F. Doherty.' This followed yet another sale of the Rumanian Box, and it forced Lustig to hurriedly catch the first eastbound train out of town, with Colonel Doherty and the police hot in pursuit. He got as far as Detroit, where in due course he was arrested under the name Charles Gromar. After that, Lustig's police file notes only: 'Discharged'. As in Grove, Oklahoma, it seems likely Victor bought his way out either with another money box, or a stash of genuine currency.

Lustig did not immediately leave Detroit, because on the morning of 11 March he complained of a slight headache and stomach discomfort. That afternoon his pain grew worse, and an ambulance was dispatched to take him from his suite at the waterfront Cadillac Hotel up the road to Grace Hospital, where he was diagnosed with diverticulitis. These were the days before penicillin, so the doctors first drained the infected area and then put the patient on a liquid diet. Although it was classified as 'a procedure' rather than a full-scale operation, Lustig was given a powerful sedative to help him get through his initial treatment. The last thing he said before the surgeon cut into him was 'Where is Skeezix?' and 'Will this hurt, gentlemen?'

Lustig was lucky; he came through without complications, although the doctors issued the usual warning about his getting more rest and exercise in the future. He complained about the $6 per night he had been charged for his private room, but it could have been worse. Seven months later, Harry Houdini was admitted to the same hospital and died there following an operation to remove his appendix.

Betty Lustig speaks both of her parents' rocky second marriage and her father's continuing vagrancy, in the formal sense of the word, when she writes of that year: 'In 1926, [we] were in New York, Chicago, Detroit, Kansas City, Montreal, Boston, London, Cherbourg, Berlin, Munich, Spain and Italy, with Victor running from the law and his wife chasing after him.' Since Lustig actually visited at least half a dozen more places than those on his daughter's list, it's again his sheer mobility that most strikes one. Brief periods at the family's new home in Brooklyn were sandwiched between moves, multiple trips across the Atlantic, and what amounted to a season pass on the transcontinental train as he shuttled around between New York and Los Angeles, with various stops en route. It may have served the needs of Lustig's business, but it was not a good formula for domestic harmony. As Betty writes: 'Finally, [my mother] gave up. Since they now never travelled as husband and wife, she had a difficult time watching him, so she stayed at home to better care for [me], but stretching her jealous imagination to its limits.'

If Roberta's material standards were improving in 1926, her personal happiness was fast deteriorating. In a sense she became a captive. Victor gave her everything she wanted except freedom, and insisted that she have an escort he trusted even when she went out to the local shops. She complained to her Kansas friend Josepha Gore that 'her life was very hard; that Victor preferred to travel alone, and it was very difficult for her, particularly since she knew there were plenty of other girls out there in places like Chicago or Denver and it tortured her to think of what he got up to with them'.

Roberta was right to be worried. Now in his late thirties, Victor showed no signs of slowing down, nor of taking his wedding vows more seriously. While in Los Angeles later that spring he met a 19-year-old woman named Estelle Sweeny who had come west to try her luck as an actress after finishing as runner-up in the annual Miss Peoria, Illinois, beauty contest. Once there an agent changed her name to Stella Swan and got her a walk-on part in an artistically unassuming picture largely notable for its bevvy of scantily clad women. It proved popular enough to then be loosely adapted into a stage show that enjoyed a brief off-Broadway run under the title *Revudeville 1926*. After that, Swan went on to enrol at the Warner Brothers school, where aspiring young actresses became apprentices to the studio; only after years of militaristic training and a series of low-budget 'B' features, if even then, could they hope to break through into the big time.

Stella Swan may have been unusually receptive, therefore, when she met the courtly, middle-aged man who introduced himself as a 'top New York producer' who happened to be in town scouting for talent to put on the Broadway stage. 'There'll be a lot of hard work ahead if you're to succeed,' he warned the wide-eyed ingénue, and she assured him that she would happily do whatever it took. In the slightly prim words of Agent Johnson of the Secret Service, 'That night he invited the girl to his hotel room and in a short time she ceased to be a virgin.'

The next stage was for Lustig to take Stella with him to Havana, then an entrepôt and playground for wealthy vacationing Americans something like today's Las Vegas, if with a better dress code and less low cultural prurience. In short order, they made the acquaintance of one Ronald Dodge of Providence, Rhode Island, a farm equipment tycoon with a weakness for the musical stage. Lustig bought his mark several well-lubricated dinners before shyly letting it slip that he was even then putting a new show together with Miss Swan as its leading lady. He estimated that the production's entire start-up cost would run to $70,000, of which he had so far raised $20,000.

While Dodge pondered that, he and Lustig repaired to a private room in their hotel in order to see Miss Swan dance, and, as a later police report put it, 'act up'. Following this closed-door audition, Victor invited both parties to join him on a short stroll to have lunch down on the beach. By the time they arrived there they were being followed by an excited mob of teenaged boys, which Lustig pointed out was further irrefutable proof of his protégé's magnetic appeal to the opposite sex. He did not mention that he had been surreptitiously dropping cigarettes and coins behind them as they walked. As a result, Stella Swan experienced some-thing novel – an audience who apparently appreciated her for her natural beauty, not just for her appearance in a stylised loincloth or a spangled G-string.

Soon Ronald Dodge was begging to be allowed to put up the outstanding balance of $50,000, while Lustig, instead of the crude hustle of lesser con men, solemnly advised him of the risks involved in any such theatrical venture. The warnings served only to further fan Dodge's eagerness to part from his money in this way. In short order the two men consummated their partnership over the course of another lavish dinner at their hotel. About halfway through the meal, a bellboy walked up to their table, bowed, and told Lustig that there was an urgent phone call for him from London. Victor tipped the boy generously and excused himself from the table. When he returned a few minutes later he appeared to be calm but quietly happy with himself. 'It seems we may open simultaneously in the West End,' he announced, mentioning a British royal family member who was now apparently keen to back the production. In his own excitement, Dodge did not stop to consider that it would then have been around three o'clock in the morning in the English capital.

The inevitable happened. After a further dinner or two, the $50,000 changed hands from Dodge to Lustig, closely followed by the latter's own passing from the scene. Later that day, Victor had promised to hire a pleasure boat on which all three interested parties could meet to toast their coming international smash while they cruised lazily around the Gulf of Mexico. When Ronald Dodge, Stella Swan and several other invited guests arrived at the harbour they found that Lustig had already weighed anchor. The truth seems to have dawned on his primary investor soon after that. Dodge greeted the fact of Lustig's defection with that mixture of rage and self-reproach characteristic of Victor's marks over the years. Back in Providence, he wavered about whether or not he should report the matter to the police, but in the end he seems to have decided that to do so might raise awkward questions for him at home from his wife. Rightly, he may also have felt that there was little realistic chance of his ever recovering his money.

Dodge did, however, return to Havana some weeks later, where he found the former Illinois beauty queen forlornly working in a dockside gentleman's club. He made an appointment to meet her backstage, where, to again quote Agent Johnson's evocative words, 'The [other] dancers grinned and turned to walk away, rotating their bottoms from habit as he led the stricken girl to a seat.' In these poignant circumstances, Dodge gently explained to Stella that there never had been any Broadway production of the kind Lustig had described, and that they were both the victims of a monstrous hoax. Even then, the aspiring starlet's reaction was one of piteous disbelief. 'He played us,' Dodge repeated. Stella was still incredulous. Gently sobbing to herself on a bench at the back of a Cuban strip club, she simply didn't want to believe what she heard. Up until then the young actress still seems to have clung to the hope that it might all have been some sort of ghastly mistake. In the end Ronald Dodge gave her $200 out of his own pocket, and she returned to her former life in Peoria.

After that, Lustig evidently deemed it wise to spend several weeks living under an assumed name, first in Vienna and then in London. While in the latter he soon became a focus of attention as he promenaded around the Langham Hotel in his specially made platform-heeled boots and elegantly cut frockcoat. The teenaged future spy Guy Burgess, who managed to spend his weekends at the Langham while down from Eton, later described him as 'beautifully shod, if with a hint of the pantomime Englishman', though he had to admit that Victor 'had a wide array of admirers'. According to Betty Lustig, her parents would soon go on to divorce for a second time. 'My mother married Doug Conner, a man unworthy of her in every way, and Victor married a Sue Miller [*nee* Qudback] in Chicago. These two people, who would always love each other, let stubbornness and jealousy lead them further apart at every step.' Betty herself was soon installed at a Catholic girls' boarding school in Pittsburgh, where Victor frequently appeared in order to give the 6- to 13-year-old students inspirational talks on business morality, as well as donating $2,000 for the purchase of improving books for their library.

Despite these laudable initiatives, her father 'had many lovers', Betty admitted. Both Irene Kreusch, who briefly resurfaced in 1926, and Billie Mae Scheible were still intermittently on the scene. He also continued to see something of the screen star Ruth Etting, notwithstanding her own marriage to the psychotic 'Moe the Gimp' Snyder, a man next to whom Al Capone possessed almost regal dignity. Yet another partner of Lustig's, a Los Angeles showgirl named Rina Landon, would live long enough to tell a newspaper reporter in the 1980s that she and Victor had been in bed one night in 1926 at the Hollywood Roosevelt Hotel when there was an angry thump at the door. Watching her partner calmly produce a semi-automatic pistol and walk with it to greet their visitor, she exclaimed, 'You never told me you kept a loaded gun under your pillow!' Always keen to avoid violence if he possibly could, Victor merely spoke a few emollient words through the locked door, evidently persuading the caller that it was all a case of mistaken identity. The young woman heard the other party's footsteps disappear down the hallway, followed by Lustig announcing in the same level tone that perhaps they should gather their belongings and leave the building by way of the fire escape.

Later in 1926 Lustig was bold enough to again risk a play on an organised crime boss. This was Jack 'Legs' Diamond, a 29-year-old Irish American mobster with a controlling interest in several New York-area speakeasies. Lustig and his old travelling companion Dapper Dan Collins entered into an arrangement to supply brand-name liquor to Diamond's establishments, but then switched the

Jack 'Legs' Diamond during one of his many court appearances.

labels so that he in fact received a mixture of juniper oil cut with a dash of high-octane gin brewed up in Dapper Dan's bathtub. The two co-conspirators were lucky to be able to leave town before their patron – an energetic individual, whose nickname derived from how fast he could run – was able to take revenge. Diamond, whose sentimental side once led him to present young Betty Lustig with a pet goat, met his end just five years later, when two business competitors entered the small New York hotel where he was staying. One of the men held the victim down while the other one shot him three times in the back of the head.

Whether to let the heat cool down after his bootlegging escapade, or simply out of lifelong habit, Lustig was again on the move in late December 1926. He spent Christmas of that year in Amarillo, Texas, where he arrived carrying two identical monogrammed suitcases. One of the cases contained genuine US government Liberty Bonds, and Victor stuffed the other one with torn up strips of newspaper.

Lustig's mark was Amarillo's widely despised sheriff, 52-year-old Roland 'Whitey' Jones, who combined his law-enforcement duties with a financial stake in a popular downtown brothel, among other such nearby businesses. A stocky, primitive man with bald head and gross features, Jones gave off an aura of pure villainy. His speech was peppered with racial slurs and other obscenities, and he especially relished the chance to detain a black man – or woman – overnight in his jail. One teenage victim had died while in the sheriff's custody, allegedly after he violently raped her, although the death certificate listed merely 'Failure to respire' as the critical event. Convinced that the Negro was plotting against the Aryan world, Jones had an endless litany of abuse at the tip of his tongue.

Using his assumed title, Lustig quickly secured an interview with Sheriff Jones on the Monday morning of 3 January 1927. He told the lawman that he had $80,000 worth of Liberty Bonds with him and that, due to a temporary embarrassment demanding ready funds, he would be willing to part with this treasure for only $60,000 in cash. The sheriff inspected the bonds and quickly agreed to the deal. When the two parties met again the following morning Lustig once more flipped open the monogrammed suitcase, which by now had a few genuine Liberty Bonds on the top and, unbeknown to Jones, the strips of worthless newsprint underneath. In a further stratagem of which the sheriff was unaware, Tony the chauffeur was stationed in a Rolls-Royce at the rear of the building, holding the other suitcase with the majority of the bonds in it, ready to leave at short notice. After a cursory inspection, Jones smilingly handed over $60,000 in cash, and accepted what amounted to about $500 in government deeds in exchange. Lustig stayed long enough to propose a brief toast to their mutual prosperity. Following that he excused himself from the sheriff's office and without further ado joined Tony in the Rolls, instructing him to gun the engine and not stop until they crossed the state line.

They seem to have made it as far as Indianapolis, 900 miles away, because two days later Lustig was arrested there under the name of Albert Phillips on a charge of vagrancy. This was a rather broad legal term at the time, and could apply to anyone moving around from place to place without an obviously legitimate means of support. As usual, he was soon back in circulation. The note in Lustig's growing police file says that he was detained in Indianapolis on Thursday afternoon and that he was 'ordered out of the city' on Friday morning.

He lingered in the general area, even so, because before long he was in trouble again in his old haunt of Crown Point, roughly 100 miles to the north. The charge sheet this time read: 'As Albert GRAUMAN, wanted for Grand Larceny – Apprehended'. Just as had once before, Lustig escaped from local custody, apparently after bribing a prison guard. He was caught again three days later while strolling around the town wearing a Canadian army tunic adorned by a 1918 Victory Star, with oak-leaf cluster, pinned to his chest. He had obtained the medals from a pawnbroker in Shawnee,

Kansas. Once again he either talked or bought his way out of trouble, because the file reads, 'Recaptured', immediately followed by the notation 'Released – Not Wanted'.

Lustig was soon back again in Europe, where he proceeded to liberally distribute bogus US War Bonds around the Riviera before the hard-nosed Toulon police came for him. Even then he kept his nerve. When the arresting officers announced that they meant to deport him back to the United States, he told them, 'This is a diplomatic matter, *monsieurs*.' Among other things, Lustig had a deserved reputation as an unusually proficient barrack room lawyer. It was a notable fact of his long criminal career that he rarely felt the need to engage the services of a formally qualified attorney. Such was his aura of inner confidence, of someone possessing boundless insights into legal issues of the utmost complexity, that many provincial law-enforcement professionals, some of them judges, seduced by his poise and general self-assurance, would indulge him. Lustig calmly informed the competent officials in this case that he was a dual Franco-Czech national, and that as such it behoved the Toulon force to contact the US State Department in the matter. Provided that body formally requested his extradition, and, further, should the foreign ministries in both Paris and Prague grant the application, then he was at their disposal. The flustered gendarmes glanced at one another, and then at Lustig, and back at each other again. After conferring further on the matter, they opted for the Indianapolis formula. Lustig was asked to leave their jurisdiction of his own accord within twenty-four hours, and given to understand that his presence in the city would be more sparingly tolerated in the future.

A rude shock awaited Lustig when he returned across the Atlantic on board the RMS *Mauretania* in the first week of May 1927. A small pilot boat met the ship a mile outside New York harbour and, as the passengers leant over the railings to watch, two middle-aged men in dark suits and black wingtip shoes made their way with some difficulty up a rope ladder to the deck of the liner more than 100ft above them. The pair were members of the United States Secret Service, and they were there to speak to Lustig about the matter of some phony Liberty Bonds that had been changing hands up and down the east coast.*

The senior of the two federal agents who boarded the *Mauretania* that spring morning was a 45-year-old, thickset New Yorker named Peter Anthony Rubano. He was to play an increasingly significant part in Lustig's life over the course of the next several years. Cold, stern and incorruptible, Rubano had been raised in the South Bronx, the oldest of fourteen children of Catholic immigrant parents from Italy. He had first made his name in law enforcement in 1910 by tracking down Ignazio 'the Wolf' Lupo, a Sicilian-born mobster wanted for a variety of robberies, beatings and murders around upstate New York. The Italian government was so relieved at the news of Lupo's arrest that it presented Rubano with a medal. He went on to serve with distinction as a US army officer in France during the First World War. In one engagement Rubano was said to have turned his Maxim machine gun on a German infantry column and 'played upwards of 100 bullets into the advancing enemy ranks, as precisely as one might play the hose upon one's garden'. General Joffre, the former commander of French forces on the Western Front, had later awarded him a gold watch as a token of his nation's esteem.

In February 1919, Rubano was back in his civilian job at the head of a task force that rounded up a gang of seventeen foreign

---

* An alternative version suggests that Lustig himself had pre-emptively sent a wire inviting the Secret Service to meet him on board the *Mauretania*. According to this theory, he did so in the belief that he could talk his way out of trouble with the representatives of the federal government more easily than with the local or state authorities who might otherwise have wished to interview him about certain outstanding matters within their jurisdictions. The files of the US Treasury Department, then the agency responsible for the Secret Service, read: 'Multiple sources confirm "Count" Victor Lustig will travel on RMS *Mauretania* [and] Representatives will meet him to ascertain if he will furnish data on [the Bonds] ... The purpose of this is to establish the truth or falsity of his claims to have been absent from the United States during the time various US peace officers have complained of his activities. No arrest warrant has been issued at this time.'

The incorruptible agent Peter Rubano, extreme right, guarding Marshal Foch and others at a conference in Washington DC.

anarchists accused of un-American activities, including a threat to assassinate President Wilson. Later that year, he personally defused a parcel bomb that had been sent to the office of Mitchell Palmer, the crusading US Attorney General, who, as we have seen, was in the throes of deporting large numbers of suspected Communist subversives. The government rewarded Rubano for this act by sending him out on a speaking tour of the country to arouse it to the Red Menace. By now married with two teenage children, who addressed him as 'sir', he was a tough, laconic character who seemed to have stepped out of Central Casting as the ideal of a 1920s G-man. One admiring adversary said of him: 'He was made of steel ... When he shook your hand, it stayed shook, as if he was making an arrest, and his voice cut across a crowded room. No one ever took liberties with him.' Even J. Edgar Hoover, usually sparing in his praise of a subordinate, later wrote: 'This agent occupies a

position in law enforcement second to but few. With close application, and an avoidance of all distractions, [he] keeps everything
pertaining to his business in so methodical a manner that he attacks
the criminal type with surgical precision.' For the next eight years,
Rubano would diligently pursue his principal quarry with a deep,
unwavering compulsion that went far beyond a mere professional
duty. The power of his obsession was such that he could communicate his extreme, even monomaniacal, ambition to the members
of the small squad, many of them juggling the competing demands
of wives and children, who willingly joined him in his mission. In
short, he became Lustig's Captain Ahab, driven by a quest for justice and revenge against the man he described as the most fiendish
deceiver in America.

The first battle of wits between the two parties on board the
Mauretania ended in an effective draw. James Johnson, who went
on to become one of those assigned to Rubano's force, wrote of
the encounter:

> Lustig was most co-operative and talked a great deal. But,
> strangely, little useful information seemed to be forthcoming.
> Rubano ordered lunch sent in, and after that continued the
> questioning. He was determined to pin the confidence man
> down ... The fourth hour of questioning passed, and the fifth
> and sixth. Lustig showed no signs of fatigue or even of resent-
> ment when the questions became sharp and personal.

It was a stalemate. A veteran charmer, Lustig politely denied
knowing about any funny money circulating around the US,
while regaling his two guests with suitably edited recollections of
his youthful adventures in the likes of Vienna and Paris. After this
burst of studied geniality he again repeated that he alas had little
personal familiarity with the world of Liberty Bonds or any other
such instruments. He wished he could be more helpful, but there
it was. The upshot of the meeting was that towards nightfall Victor

walked down the gangway of the *Mauretania* a free man and vanished into the streets of New York. The official file reads: 'After several hours, [we] could not draw him into a serious sustained discussion of any specific criminal activity.'

But perhaps the main reason for Lustig's reticence on the subject was that he couldn't dispute just a few of Rubano's assertions without admitting the truth of many others, and the government man had hit dangerously close to home when he raised the question, for instance, of certain off-track betting irregularities at the Saratoga racecourse, or the alleged psychic powers of a medium believed to have practised on the New Jersey shore. According to his brother Emil, Victor was 'much relieved in mind' to finally take his leave of Agent Rubano that spring day in New York. 'He had detected something in his inquisitor's eye, and it greatly troubled him,' he wrote.

Nonetheless, there remained the question of sustenance. Victor still had an impressive number of bills to pay and mouths to feed. As the summer of 1927 wore on, the United States economy showed increasing signs of strain, eventually prompting the Federal Reserve Bank to significantly reduce the nation's short-term interest rates early in September. Like many con men, Lustig was a firm believer in the need for financial risk prevention, and the maintenance of sound economic fundamentals at the state level. Complaining that he had been robbed of many thousands that year on the stock market, he soon set about recouping his losses. After burning yet another provincial sheriff for $15,000 by means of his Rumanian Box, Victor went on to invest some of the proceeds in a scheme to relieve a mark named Steven J. Stone, a wealthy insurance executive from Albany, New York, of his life savings.

Lustig told Stone that he owned a number of silver mines in a remote part of Colorado. They were all fabulously productive, and would remain so for many years to come. But there was a problem. He, Victor, was an incorrigible gambler, and in one recent disastrous night he had lost many thousands at poker. As a result he found himself in need of ready funds, and thus had no option but to sell a controlling interest in one of his mines for $80,000, or $2 million at today's prices.

Of course, Lustig didn't expect Stone to simply take his word for it. He also produced authentic-looking deeds of ownership, and equally persuasive 'officially audited' statements of current and projected income. The documents had been run up by a printer friend of Emil Lustig in the back room of his shop in Throgs Neck, New York. Newspaper articles were similarly furnished that represented Victor as one of the great precious metal magnates and social benefactors of the day. They, too, were forged. Acclaimed as a major local entrepreneur, Lustig shyly admitted, the *Denver Post* had even named him their Man of the Year. He had been a fool at the card table, he acknowledged, but all he needed were some modest funds and the opportunity to keep his hundreds of hard-working employees and their poor families from starving. In a wrenching detail, Victor added that he had left his house one morning not long ago and found a little old lady waiting for him on the street with a bunch of handpicked flowers tied together in a plain newspaper wrapper clutched in her hands. Her subsequent presentation to him, and those of many other such worthy people, contributed to his determination to continue to provide for their welfare, whatever the cost.

The old woman had told him that she was a widow and that her son was employed in one of Lustig's mines, where he made enough money to support both her, the son's wife, and the couple's seven young children. Victor was a saint, the lady had continued, pressing her ragged bouquet into his arms. His largesse had made him the toast of the tight-knit local community, it seemed. Lustig told Stone that it would break his heart to close down even a single mine, and that he would do whatever it took both to avoid any layoffs and to continue to offer certain vital services to his employees, ranging from day-care nurseries to adult literacy classes for his undereducated workers. The $80,000 he was asking was 'practically a steal' he added, without apparent irony.

Stone duly parted with the money, at which point Lustig and his family took the next available fast train out of town to Detroit. After that Victor spent some extended time in western Canada under the name of Van Gross, an itinerant Catholic lay preacher. Six months later, a story in the *New York Herald Tribune* had the lead 'The Relentless Steven Stone Still Searches Every Major City in the United States for Count Lustig'. Victor was eventually arrested in Omaha when he tried to dispose of another bogus mine in the same way, but he manoeuvred his way out of trouble with a $20,000 bribe and the promise to leave town within sixty minutes.

Lustig hastily moved his primary residence back to Chicago, where he now generally went under the name of Miller. He and his new 27-year-old wife Susan, a lithe former model with long auburn hair, rented a modest brick home near that of his old friend Ernest Hemingway's family in the western suburb of Oak Park. He also established an innocuous-looking, three-room downtown office on State Street that contained among its effects a large portrait of President Coolidge flanked by a furled American flag on a brass pole with a plastic eagle on top. A tray of business cards fanned out in the vestibule read:

ROBERT V. MILLER ESQ.

Imports and Exports. Foreign by birth, American by choice.

Pushing further into Lustig's inner office, the visitor would have seen solid, confidence-inspiring furniture in dark mahogany, a faux marble fireplace, and shelves full of biblical texts, classical poetry anthologies and bound academic journals whose dark leather spines and faded gold lettering signalled a certain gravitas. The caller wasn't to know that his host had purchased the books as a job lot in order to better furnish the premises.

Installed behind a heavy oak desk reassuringly decorated with framed family photographs, Lustig himself was a genial, avuncular figure with a steady gaze and a warm grip. For the next few years he often used this setting as a convenient rendezvous for talking shop with his brother Emil and associates such as Dapper Dan Collins, as well as for entertaining lady friends and even one or two friendly local journalists. Victor was rarely troubled while in residence there. The profits from the Rumanian Box provided him with a tidy annuity and allowed an ample spare margin for distribution to the forces of the law. Every now and then a representative from Chicago's city hall or the police department would pass into Lustig's inner sanctum and leave again a few minutes later with a well-stuffed envelope secreted in an inner pocket. Victor never resorted to physical violence, and rarely if ever stooped to crude theft. Although prevented, whether through choice or necessity, from enjoying full US citizenship – at least once failing to show that he was of the necessary 'good character' to qualify for naturalisation – he was in every other outward respect a model of the exemplary small American businessman. Even at a time when Al Capone could advertise himself as a humble secondhand furniture dealer, it was a notable feat of reinvention on Lustig's part.

He also planned ahead. Lustig had half a dozen different European passports ready in his office safe in the event of a hurried overseas departure. Tony the chauffeur was instructed to always ensure a car was fully fuelled and ready to go at a moment's notice. Victor kept bundles of cash in different foreign currencies in left-luggage lockers located in train or bus stations scattered around at least five US cities. He even maintained a fully furnished apartment in the remote hilltop village of Skidel in the Lithuanian–Byelorussian republic (today's Belarus). The only amenity the place offered was safety. It was a quiet little community with no industry and few if any foreign tourists, and at the time its host government still had no extradition treaty with the United States.

Later in 1928 Lustig pulled off another variant of his silver mine scam. His latest mark was a wealthy Texas rancher named Ray Murdoch who lived in the dusty border town of La Joya on the northern bank of the Rio Grande, about 200 miles from San Antonio. James Johnson had now been assigned to the Secret Service's newly formed Lustig task force under Peter Rubano's direction, and wrote of the scene:

Murdoch … began to speculate in stocks, apparently buying them from a mail-order brokerage house in New York. His account was respectable in size, and so he was not at all surprised when the home office sent one of its customer-relations men down to Texas to see him personally and offer further service and advice.

Lustig, the honest broker in question, introduced himself to his unsuspecting client as George Simon. He told Murdoch that his account with the firm was ticking over nicely. With careful management, it would continue to return a yield of around 4 per cent a year. From there it was not difficult for Lustig to interest the Texan in an altogether more ambitious money-making venture. All Murdoch needed to do was invest a trifling $20,000 in share certificates issued by an entity called the Handleman Gold Mining Trust, and his only problem from then on would lie in having to rent extra storage space to accommodate all the cash that would roll in. 'I have the name and address of the mine's largest shareholder, a Mr. Jackson DeMuth,' Lustig confided. 'The man's in poor health, living in a small hotel in Brownsville, and wants to unload his stock while he still can. If we move quickly we may still be in time.' Murdoch listened to this pitch and then gave it as his opinion that it was a stroke of 'goddamned genius'. Lustig modestly shrugged off such an accolade, merely repeating his advice that they should act in the matter with all due speed. It was the classic grifter's set-up: find your mark, inform him of what very little upfront cash would be required to become fabulously wealthy, remain calm, and then encourage the sap to sign up without further delay.

Lustig and Murdoch separately drove the 70 miles to the bedside of the stricken Jackson DeMuth, who feebly agreed to sell them his shares. It would have been surprising had he done otherwise, because he was in fact an unemployed actor Victor had engaged for the occasion. DeMuth duly handed some impressively engraved deed certificates to Lustig, and Victor in turn passed them to Murdoch. These documents were also the work of Emil's friend in his print shop at Throgs Neck. After that the money changed hands, and the parties exchanged celebratory toasts. The upshot was that a beaming Murdoch emerged from the hotel just as night was falling over the quiet town of Brownsville. Apparently he was in a rush to drive home to La Joya, or perhaps it was already too dark for him to see properly, because he failed to notice the mortally ill Jackson DeMuth walk briskly out of a side door of the hotel and climb into a waiting tan Rolls-Royce with the man he knew as George Simon beside him in the back seat and a uniformed driver at the wheel.

On 11 December 1928, Lustig called by appointment at the home of a Boston dry goods magnate named Thomas Kearns, who was apparently amenable to sinking $16,000 in yet another spurious mine operation. But this time around something went wrong at the kill, and at the last moment the mark requested more time to consider his investment. Since he needed the money, Lustig waited until Kearns was out of the room, then picked the lock of a desk drawer, helped himself to all the cash lying there, and left town. Although Victor had no moral reservations on the point, it was a rare instance of a straightforward act of theft on his part. It also brought him disproportionate grief. Although the money helped solve his immediate liquidity problems, it did him more harm than good in the long run, as Kearns joined the growing list of those who made it their business in life to track him down. Each day's mailbag at Peter Rubano's office in the Treasury Department brought more invective from those of Lustig's victims who cursed his name and demanded his arrest. He would rarely again go out without carrying a loaded gun, except when it came to reading the children morally uplifting stories at Betty's convent school.

Just a week later, Lustig's family accompanied him on the SS *George Washington* to enjoy a sentimental Christmas in Vienna. While there he took 7-year-old Betty on the train with him over the Czech border to the small town of Vestřev, near Hostinné, and treated her to a guided tour of some of his childhood haunts. Together they walked hand-in-hand to his mother's grave in the ancient church-yard on the muddy banks of the Kalensky river, next to the town's main drainage canal. After placing a wreath on the plain wooden marker, Victor stood silently for several moments. Afterward, still quiet and thoughtful, he led Betty around some of the sights, such as they were, of Hostinné itself. The place had barely changed in forty years, he remarked approvingly, as they passed through a town lined by cobbled streets of modest beauty, hilly and wooded, dotted with small farms and crude stone cottages inhabited by generations of hard-working, frugal peasants. He recognised an old school friend named Rudel, a paper mill machinist, and they chatted briefly. It had all been an idyllic day, Victor announced back in the family's grand Vienna hotel, although his nostalgic journey was to end in unortho-dox fashion. Lustig's police file notes:

January 7 1929, arrested, Vienna, Charged [with] Tentative theft – possession of false deeds and checks, and fake passport.

Deported.

Speculative fever was still raging unabated in the American stock market that winter. After a brief but vertiginous fall in the summer of 1927, Wall Street prices had climbed again even while business activity as a whole faltered. There would be another sharp correction to the market on 26 March 1929, but on that same Tuesday afternoon several of the nation's biggest banks announced that they would do whatever it took to make credit available at no more than 7 per cent interest, and as a result the threatened panic was averted. During the week of 1 April, more shares changed hands than in any previous week in the 137-year history of the New York stock exchange. As the historian Frederick Lewis Allen remarks:

> One did not have to listen long to an after-dinner conversation, whether in New York or San Francisco or the lowliest village of the plain, to realise that all sorts of people to whom the stock ticker had been a hitherto alien mystery were carrying a hundred shares of Studebaker or Houston Oil, learning the significance of such recondite symbols as GL and X and ITT, and whipping open the early editions of afternoon papers to catch the 1.30pm quotations from Wall Street.

In 1929, share certificates traded exclusively in paper format. For the most part, they were neither fussily detailed, nor particularly sophisticated in design. The scope for forgery was immense, and limited only by the forger's access to adequate supplies of suitable paper and ink. Producing fake deeds and passing them off on gullible investors proved almost as lucrative to some people as the legitimate exchange of scrip did to others.

For once casting modesty aside, Lustig later boasted that he had forged and sold over 200 financial instruments in the twelve months beginning in June 1928, and that they had earned him around $60,000 in net profit. This represented a significantly better return than the $1,800 annual average salary the typical skilled blue-collar worker then brought home. As he approached his 40th birthday, Lustig was a seriously wealthy man; he needed to be, and never felt himself wholly secure – exploiting others was a kind of addiction to him – but by the standards of most modestly educated immigrant Americans, let alone of those like his friend Rudel back in the old country, he had little of which to complain. He was shrewd, ambitious, imaginative, careful without being mean, and preferred to do business without unduly troubling the Bureau of Internal Revenue.

Lustig was back in Europe in July 1929. We know this because he was arrested on the 19th of the month while staying in a penthouse suite at the Hotel Le Meurice, about a ten-minute walk upriver of the Eiffel Tower. The Paris authorities used the time he was in their custody to exchange several wires with Agent Rubano and his colleagues back at the Treasury building in Washington. Some eighteen years later, Lustig wrote rather plaintively to the City Attorney of Boston:

Dear Sir

I was arrested in Paris, France, in 1929, and held for three months. After that, some of your men came after me and had a Washington extradition warrant against me. I was extradited to your town and held for trial … I got out on a $15,000 bail put up by a New York company … Today I have a detainer from your office. I hope you can let me go as I am now about 58 years old [and I wish] to go home to my native country. I have several injuries that will remain permanently. I hope you can let me go.

In time the French police escorted Lustig to a second-class cabin back on board the SS *George Washington* and shipped him home to New York. He arrived there on 6 November 1929. The US stock market had finally crashed just eight days earlier. As shares dropped vertically with no one buying, traders were sold out as they failed to respond to margin calls, mobs gathered outside on Wall Street, and by the end of the day even some of the best-managed investors in the country had lost millions. Among other things, the crisis brought a temporary end to the market for forged stock certificates. Lustig took this enforced professional hiatus in his stride. Peter Rubano and his associates had been there to meet the *George Washington* on arrival in New York. As Rubano slapped the handcuffs on him, Victor merely smiled and told his nemesis, in a line he may possibly have rehearsed: 'Thank you for paying my passage. The accommodations were excellent.'

Rubano escorted the prisoner to the Massachusetts state line, where he was transferred to the custody of the local authorities. Eventually an interview was arranged at the Boston police headquarters, which Thomas Kearns also attended. Kearns had protested that he did not want to be in the same room as 'that bastard', but the city attorney's office insisted. It seemed that they finally had Lustig where they wanted him, but, just two days later, a curiously benign judge granted him bail. Skilfully playing the legal system, the accused then bombarded the court with writs and petitions, eventually filing 3,028 closely typed pages of documentary evidence, the essence of which was that it was all a case of mistaken identity. In due course the same judge ruled that Lustig's $15,000 bond should be forfeited as a contribution towards the 'transportation and subsistence costs' in the case, but set the defendant free.

On his return to Chicago, Lustig opened his 1929 accountant's ledger, with its five neatly ruled rows headed Assets, Liabilities, Income, Expenses and Capital, and reviewed his immediate career prospects. Optimist that he was, he was still forced to include several items in the debit column. Might he yet have to pay a price for the Thomas Kearns affair, for instance? Would Ronald Dodge, the spurned Broadway producer, continue to take an interest in his whereabouts? Several individuals were still seething from their purchase of the Rumanian Box, or of non-existent mining rights. And what about the indefatigable G-man Peter Rubano and his dedicated force? It had not been a bumper second half of the year for generating new business, Lustig was forced to conclude. The stock-forging racket had been good while it lasted, but Wall Street no longer seemed quite so attractive a proposition once ruined investors started leaping to their deaths there.

Summing up the situation, Lustig wrote in his ledger on 19 December 1929: 'I end the year with wonder that this could all happen [and] thanks that my family are safe.' On Christmas Eve he was arrested while trying to walk over the international border from El Paso into Juarez with a pocketful of counterfeit Mexican currency, and spent most of the holiday week locked in a rural Texas jail cell as a result. Once again he played the system to his advantage. As Victor had technically neither left the country nor broken any state laws – or at least none that were currently on file – a judge ruled that he was free to go, on condition that he appear for his next scheduled hearing in Boston. On leaving the El Paso courthouse, Lustig demonstrated his puckish sense of humour with a short entry in the city's guest book. It read: 'Anyon [*sic*] who visits Texas will see why it is known as the Friendship State. I will return.' Then he belatedly crossed over the border into Mexico, this time by chauffeured Rolls-Royce.

Business may have been tough, but Lustig had a talent for dressing up his various scams, and even the squalid constraints these sometimes imposed, with a paradoxical touch of gravitas. He made each swindle seem like a momentous advance in human ingenuity, as shown by a list he took the trouble to draw up that year that came to be known as the 'Ten Commandments of the Con'. Rule number seven read: 'Never pry into a person's personal circumstances (they'll tell you eventually).' Number eight advised: 'Never boast: just let your importance be quietly obvious.' It was almost as though Lustig viewed himself as an instrument of God when it came to matters of crime and deception; that this knowledge was not for his benefit alone, but that the Almighty had placed him in a special position for conveying his insights into the human condition to a world that badly needed them. By striking this note, Victor was clearly differentiating himself from the common hustler. The obvious pride he took in publishing his list was almost certainly not untainted by an implied, though debatable, aspiration to legitimate business-philosopher status.

Another sign of Lustig's pre-eminence in the field was the ever-growing number of imitators he inspired. We've noted the activities of 'Count' Boris Dobrzynski, 'that chirpy little bird', according to the *New York Herald Tribune*, who relieved 'socially anxious Americans' of 'many tens of thousands' with a device much like the Rumanian Box. Another clone was a man with a long face marked by a deep scar on one cheek, and in general drenched in a mortuary gloom, who circulated around the drawing rooms of the Upper East Side and other such enclaves calling himself Prince Jakub Arnaudoff. To his credit, the prince was actually a former Polish cavalry officer who had fled to London in 1914 and offered his services to the British army, before emigrating to the United States after the war. On the debit side, he then spent much of the 1920s impersonating everyone from Buster Keaton to Calvin Coolidge. He was eventually deported for 'tending to degrade American public life', as the formal complaint put it, after posing as the assistant director of the National Recovery Administration, allegedly responsible for collecting dues from a number of large labour unions. In time James Johnson of the Secret Service drew up a list of twenty-three Lustig copycats. While he considered eight of the men 'particularly skilled in his field', he concluded that 'none had qualifications superior to the original'.

However flattering his reputation, Lustig knew that the forces of law and order were steadily closing in on him. In January 1929, in apparent reprisal for the bootlegged alcohol episode, 'Legs' Diamond had anonymously provided the Secret Service with certain details of his former colleague's preferred aliases and hideouts. Even as Victor continued to restlessly move around from one town to another, Peter Rubano and his task force hunted him mercilessly. The Lustigs' family maid once woke young Betty in the dead of the night, and told her to quickly pack a suitcase. A few minutes later the child found herself being driven at wild speed to the train station in downtown Chicago. Before long, Betty, the maid and the family dog were installed under assumed names in a compartment on the 'El Capitan' transcontinental express to California. It says something for the lifestyle she had come to accept that nothing about this struck the 7-year-old girl as particularly out of the ordinary. At dawn the train made its first scheduled stop in Des Moines, Iowa, and Betty glanced out the window. She later wrote of the scene:

> [I] saw a woman in a white nurse's uniform pushing a wheel chair. In it was my father. I recognised him and I wasn't surprised by what I saw. I had seen many such curious scenes before when [we] were moving. He was in the wheel chair with his leg in a cast, his arm in a sling, a wool blanket wrapped around him and his head down on his chest with a felt hat pulled down to his ears.

'Ah, Skeezix,' Lustig said calmly, as soon as he was on board the train, and the blinds in their compartment were drawn. He rapidly discarded the cast and the sling, also not seeming to find the scene especially unusual. 'I held on tight to him and didn't say another word,' Betty recalls. On arrival in Los Angeles they put up for two months at the home of an unnamed 'beautiful movie star', who may conceivably have been Clara Bow, on Pacific Coast Highway in Malibu. Betty remembered the place as a 'vast pile of towers and turrets' with a palm-shaded swimming pool, 'lots [of] Filipino servants, and an English tutor for my schooling'. But this interlude also ended abruptly when Victor shook his daughter awake early one morning and announced that she and the maid were to be driven post-haste back to Chicago. Betty once tried to count the number of times that she and the family had criss-crossed the country. 'It must have been at least seventy-five,' she concluded.

Lustig himself saw in the 1930s from the comparative safety of provincial Mexico, where he spent the winter months as the guest of a young woman known only as Araceli in her small, whitewashed home in the coastal town of Manzanillo. When the cold weather came, Victor rejected his companion's suggestion that he buy a suitable coat for himself in the local market on the grounds that he had once been cheated there when he shopped for groceries. Instead they took a taxi nearly 500 miles to Mexico City, where he bought them both expensive new wardrobes. The couple stayed on in a hotel there for several days during an ensuing snowstorm. Lustig seems to have been relatively content in his southern exile. As soon as the weather allowed, he went back to the picturesque seaside house, whose shuttered windows opened on to a cobbled courtyard, where he particularly remembered the flowering apple and cherry trees, lilac and rose bushes, and long walks down to the crescent-shaped beach. It was an idyllic respite from his usual routine of repeated crime and flight, but it, too, ended in familiar fashion.

One morning in early May, Lustig's hostess woke up to find a note telling her that he had unfinished business north of the border, and that it was best that she remain behind. That was the last Araceli ever saw of him. A year later, she went on to marry the Assistant Attorney General of Mexico.

7

GOING SOUTH

Before long Lustig had to face another crisis. Except for a few
modest scores with the Rumanian Box, he was close to the end
of his resources. In March 1930 he and his already long-suffering
wife Susan moved to a smaller, two-bedroom timber house in the
inner Chicago suburbs. His neighbours there were working-class
men and women with jobs on the railroad or packing meat in
the downtown stockyards. Victor complained that the new home
was 'infernal', with trolleys rattling up and down the narrow street
and people who were physically or mentally ill 'howling away like
wolves' in the night. Lustig was almost certainly the only local
resident with a Rolls-Royce parked outside his front door. He
called himself Miller on the lease, but the Chicago shopkeepers
knew him as Schaffer, Gardner, Gross, Lamar, Kessler or Duval,
among several other names. Although modest from the outside,
the Lustigs' home had the latest conveniences, including one of the
area's first indoor lavatories in a private residence. After installing
gas heating, Victor donated the building's old coal fireplace to the
needy through a local church.

On 21 May 1930, after returning from Mexico, Lustig registered at the central Chicago courthouse as the law required, this
time listing himself as 'Salesman'. Still able to afford the luxury of
good intentions, he took the opportunity to donate to the city's

charity for the widows and orphans of slain police officers, and to attend their annual fundraiser in a downtown hotel. But in less than a month Victor left this refuge of comparative respectability and disappeared back into the underworld of itinerant crime. He left behind no word with his wife, and on his court form there was a blank for 'Secondary addresses', while 'Unknown' marked the question: 'Additional means of support'. In early June he was staying in a common lodging house in Philadelphia, although he also appears to have seen something of his friend Billie Mae Scheible at her nearby establishment. He was described as 'well dressed' for his court hearing in Boston on the 27th of the month, which suggests he at least had a roof over his head and money in his pockets. After relieving him of $15,000, the judge ruled that the defendant had no further case to answer in the Thomas Kearns affair, and let him go.

Even Lustig's elastic mind had trouble wrapping itself around the problem of how to make an adequate living in the depths of the Great Depression, but his admirers and detractors both gave him credit for persistence. With little or no prior experience in the field, he now went about bilking the fine art world of several thousand dollars. Victor must have taken the train out of Boston almost the moment the judge there released him, because he was back in California just six days later. The morning after watching the Independence Day parade in downtown Los Angeles, he knocked on the door of the curator's office at the Museum of History, Science and Art a mile or so away in Exposition Park. Lustig told the man who greeted him that he had the good fortune to have known Claude Monet, who had died in 1926, and that the great artist had made him a gift of one of the preparatory sketches of his celebrated series of oil paintings of the flower garden at his home in Giverny in northern France. With little more discussion than that, the curator invited the impeccably dressed stranger to return the following Monday morning with the piece in question. When he did so, Lustig unrolled a small sheet of paper showing a pencilled sketch of the famous Japanese bridge and surrounding water lilies. He added that Monsieur Monet himself had asked that the work be offered only to an institution able to display it for as many 'ordinary' people as possible who could enjoy it the year round, which is why he, Victor, had brought it to southern California. His presentation was remarkable in many ways: according to a later newspaper report, it was 'fluent and smooth, [and] astonishingly convincing in every regard, with a ready answer to every question asked of him'. But perhaps most surprising of all was the ringing endorsement that quickly followed the experts' appraisal of the work they excitedly passed among themselves. Lustig, who had paid a starving art student living above a Chicago fish warehouse $200 for the canvas, left the gallery $6,000 richer.

Twelve months later, New York's Museum of Modern Art staged the first full-scale exhibition of Van Gogh's paintings on American soil. Amidst the famous landscapes and still lifes, visitors noticed an unusual item displayed in a blue velvet-lined box. A professionally engraved card next to it read: 'This is the ear which The Artist cut off and sent to his mistress, a French prostitute, December 23, 1888.' There is some dispute surrounding the true identity of the mastermind behind the hoax. Although most sources favour the claims of Hugh Troy, an American painter known for his practical jokes on the academic establishment (he once used a rhinoceros foot wastepaper basket to make tracks in the snow around the grounds of a New York university, sufficient to cause a minor panic on the campus), Lustig later confirmed that it was one of his, and that the 'ear' had in fact been fashioned out of a lump of dried beef. For once there had been no pecuniary motive involved. 'I did [it] purely to demonstrate the folly of the gentlemen of that world who would deign to lecture us,' he remarked. 'Even as a child, I observed that the greater a man's so-called learning, the easier he is to bamboozle.' This core conviction would grow only more pronounced with the passage of time.

As he had since adolescence, Lustig was soon busy looking for the next angle. Money was increasingly an issue. Wall Street was effectively out of commission, and he now had dependents in at least three American cities. James Johnson reported in 1930:

> Cash was becom[ing] a problem for Lustig. It came to him in great chunks but seemed to disappear as fast as an ice cake in the sun ... A sales clerk who made seventy dollars a week and had geared his life to that income was less in need of funds than he was.

With no particular set-piece play to hand, Lustig improvised with several petty scams. For sheer variety, his criminal impostures would take some beating: In 1930 alone, he posed as a rabbi, a priest, a real estate magnate, a hotel bellhop, a pilot, a surgeon and a member of President Hoover's kitchen cabinet. On 12 October, the New York police came to interview him after his sometime associate 'Legs' Diamond was shot five times while eating breakfast in his suite at the city's Monticello Hotel. He survived, but was gunned down in a different hotel just a year later. Lustig told the detectives that he knew nothing about the whole business. For once this was only the truth, 'and the law left quietly after just ten minutes,' he reflected. Yet the relief was tinged with real anxiety about the Diamond affair. 'Might I be next?'

The Secret Service's Peter Rubano approached his work methodically, much like a bricklayer, patiently establishing one fact after another, but even he reeled under the weight of all the documentary evidence in the Lustig case. After a week spent combing through the thousands of pages of accumulated court testimony, he admitted, 'The task confronting [us] is such a monstrous one that I am staggering a bit under it.' Even so, he relished the scrap. Reading an account of how Lustig had allegedly swindled an elderly couple in Texas out of their life savings, a colleague reported that Rubano 'turned beetroot-red and slammed the desk with his fist'. Clearly, the whole matter was not going to end amicably. Lustig's subsequent decision to get into the financial counterfeiting business saw Rubano figuratively spitting his teeth into his hand and noting that it was morally reprehensible that anyone should undermine the currency of the United States in this way. 'It is the land that [took] him in,' he wrote, with some asperity, in a report later in 1931. It apparently did not occur to Agent Rubano that Lustig might have similarly scammed the central banks of at least half a dozen other states, and that he made no distinction in matters of race, creed or gender when it came to soaking individual citizens of their money.

Back in the days when he was switching the labels on Dapper Dan Collins's bathtub gin, Lustig had met a balding, bespectacled Midwestern drugstore clerk named William Watts. A period photo shows a pale young man with a long, lean face, a beaky nose, and a somewhat wistful air. Watts's shy and self-effacing façade was only half the story. He was a bachelor, obsessed with cleanliness, and in his early thirties still lived in his boyhood room at his widowed mother's house in Omaha. He also led a double life, as what one magazine writer called 'the master counterfeiter of the modern age'. A meticulous craftsman, Watts had ascended quickly through the underworld, showing a flair for turning out everything from bonds and wills to university diplomas, and latterly $100-bills, the last of which he produced on a geometric lathe installed in the basement of his mother's modest bungalow. James Johnson described him this way:

> In the 1920s Watts helped run a Nebraska drugstore. About 1925 he popped up in Chicago working for Capone. He counterfeited Irish and Scotch whisky labels for the mob's rotgut. The job was so good that the Internal Revenue boys couldn't tell them from the genuine. Except by sampling the contents, of course.

Lustig soon treated Watts to one of his trademark charm offensives, taking him to expensive dinners, introducing him to the girls at Billie Mae Scheible's establishment, and in time renting him a pied-à-terre, under the name Ramsey, in a large rooming house on Palisade Avenue in Union City, New Jersey, with sweeping views across the Hudson River to Manhattan, where the Empire State Building rose up over the winter of 1930–31. It was the provincial pharmacist's first real taste of independence, or of apparent friendship. Young Betty Lustig sometimes accompanied her father to visit Watts. She remembered the notorious counterfeiter as 'a nice man who lived alone, or at least no one appeared to be living with him when we saw him. He loved good music and he and Victor exchanged music notes or listened to records together.' Watts once gave the 8-year-child an engraved ring, and she liked to sit by the riverfront window stroking her host's hairless cat while he and Lustig talked shop.

The Secret Service, which had chased counterfeiters since 1865 (protecting presidents became part of their job only in 1901) had first noticed Watts's activity in December 1926, when a phony $100 bill turned up in a bank clerk's drawer in St Louis. The teller remembered that a neatly groomed man with thinning sandy hair, who told her he was in town for a druggists' convention, had passed her the bill and asked that she exchange it for ones of smaller denomination. Her manager referred the matter to the bank's auditors, and after several days' investigation Watts's name had surfaced on a list of possible suspects. No one in authority seems to have followed up the lead, however, because Agent Johnson reported, 'The story didn't get much attention, although the bureau in Washington kept the funny bill for future reference.'

Still needing ready cash, Lustig was willing to tackle almost any reasonably lucrative project, no matter what risks were involved. The deal he now struck with Watts was to move the all-important lathe and other printing equipment 1,200 miles across the country from Omaha to Union City. After that they would bring in adequate supplies of suitable paper and ink. Special copper plates would be used to fabricate the thin security ribbon threaded through each genuine banknote. After the various seals and serial numbers were stamped on using a platen press, Watts would finally hang the bogus currency up to dry by pinning it to a clothes line strung across his bathroom. Lustig then paid him $30 for each finished $100 bill. Using out-of-town banks, Victor made several dummy runs to ensure that there were no unforeseen problems. He had survived as long as he had in part because of a shrewd understanding of the way in which such institutions did business. When that exercise proved satisfactory, Victor approached his old colleague Dapper Dan Collins to act as his main distributor, paying him, too, $30 for each bill successfully exchanged for legitimate currency, thus netting him a handsome $40 for each transaction, which translated into about $800 a day, or the equivalent of about $200,000 ($5 million at modern prices) each year in clear profit.

On 1 July 1930 Lustig filed his required United States Census form, listing his occupation as 'finance' rather than 'salesman'. Several days later his daughter Betty came to spend the rest of the summer with him in Chicago, where they frequently set off for weekend trips to Lowell Park, a 200-acre beauty spot located about an hour's drive west of the city. Although Victor restricted himself to peeling off to a striped tank top suit and crouching on a wooden stool he carried with him down to the beach, young Betty often ventured far out into the Rock River. She later remembered how much she had admired the wavy-haired teen-aged lifeguard, known only as 'Dutch', who on average once a day leapt gracefully down from his platform and pulled some stricken swimmer to safety. A legend later arose that the young man in question had sometimes come to the rescue of pretty girls who were in no danger of drowning. Betty thought it all a 'heavenly' interlude when, for a few weeks, at least, she had been able to live

Ronald Reagan in his lifeguarding days.

in more or less the same way other children did. Lustig later called it the last truly carefree summer of his life. On the final weekend before the new school year began Betty took a souvenir snapshot of her handsome lifeguard friend, who soon moved to California and became Ronald Reagan.

Lustig was a cultivated as well as protective parent. From him, Betty learned to read voraciously and appreciate music and art, even if some of the old masters her father proudly displayed on his living room wall were of suspiciously hazy origin. Her time at convent school, though medievally strict, at least had its consolations:

My father visited me often and became a good friend of the mother superior, who spoke German and liked this young [*sic*] countryman of hers who had his daughter in her care. Victor liked her, too. He said later that the one person in the world to whom he would entrust his life was that mother superior. [And] he did. It is known, although it is not in the convent annals, that she harbored him one night and saved him from arrest.

It would be wrong, even so, to describe the Lustigs' family life of the early 1930s as one of sound Catholic values, or to confuse Betty's happy summer memories with any longer-term sense of contentment or stability. 'When I brought a friend home to visit, I got a terrible shock,' she remembered. 'I realised that I didn't live the same way as other girls.' Apart from anything else, her father was now married to another woman, and her mother to another man. As is well known, bonding with a partner's children can be hard enough to bring off at the best of times, requiring a high degree of tact and passing familiarity with the concept of self-abnegation. It has to be said that neither Betty's stepmother nor stepfather quite conformed to this ideal, and so far as she ever let herself go emotionally it was with a series of animals and household pets – her best friend at boarding school was her pony Scarleg – with which she could abandon herself in a carefree display, an uninhibited effusion of irresponsibility, happiness and love. Betty later wrote that at around this time she had prayed 'Please, God, let my mother and daddy be back like we were. Please, God, if you do this, I promise I will be good' each night until she was 15 years old, at which point she finally stopped because it didn't work.

Meanwhile, Lustig seems to have made time for business even while accompanying Betty to those idyllic summer weekends at the beach. On 15 July 1930 he was arrested in New York, under the name Miller, and again charged with vagrancy. He paid the court another $2,000 and left town early the next morning for

Atlantic City. They promptly held him there, too, although the file reads: 'Fugitive – Discharged. Not Wanted.'

The head detective who felt Lustig's collar in Atlantic City later noted that he had seemed 'cool and reserved' at first, but increasingly uneasy once back at the station. 'Appearance: twitchy. Peculiarity: Racing speech', he wrote in his report.

The court might have ruled in the matter, but Lustig knew that Thomas Kearns, the Boston tycoon whose petty cash he had filched nearly two years earlier, was still on his case. Kearns had no more potent ally in his mission than Peter Rubano, who now had nine Secret Service agents as well as secretaries and other support staff at his disposal, almost exclusively dedicated to bringing Lustig to justice. His associates noted the unrelenting lawman as a disciplinarian. He insisted that certain rules be adhered to strictly: the men under his command were to wear suits and ties while seated at their desks, and to always carry a raincoat and hat with them when out on the road; undue noise, whether argument or enthusiasm, was not tolerated in the squad room; and government property was to be respected. 'There will be no standing on the chairs,' Rubano announced.

Perhaps it was no wonder that Lustig felt a growing sense of apprehension about the future, or that he continued to restively move around from one place to another, establishing a new alias in each town. So thoroughly did he erase his tracks that Peter Rubano had only one tenuous clue as to his whereabouts that winter. On 14 December 1930, Victor was arrested in Oklahoma City, under the name John Kane, and charged with 'Occupying a room for immoral purposes'. Released on bail two days later, he again headed across the Mexican border for the Christmas holidays. With Lustig temporarily out of his jurisdiction, Rubano backed off like a reversing steamroller.

While the Secret Service languished in Washington, the subject of their attention went about relieving men and women south of the border of their money. The spirit of seasonal goodwill, to the extent that he felt it at all, did not last very long. On 2 January 1931, Lustig was arrested in the western Mexican city of Guadalajara, charged with 'lewd conduct with a female not his wife [and] insubordination against higher authority'. He was cursorily examined by a police doctor, who gave a coldly objective account of the prisoner on the eve of his 41st birthday: 'Height 1.67, long, scarred face. Likely gout. Sinus problems. Dental work indicated.' Set against this starkly clinical record of middle-aged disrepair, the Guadalajara police report adds: 'Beautifully dressed. An insinuating style, and very talkative with officers … Told them he was here purely for pleasure.'

It took the Mexican judicial system until early February to decide what to do with the exotic stranger in their midst who claimed to be a Czech nobleman of some sort simply in search of a little winter sun. International communications were then a more rudimentary affair than they are now, and as a result the local magistrate wasn't to know many of the details of Lustig's colourful past. If anything, he seems to have suspected the accused man of being a spy. What else explained the circumstances of his arrest? How had he come by the $7,500 found sewn into the lining of a suitcase stashed under the bed in his hotel room? Lustig said that he had earned it through his legitimate dealings on the New York commodity market. But why did he also have three different passports? Such things were quite common for citizens of the contiguous European states following the unpleasantness of 1914–18, Victor explained smoothly. And what about the scantily clad local *señorita* found in his company? A wholly respectable young lady whom he had been interviewing for a possible position as his daughter's governess back in the old country, Lustig said, adding that he had assumed the woman's fetching if admittedly sparingly cut dress was merely some charming native costume. He had had a thoroughly enjoyable stay in Guadalajara, he continued, but he felt sure he had trespassed on the city's hospitality long enough. They would be worrying about him back home. He was already overdue at his small family estate. If the court would indulge him, he would board the next available train to Los Angeles, proceed to New York, and take ship from there to Le Havre, where his faithful chauffeur Ludwig would be on hand to drive him to his modest ancestral seat near Prague. Faced with this oratorical onslaught, the provincial Mexican judge let Victor go, with the request that he embark on his journey without delay.

Perhaps interagency intelligence-sharing wasn't totally deficient, however, because the police were waiting for Lustig when, just a few days later, he crossed the frontier into Eagle Pass, Texas. The local sheriff's report read: 'The alien "Count" VICTOR LUSTIG, alias Miller, alias Mergler, alias Schaffer, etc, entered the United States while not in possession of an unexpired immigration visa.' Lustig's first instinct on his arrest was to lie, claiming that his US passport had been stolen from him in Mexico, and that he would certainly apply for a replacement the moment he was able to do so. When that failed to persuade the Eagle Pass authorities, he changed tactics. If the chief of police went to the local train station and opened a certain numbered locker, Lustig confided, he would find a bag containing $8,000 awaiting him there with his name practically written on it. The lawman did as his prisoner advised. Corruption was then endemic in the American justice system at all but the most exalted levels, and Eagle Pass, Texas, it has to be said, was sadly far from that ideal. The following morning, posing as one J.R. Richards, Lustig once again walked free. A dusty Greyhound bus deposited him 60 miles away in Del Rio, an even smaller community with a few unprepossessing miners' shacks and equally modest stores set on a treeless slope, outlined bleakly against the grey sky. Even then, Victor tried to interest the town's Baptist minister in a Rumanian Box, but succeeded only in spending another night in the local jail. When later coming to compile Lustig's official criminal file – a document eventually running to some 1,400 pages – Peter Rubano said tersely of this last incident: 'Held for a time. Released. Case never tried.'

Being Lustig, he was arrested again even before he made it over the Texas state line, this time charged with 'Possessing distinctive papers, Section 264, Title 18, U.S. Code', although a familiar note adds: 'Indictment dismissed.' By now the various court appearances were coming at ever more frequent intervals, and Lustig wasn't the only one with the law on his tail. Dapper Dan Collins was in and out of jail at least four times in the early 1930s, on a variety of charges involving swindling, smuggling, blackmailing and plain theft, although in between times he still managed to fence impressive quantities of bogus $100 bills around the eastern seaboard. Before long Victor himself was apprehended again, in Hartford, Connecticut, in connection with 'illegitimate currency sabotaging of First Citizens Savings Bank', as the complaint formally put it. He was questioned unusually gently and held overnight in a cell that he blustered was 'no worse than a Kansas family hotel room'. A judge, calling it all a case of mistaken identity, released him from custody the following morning. So far from having distributed the phony bills, he ruled, Lustig had innocently pocketed one of them the bank teller gave him, before properly surrendering it the moment he realised the error. The chief of the Hartford police apologised to Victor on behalf of the department, and asked him if he might be willing to give a short lecture on forged currency recognition techniques to the same officers who had just arrested him. The talk was 'highly illuminating', the *Hartford Times* reported.

While Lustig went around the world ruthlessly treating individuals and their financial institutions like so many private ATMs, he became 'gentler, more sincere and attentive' to his own family. Until then he had hardly ever talked to young Betty about her mother. Now, during a walk he suddenly said, 'You can be proud of your momma. It was I who made the mistakes, not her.' A very sentimental gangster, Victor was attuned to his 10-year-old child's fantasy world. He loved to tell fairy tales, and taught Betty to ski, skate, and even in time to play competitive pool. One of his party tricks was to balance an expensive crystal glass on the tip of his nose; he also balanced sharp knives in this way, then gave them a sudden flip and caught them in his hand. Lustig wasn't the first habitual criminal to have an engagingly childlike side to his character, but in his case it was unusually pronounced. One might tentatively conclude he wanted to give his child a significantly different start in life than his own threadbare boyhood. He later wrote to Betty while at a crisis in his affairs:

My dear little honey … I am on my way far away, and I only want to say good bye before I go. So, when you get big you can come to me, but always remember that you have a daddy that loves you and always will, even if you never see him again … From your papa who will never forget you.

As he loosened up in his forties, at least in his family life, Lustig further developed the two skills that were to sustain and dog him throughout his career: his genial capacity to charm people when the situation demanded; and his incurable fondness for spending their money.

The police again came for Lustig on 25 June 1931, and he spent the next three weeks in a St Louis jail cell. He had been staying at the city's Coronado Hotel, where he was registered as Robert Duval, and the charge sheet read: 'Accused of being a fugitive and confidence man … Booked on fraud, imposturing and mutilating Government Obligation … Found with $36,000-worth of U.S. Liberty Bonds, the ink upon them palpably wet.'

This latest collar had been affected by one of Peter Rubano's undercover men, who went to Lustig's hotel room posing as a buyer. The subsequent police report was impressive: 'This man is an internationally known confidence artist, and is wanted in Spokane, Wash, Crown Point, Indiana, Los Angeles and San Francisco, California, Detroit, Mich, Denver, Col, and multiple other areas.' Nonetheless, the file adds: 'The charges were dismissed on July 18 1931 by US District Attorney. Accused was then held for the US Immigration authorities, but gave bond, which he forfeited.' Lustig was fast developing a mystique of invincibility; no matter how often he was arrested, the difficulty lay in persuading an incorruptible judge not to release him again. When the weather turned cooler in September, Peter Rubano wrote in his case report, 'I presume to say I know [Lustig's] habits. Our bird has flown south … The Count, in my opinion, is somewhere under a bluer sky than Washington.'

Rubano's nose was correct: Lustig had migrated back to Florida, where he spent the early autumn busily circulating bogus Liberty Bonds and forged currency. He rarely if ever resorted to strong-arm tactics in the execution of his crimes, but Rubano now made a note in his file of a surge of 'expropriations' around Miami. These were armed robberies of banks or large retailers, carried out by individuals 'who [gave] signs of working on behalf of a higher intelligence'. The most notorious was a hold-up of the Sweetheart Groves Credit Union on 13 October, in which Lustig was suspected of being involved behind the scenes. By that point the local sheriff was also keen to interview him about some irregularities in the accounts at the nearby Hialeah Park racecourse, which was being extensively renovated after suffering hurricane damage. One of the contractors complained that he had been paid with dud $100 bills, and in time several of the serial numbers were matched to similar notes in circulation 1,200 miles away in New Jersey. Although the authorities couldn't make a case against him, Victor found it expedient to move his activities from Florida back to Texas.

With a certain inevitability, Lustig was arrested almost immediately when he checked into the Holmes Hotel in Fort Worth, where he was registered as 'G.R. Warner, representative of Warner Brothers Studio'. The charge sheet reads, 'Investigation on general principles – confidence man.' Released the next morning, Lustig took a leisurely road trip through the south-eastern states, promiscuously exchanging bad $100 bills for good ones along the way, before returning for Christmas in Miami Beach, where he reinvented himself as Baron Robert Wagner. The local police came for him on New Year's Eve. Lustig had gone out to dinner, accompanied by his driver, a 20-year-old lady friend and his visiting daughter, as he often did, but this time they were accosted by three uniformed officers with drawn service revolvers. Victor went quietly, after telling his chauffeur to make sure the two young women got home safely. Booked in for 'investigation – suspected confidence game', he was once again released early the next morning.

That wasn't quite the end of Lustig's immediate problems, because the Department of Labor in Washington DC soon redoubled its efforts to deport him. An almost regal-sounding proclamation went out from the agency on 5 January 1932:

> I, Turner W. Battle, Assistant to the Secretary, by virtue of the power and authority vested in me by the United States of America, do hereby command you to detain and remove this personage to Czechoslovakia, at the expense of the Immigration and Naturalization Service, including that of an armed attendant, as necessary.

This was another target on Lustig's back, but, then as now, Americans were confronted with numerous challenges and confusions in the practical workings of their government. While the Department of Labor wanted Lustig removed post-haste from the country, their colleagues across the street at the Treasury building lobbied for him to be locked up for a very long time indeed in a federal prison. 'Our Office … will pursue all outstanding warrants against [this] individual, whose crimes continue to pose a threat to public safety. This Department believes [his] trial, admission of guilt, and incarceration represent the only satisfactory outcome.' For its part, the Secret Service showed no sign of relenting in its terrier-like pursuit of its quarry. Even the unflappable Lustig found Peter Rubano's sheer persistence alarming, telling his brother

Emil: 'Give me a fair fight, one on one, and there isn't anyone or anything I won't face. But this man isn't human. I'm being hunted by a hell hound.'

Perhaps as a result of these attentions, in March 1932 Lustig saw fit to return for an extended visit to Europe. Toting a crested Prada valise identifying him as Victor Mergler of Kansas City, he made his way to a first-class cabin on the Anchor Line vessel SS *California*, sailing from Baltimore to Glasgow. He was travelling alone, although once on board he quickly made the acquaintance of a fellow passenger named Joan Dupont. Recently widowed, she was going to Paris for the spring to help recover her spirits. Lustig's antennae must have quivered when he saw the still only early middle-aged lady come on board at the head of 'a great conga-line of maidservants, stewards [and] porters' bearing trunkloads of what he assumed to be expensive furs and jewellery. That same night he presented her with an accomplished charcoal drawing, so struck had he been by the scene, of her arrival on the *California*. Overall the work did not impress Mrs Dupont, who it turned out was a fine-art connoisseur, but she admitted that it was executed with some care. It's possible her chief emotion was merely one of surprise at the stranger's boldness. Taking her review in his stride, Lustig bowed politely and withdrew to his cabin. That might have been an end of the matter, except that on her eventual arrival at the Hôtel de Crillon, of all poignant places, Joan Dupont found that her accompanying luggage – though exact proof of its extraction was lacking – had been reduced in number by one medium-sized portmanteau, containing clothes, a pearl necklace, and assorted currency.

Lustig meanwhile made his way to London, where for once he put up not at the likes of the Carlton or the Ritz but in an anonymous-looking family hotel occupying two corner houses in a quiet side street near the British Museum. We can't know if he had actually purloined the contents of Joan Dupont's suitcase, but, if so, he soon seems to have been in need of additional funds. To make good the shortfall, Victor consulted the business pages of the London phone book under the category of gentlemen's outfitters and placed a call to an establishment who advertised their willingness to travel to a customer's residence with a selection of swatches for his perusal. When the firm's junior assistant arrived at the hotel, Lustig invited him upstairs, poured him a drink, and briskly leafed through the samples his visitor had brought him. He was obviously well acquainted with the world of bespoke tailoring. In one of those rare moments when the curtain parted fleetingly to reveal the wizard working the levers, Victor had once remarked that he never wanted to let a business opponent see him slouching around in casual dress. Any sign of weakness was the quickest way for them to size you up and take advantage. 'It is all about perception,' he added.

Lustig probably noticed the salesman's face brighten up as the order reached £200. The young man was getting a commission. After their business was concluded, Victor shook his visitor's hand and casually mentioned that he would like to cash a small cheque downstairs at the front desk. The management was being tedious about this, he added, on account of his being a stranger in town. A few moments later, the tailor's assistant was on the phone to his supervisor. He reported on both the sizable pending order he had just taken from Lustig, and on the latter's temporary shortage of ready funds. There was little need for any further discussion. The supervisor rang the hotel manager and told him that his firm was only too happy to vouch for their guest Mr Mergler. Later that day Lustig successfully cashed his cheque, then returned upstairs, waited until nightfall and left the hotel by means of a convenient drainpipe. In subsequent evidence the young salesperson who had called in with the swatches described the man he had met as 'very smart and educated'. On first entering the stranger's room he had noticed three things: his host was European; he was a 'gent'; and behind him on the desk was a framed photograph of Herbert Hoover, inscribed 'With my deepest thanks and warmest esteem' over the US president's signature.

This story says something about its time, when a toff was usually or always to be trusted, and no one was yet in a position to do a simple internet search of anyone else's name. But it also speaks to Lustig's proven talent for adapting the scammer's stocks-in-trade of deception and manipulation to a given set of circumstances. Had he ever chosen to put his mind to anything resembling honest business ends, he might well have died a rich and respected man.

Weeks after returning from Great Britain, Lustig became embroiled in one of the most violent criminal incidents of the 1930s. Even the hard-boiled detectives of the New York homicide bureau were shocked. In the early hours of 22 July, two Russian-born American citizens, Longin Kovtoun, 48, and Kurt Lamprecht, 42, were found bound and gagged, their bodies 'riddled with shot, and otherwise marred', to quote the police report, dumped face down in a thoroughfare near today's JFK Airport, known, with grim aptness, as Cemetery Lane. According to the *New York Herald Tribune*: 'Both men had been drilled through the head. Their hands were tied, and their mouths were sealed with adhesive plasters. Their bodies lay side by side on their stomachs. There was no sign of a struggle. The assassin or assassins were obviously well versed in their trade.'

The police investigation turned up a number of curious details about the deceased men. For one thing, both went by a variety of aliases, among them Count Boris Kuntsov, Prof. Arcady Szparkowski and Prince Cornelius Hackenbush. These may have sounded like characters in a Marx Brothers film, but the more the detectives looked into the whole business the less they were amused by it. Despite respectively working as a tailor and an office clerk, Kovtoun and Lamprecht each maintained a large house in a fashionable part of Manhattan. Kovtoun had traces of heroin in his system, and an associate told police that he had known the tailor to pull burglaries, practise confidence tricks and even pimp his young wife to support his habit. Lamprecht, for his part, was seemingly a student of the Rumanian Box, because police found detailed sketches of the device in the dead man's notebook. Even more curiously, there were torn up shreds of a US banknote in Lamprecht's stomach – a detail that was not discovered until a mortician came to prepare the body for burial.

'Little more was known about the victims,' the *New York Times* later reported, 'except that, like Count Lustig, they affected the Continental manner, dressed much the same as he did, and had the same smooth hands and perfectly manicured nails.' The sorely abused Mrs Kovtoun told authorities that her husband had often spoken of his good friend Victor, and that she believed the two men had each in some way been plotting to restore the Romanov dynasty to the throne of Russia. On a more immediate note, she added, Kovtoun had recently withdrawn $200 from the family's insurance policy, and taken this with him to meet someone who had promised to alchemise the cash into $30,000. As a result, Lustig was invited in for questioning by the New York police's Special Operations Bureau (SOB) on the sweltering hot Friday afternoon of 12 August, in order to help explain how, exactly, he had come to know Kovtoun, and, for that matter, why the initials 'VL' were jotted down alongside the sketches of the Rumanian Box found in Lamprecht's journal.

Lustig remained unruffled. He told the police that he had never had the pleasure to meet Lamprecht, but that perhaps he had been one of those White Russians with a lingering aversion to the late Bolshevik leader Vladimir Lenin – quite possibly the 'VL' of his diary, he helpfully suggested. Kovtoun and he were acquainted, Lustig acknowledged, but only in the most benign and altruistic manner. The poor man had had something of a bad reputation, Victor explained. People considered him eccentric. He rode a loud motorcycle around town, and had made some poor choices in his private life. Lustig had tried to help him. 'All I did was advance him a little coin,' he insisted. Besides, Lustig added, slipping back into the slightly stilted tones in which he habitually phrased his written statements, before affixing his most florid signature to them, he had been otherwise located during the week of 18 July 1932, entertaining his young daughter 900 miles away in a rigidly selectioned place of lodging at Lowell Park. The officers could ask about him there. They did. A witness said that he had seen Lustig and his child eating dinner together in the resort's beachfront cafe on the late evening of 21 July, and that they had been there again for breakfast on the 22nd. Betty herself told the authorities that she was certain her father had been in the same small cabin as her in the intervening hours, if only because she could hear him snoring in the next bed. The police knew that Lustig was a trickster of legendary proportions, but also that he had little or no known history of violence. In the blunt words of the SOB report: 'This individual is an international flimflam artist and twister. He lives outside society's normal conventions. But he is not the type to take the plunge beyond fraud and imposture and flush his life down the pan for a double homicide.'

The New York police eventually came to believe that Kovtoun and Lamprecht had been tied up with a counterfeiting ring operating somewhere out of New Jersey, and that one or more of their business associates was responsible for the horrors at Cemetery Lane. No one was ever brought to trial for the crime, and the file on Lustig's interrogation ends: 'This man could almost certainly not have been present at the scene … He claims to work in the import-export sector, and [is] domiciled in Illinois. He is married to a woman named Qudback. They live together on and off in Chicago.'

Noting that 'there [were] no known outstanding complaints' against him, the police released Victor without charge.

Forty-eight hours later, Lustig drove out with his brother Emil to visit William Watts in Union City. He discussed his future plans en route. Victor told Emil that the heat was now well and truly on them in Washington, and that it might be best for all parties to keep a low profile in the immediate future. Once in the rooming house on Palisade Avenue, Lustig asked Watts how much counterfeit money he currently had on hand. In reply, Watts silently opened a closet door in his spare bedroom and shone a torch on two identical locked metal suitcases pushed back against the wall. Still without speaking, he released the catches and flipped them open. Each case was stacked to the brim with $100 bills. Lustig cast a seasoned eye over this truly fabulous treasure. 'You've got about 6 million clams there,' he remarked evenly. At the time a new family car cost about $500, and you could rent a comfortable city apartment for $20 a month. Glancing around the rest of the otherwise sparsely furnished bedroom, Lustig saw that Watts's first experience of unsupervised living had been sadly deleterious to his housekeeping standards. The floor of the room was covered with empty pill vials and paperback crime novels. Two sets of sheets were nailed over the windows in place of curtains. The place smelled, and not just of Watts's chemicals. Lustig saw bugs on the floor and a line of ants around the baseboard. Watts himself appeared not to have recently exerted himself when it came to baths or razors. It must have been a distressing spectacle to one of Victor's fastidious nature. 'Perhaps we should shut up shop for a while,' he said, echoing his earlier comments to Emil.

This represented only a temporary lull in Lustig's hectic criminal activities. The warrants against him were steadily piling up, and back in Washington Peter Rubano and his crew were working under increased pressure from the FBI. J. Edgar Hoover began 1933 by firing off a memo to William Moran, director of the Secret Service. Lustig 'could not possibly have acquired large amounts of cash by legitimate means', he began, reasonably enough. 'The subject has a long history as a confidence man. He must be apprehended. Bureau is putting every means available at your disposal,' the portly FBI chief wrote on the morning of 1 January, his own 38th birthday. Lustig himself turned 43 that week, and admitted that his health was becoming a worry. A later physical exam reported: 'Began to take hormone injections in 1932–33. Complained of poor functioning of intestines, and swollen sinuses. Electrocardiogram at that time indicated a worsening of heart condition. Also reported regular headaches and a hoarse throat.' Mentally, however, 'Subject exud[ed] a vigor and enterprise, pressing forward with high-energy plans extending to either coast.' This was the dynamic Lustig of Eiffel Tower days. The doctors concluded: 'His spirit was at no time broken … Others might have paused and desisted. He did not.'

Lustig may have retained his brimming self-confidence, simply moving on after each con and reinventing himself in a new town. But by now the authorities were at last beginning to pool their resources against him. On 23 January, the Milwaukee chief of police wrote to Rubano's office in Washington: 'Party known here as Victor Gross is wanted locally for Confidence Game.' A week later it was the turn of the Detectives' Bureau in Chicago: 'Victor LUSTIG, aka Gruber, aka Gross, wanted here – suspected confidence man.' Later in the month the sheriff of far-off Spokane, Washington, a town already fleeced by Lustig seven years earlier, joined the chorus. A C.H. Baxter had 'willfully deprived individuals in this parish of $48,500', the officer complained. $40,000 of this had been 'extracted by slick claims of future wealth opportunities', while the balance of $8,500 in $100 bills 'were all forgeries distributed to banks, retailers, and the front-desk girl of the Davenport Hotel'.

On 30 January 1933, Paul Niehaus of the Secret Service was instructed to go under an assumed name to a restaurant near Times Square to sit down for lunch with 'our bureau's number-one enemy', and to greet him 'without either causing or exhibiting alarm'. This taxed Niehaus's acting skills to the full when Lustig eventually arrived looking like a Victorian-era foxhunting dandy, wearing a short-fronted plum tailcoat, tight white breeches and buckled shoes, while peering at his companion through an antique quizzing glass. He appeared to be about eighty years and thousands of miles out of place, and did not seem much like a modern gangster hoping to engage in some clandestine activity. Lustig never paused to explain the logic behind the dowager style, nor to apologise for having arrived at the restaurant nearly an hour late. He had long been liberated, it seemed, from such tedious conventions.

Niehaus was there as part of an elaborately arranged sting operation, hoping to steer Lustig around to the subject of counterfeiting. But the interview did not go as intended. As the government man later reported:

> Subject created a climate of warm friendship so rapidly that one felt one had made his acquaintance years earlier ... He at no time spoke [of] currency, or financial instruments of any kind, but restricted himself to pleasantries about the weather and prospects of the New York Yankees ... Later asked me if I was married, and on hearing that I was not promptly offered to introduce me to his sister.

Agent Niehaus's report concluded with the sad admission that 'nothing useful' had resulted from the lunch, although he was attaching the restaurant's bill for $11 ($260 today), which Lustig had allowed him to pick up.

Later that night Victor wrote to his brother Emil, who was in Florida: 'Following developments from Germany today. Disastrous news ... Hidler [sic] is Chancellor, [and] within less than a year I prophecy will have moulded the state into the shape he desires.' Actually it took the Nazi dictator less than two months to consolidate his power through an enabling act. Lustig proved altogether more prescient in the matter than the US State Department, which made no reference to Hitler in its daily briefing to President Hoover on 31 January 1933.

Five weeks later, Lustig celebrated a rare American bank holiday – called by the incoming President Roosevelt to calm panic in the nation's financial institutions – by taking a week's lease on a small beachfront cabin in Fort Meyers, Florida. But for the fact that he was joined there not by his wife but the glamorous Ziegfeld girl

Ruth Etting he might have been just another modestly prosperous out-of-town vacationer seeking some winter sun. Etting (who wore a large hat and sunglasses when out in public) remembered her companion's disciplined routine even while on holiday. Lustig read an improving book each morning from 8 to 10 a.m., and then went out to paddle gently in the sea. On his return he put 'a gallon of sticky green oil' in his hair, and dressed in a fresh white shirt with generously cut shorts and long black stockings that left only his pale kneecaps exposed to the sun. He chewed Wrigley gum, doffed his straw hat to ladies, distributed boiled sweets to passing children, and enjoyed fishing for trout from a chartered boat. After lunch, he retired for exactly two hours before returning to a chair on the front porch with his book. Etting, the professional actor, thought him 'deliberate but extremely poised' in his movements. Wafting up the street 'as if tiptoeing on a rug of air', Victor slipped into the local grocery store at the stroke of six each evening. He returned a few minutes later with a bottle of inexpensive white wine (the US was just then relaxing its thirteen-year ban on alcohol sales) and a copy of the late-edition *Miami News*, which he leafed through for its horse race results. At night he thought it 'great sport' to sit outside and do card tricks for local children – much later he remembered this as the highlight of the week's stay – although he ended each demonstration by solemnly warning his young audience about big city vice and discouraging them from taking up gambling. The greater the scope of Victor's crimes, the more decorous his personal life.

Lustig later insisted that he had not been bothered in the least by the reports that reached him of Peter Rubano's task force, a claim refuted by Ruth Etting in a letter written to her fellow actress Joan Blondell in April 1933. 'He liked to go through the crime pages of the newspaper, and [I] saw him make notes there,' she recalled. 'He told me he was looking for names he recognized, [and] especially those of police officers that he viewed with keen interest and no trace of resentment.' Lustig was far too experienced in the ways of law enforcement not to know that any halfway effective counterfeiting operation was bound to attract the malevolent attention of the Secret Service. He might have been alarmed, even so, by James Johnson's account of a meeting that spring of sixteen darksuited men in an attic room of the Post Office Building on Ninth Avenue in Manhattan, where they had recently moved from their old quarters in Washington. '[Rubano] opened an envelope and removed a hundred-dollar bill from it,' Johnson wrote:

> It made the complete circle of the table without any of us saying anything. We were stunned, for this was the best counterfeit we'd ever seen. It would fool anyone but an expert … 'I think you can now see the reason for [this] assignment,' Rubano said. The counterfeit bill lay on the table in front of him. He tapped it with a blunt finger. 'Find those plates,' he said.

Of course, Lustig couldn't stop breaking the law – it was what he did – regardless of any future consequences of his actions. He'd already advised William Watts to scale down his supply of counterfeit money, and warned associates like Dapper Dan Collins not to parade their wealth. He took his brother Emil out to a modest dinner one night in May 1933 and said: 'You need to keep all this quiet even from your wife. Don't put on any more style. They're watching us.' He made a fetish of secrecy, but that didn't mean he suddenly went straight, particularly when what he saw as a higher cause was involved.

One warm Friday evening early in May, a well-dressed man presented himself at the side door of the imposingly Gothic German chancery building at 1435 Massachusetts Avenue in downtown Washington DC. He told the clerk on duty in the front office that he was in the paper-manufacturing business, and would like to speak to a consular officer about the possibility of opening a factory – with substantial local employment opportunities – in the Ruhr Valley. It was a plausible enough story, and the clerk left the stranger alone for a few minutes while he went off to fetch a senior colleague in another room. Although public buildings weren't then troubled, as they were later, by security cameras, if they had been they might have noticed the visitor deftly insert a tiepin in the lock of the clerk's filing cabinet, open it, remove several documents and pocket them, before, seemingly as an afterthought, help himself to a bundle of cash, then walk smartly back out into the crowds hurrying home for the weekend on the busy street. He had made no apparent effort to conceal his theft, and the embassy officials notified the local authorities that same night. It has to be said that the Washington police did not distinguish themselves. They failed to make an arrest in the case, or even to identify any suspects, although a few days later a plain brown envelope without a return address reached the desk of Cordell Hull, the newly installed US Secretary of State. It contained a copy of a wire from the Foreign Ministry in Berlin outlining the key themes – what we would now call the talking points – of how best to 'sell' the recent civil rights restrictions in Germany to the American press. 'When the Bolshevik menace is stamped out the normal order of things shall return,' one section read. 'Our laws are liberal. No one need fear them. Germany is a tolerant place. But first we must crush this Communist-Jewish underworld.'

It's not known how far, if at all, Lustig made the distinction between 'black' and 'white' crime, the one purely for personal gain and the other in the wider interest as he saw it. But it's certain that he was in Washington that muggy spring night, and that he later wrote to Emil, 'This has been a *most* useful day.'

8

ESCAPE FROM NEW YORK

While Lustig sat down that warm spring night in Washington to congratulate himself on having done his patriotic duty, other agencies of the United States government were redoubling their efforts to put him behind bars. Although he had effectively evaded the law in towns such as Kansas City, Milwaukee and Spokane, the authorities in Chicago proved less inclined to bolster the popular myth of his invincibility. The latest warrant sworn out against him in his hometown must have seemed ominous even to a criminal of his own towering self-confidence:

> Whereas … Hon. Justin F. McCarthy of the Municipal Court of Chicago has determined that the offence of Confidence Game has been committed, and the Court having found that there is ample cause for believing Frank Gardner alias Victor Lustig guilty of such offence, We, therefore, command you forthwith to take said person into custody so that you may have his body before the Municipal Court at 26th Street and California Avenue to answer to the People of the State of Illinois for and concerning said crime, and to be swiftly dealt with according to law …

It was therefore with even more than his usual alertness that Lustig drove out to Union City, twice changing cars en route, on the dank Monday afternoon of 26 June 1933. He had come to an important decision regarding the future, and he did not intend to see it undermined by being arrested. Once at the rooming house on Palisade Avenue, Victor scanned the sleepy-looking residential street for several moments before briskly stepping to the front door, letting himself in, and climbing to the top-floor apartment. There he gave the pre-arranged coded knock, and went in to confer with William Watts.

Lustig's striking first sentence – 'I've come to discuss whether we want to make ourselves truly rich, or to spend the rest of our lives in jail' – set the tone. He went on to tell his criminal accomplice that things had changed significantly since their last meeting nine months earlier. He explained about the squad now installed across the river in Manhattan working feverishly to bring about their downfall, and the pressures on him from other police forces around the nation. He was no longer a young man, Lustig continued. He did not mean to spend his remaining years locked up in a barbaric American prison. Instead, he proposed that Watts now bring his apparatus back to full speed, and that they mutually devote the next twelve months to carefully but steadily producing counterfeit bills. At the end of that period, Lustig remarked, both they and their associates would have enough genuine currency in their pockets to simply disappear. He had given the matter some thought, he concluded, and he was now resolved to take his 12-year-old daughter with him and start a new life somewhere in Europe.

Lustig did not specifically mention his plans, if any, for his wife Susan back in Chicago, but it may possibly have been that he didn't see her as part of the new arrangements. He was an affable man in his way, but given his lifestyle, it was not to be expected that he was monogamous. There had been a distressing scene just a few days earlier when Victor returned home for dinner and found Susan slumped alone in the darkened kitchen with the gas taps on. He had quickly restored the domestic status quo, but there had then been a protracted husband-and-wife showdown the following morning. Weeping inconsolably, Susan had told him that she had had enough. She simply couldn't go through life both sharing him with other women and terrified of a late-night visit from the police, whether they were looking for her husband or, even worse, informing her that he was dead. Victor's efforts to allay her fears on the subject met with only partial success. More composed, but still weeping, Susan presented him with an ultimatum: it was either a life of continued crime, or her.

For many years, Lustig had skilfully played on the various petty feuds and turf wars that existed between individual American law-enforcement jurisdictions, and sometimes even between rival agencies within the same state. As a rule, his preferred tactic following each separate arrest had been to swiftly relocate to another part of the country and change his name. It was all part of the generous American tolerance for personal reinvention. But now that degree of latitude was denied him. Apart from the growing number of outstanding warrants for his arrest there was the matter of the sixteen sober-suited men sitting around the table in their eyrie at the Post Office Building in Manhattan, themselves a testament to the rich diversity of American life, where Peter Rubano presided 'with an air of calm dignity', one agent recalled. 'He [was] imperturbable, and so stony-faced that when he tore off and read each new teletype message you couldn't tell from his expression whether the news it contained was good or bad.'

James Johnson, one of the senior men present, remembered of this group:

We were all races and creeds, the names including Rubano, Seckler, McGuinness, Paterni, Lieberman, O'Hanley, Cheasty and Murphy. The oldest was pushing fifty, the youngest barely in his twenties. Among us were a West Pointer, three young lawyers, two former New York state troopers, an ex-bosun's mate, two members of the New York Police Bomb Squad, and a graduate of Hell's Kitchen. Those were our differences, but our sameness was the fact that we were now all agents of the United States Secret Service.

Lustig's felonies in this period came not in a great surge, but in steady waves, and his appearance on various American provincial police blotters, as one Secret Service agent said, was 'ubiquitous'. He was arrested in January 1934, in Kansas City, roughly 170 miles from the door of the Western Bank of rural Salina, and thus if nothing else keeping his promise of ten years earlier never to again operate in that same area. He seems to have again talked his way out of trouble, because the file on the incident reads 'Discharged – Not Wanted'. In March he was picked up as Robert Wagner in both Philadelphia and Pittsburgh, but again released without charge. In June it was Milwaukee's turn to enquire into the matter of 'Multiple Confidence Games, played by Gross alias Wagner', but once more the accused man walked free. At some stage Lustig appears to have drifted as far west as the small mill town of Vernon, Texas, because a local hotelier there named B.A. Winter later wrote to the authorities:

> Around [that] time a party registered in the Wilbarger Hotel that I own under the name George Warner … I entered into negotiations with him for the purchase of some telegraph and telephone stock that he represented to me he owned. In payment of this stock he was to take a diamond ring – and did take it – in exchange, but after gaining possession of same he vanished and never delivered [the stock] … I learned that a female companion who was with him at the time pawned the ring in Fort Worth, but I never could get a court action in the matter … I believe that this individual was the man known as Victor Miller, or Mueller, or Lustig.

Although June 1934 marked the deadline Lustig had set himself for finally walking away from his old life, when the time came, perhaps unsurprisingly, he found it hard to make a clean break. There were further arrests for him that summer in Memphis and St Louis, although once again he waltzed away without charge. The head of the Detectives Bureau in Chicago was almost impressed by Lustig, in a detached and professional way: 'It is remarkable how often this man seems to command the ear of a judge or court officer, and enlist them on his behalf.'

Perhaps Lustig wasn't entirely beyond all hope of redemption, however, because an Episcopalian lay preacher named Alexander M. Hadden later wrote to him reminiscing about their having met in Palm Beach, Florida, that year. 'I am glad my talking to you about "waking up" your ideas of life was not amiss … ' In turn, Lustig replied, 'I have never believed in anything, [but] I have now read several pages in the Psalms – I like them.' Admitting that his inmate might be an opportunist convert to Christianity, but still preferring to believe in his sincerity, Hadden later wrote to a prison warden: 'I really think [Lustig] with help is ready to change his ideas about living, to try God's way.'

While William Watts continued to mint currency on an industrial scale in suburban New Jersey, Lustig made the final chosen move of his life, to a modest, three-bedroomed family home located at 1614 W. Berteau Avenue in north Chicago. It was an eminently respectable, even sedate, neighbourhood. Ninety years ago, Berteau Avenue was a far cry from the vibrant, marijuana-scented ghetto it later became. There were rows of neat frame houses, each with a small flight of front steps, scrubbed and ready for inspection, and a few also boasting a wide, companionable porch where a becomingly dressed person might be seen seated in a rocking chair. On the whole the graceful, shady street wouldn't have looked out of place in the Croydon or Guildford of the 1930s, although those towns might not have enjoyed quite the same spirit of freewheeling social fluidity that prevailed here. Lustig's immediate neighbours included a vice-president of the Pulaski Savings Bank, a family of recent Chinese immigrants who ran the corner store, and the retired pastor of the nearby Ebenezer Lutheran Church. There was also at least one active member of the Chicago police department. A widow named Edith Keep, who lived in the street, left behind a memoir in which she wrote that the American press had endowed Lustig with 'almost divine powers in his criminal performances … He seem[ed] to do things that could not be explained by the ordinary laws of nature, so brilliant were the tricks and so multifold the jigs he performed.' At first sight, Keep admitted, the individual whom she met shuffling up Berteau Avenue one spring morning in 1935 seemed somewhat disappointing set against this superhuman ideal. Now aged 45, Lustig was a stubby, Chaplinesque figure with an unhealthy pallor, a puffy face, and patches of receding grey hair he revealed when courteously lifting his hat. Although far from the frock-coated dandy who had lunched with Agent Niehaus two years earlier, he was still 'friendly and approachable, with brilliantly clear eyes that seemed to snap an X-Ray picture of each person to whom he spoke'. Victor possessed such courtly charm and insinuating manners that people were instantly beguiled by him. 'He had a fast-moving brain,' Keep wrote.

Lustig had plenty with which to occupy that mind. His family life was in some disarray. He was now effectively separated from his wife Susan. His ex-wife Roberta and her new husband were making trouble for him financially. Victor was still close to his young daughter, but now saw her only for a few weeks each summer. Peter Rubano's elite team was on his case, as we've seen, and one or two regional forces were proving stubbornly interested in his activities. Surprisingly, Lustig was even worried about money. Although he was literally minting the stuff, he remarked to Emil on the fate of elderly 'businessmen' such as himself who ended up working as waiters or bottle-washers once the fruits of their labours had dried up. Some of his old associates were now in jail, he reflected, and others were already dead. Lustig was also certain there would be another war. What most troubled him wasn't the prospect of further bloodshed, but the 'blunders on our side' that allowed Hitler to grow stronger 'with each passing day of sloth' from the West. 'The British are sure all they have to do is give a tea party for him and he will fall back like a wolf who has had his fill,' Lustig wrote, adding: 'I do not believe it.'

Given all these factors, could Lustig have subconsciously – or even consciously – wanted to be captured? His letters and journals in the early weeks of 1935 dwell increasingly on the sense of futility of it all. 'We struggle,' he wrote at one point. 'We reach. And what is there at the end? A clod of dirt flung down upon the coffin lid.' A psychologist author named A.F.L. Deeson spent some years studying Lustig, and suggested that towards the end he'd experienced a sense both of despair and, paradoxically, overconfidence. 'His quick wit helped him out of no less than 48 arrests, and kept him free for over thirty years,' Deeson noted. 'But it was a gradually acquired sense of immunity which eventually let him down.' The manic depressive theory was one taken up by Lustig's first wife Roberta in her journal. 'Sometimes Vic thought he would never be caught. But [later] he was fed up, tired, and he just gave up. By then I wasn't in the wings to go to friends, or to some deposit box to get him off. That woman [Susan] didn't do her job.'

Lustig's criminal file is littered with complaints from police forces around the world. They seem to have come to a crescendo in 1935. Every few weeks trouble would again flare up for him somewhere like faraway Spokane, for instance. Lustig thought the authorities of this 'hick little town' where he'd casually clipped locals for a few thousand dollars' worth of bogus Liberty Bonds were pursuing what amounted to a personal vendetta against him. Signing his latest writ 'For and On Behalf of the People of Washington', Spokane's Sheriff Ralph Buckley made it clear that he and his department were in it for the long haul: 'Robert V. Miller, alias Baxter, alias Lustig remains Wanted by our Office for Confidence Game. The warrant is unexpired, and he will be sought whatever the time or distance involved.'

Over the next two months Sheriff Buckley sent thirty-seven telegrams and four letters to Peter Rubano and his task force at their attic headquarters in New York. Two full-time members of the squad were needed to handle all the traffic coming in about Lustig from police departments across the country. Others, like James Johnson, were out pounding the street to enquire into what he called the 'queer' money entering the tills of banks up and down the eastern seaboard.

Johnson wrote in his energetically sustained idiom:

> I began to make the rounds of bars and restaurants and pool halls and waterfront hotels and bookie joints, looking for my stoolies. During these trips I might see a half-dozen laws being broken, but my job was to arrest only one criminal – the counterfeiter. After I had contacted several of my sources, word spread that I was listening and the stoolies began to come to me of their own accord. The conversations all went pretty much like [the] one I had with a pusher named Weeper Cohen. 'I'm clean, Cap, honest, like I told ya last time,' he protested.

Even so, Johnson needed help in locating the pusher or pushers of the queer C-notes, and he was prepared to do whatever it took to make an arrest. It was the reputation of the police of the day for their occasional strong-arm tactics that seems so distasteful to twenty-first-century palates. 'And the Weeper really tried, because he understood the threat in my words,' Johnson wrote.

One of Agent Johnson's sources seems to have suggested that he investigate the activities of Lustig's brothel-keeping friend Billie Mae Scheible, because in April 1935 the Secret Service set up a system of surveillance, mail interception, phone tapping and burglary both at Scheible's main place of business in Philadelphia and her private residence in an exclusive apartment block on East 74th Street in Manhattan, where she counted a judge of the New York Supreme Court among her neighbours. Rubano himself

Billie Mae Scheible, seen in characteristic pose.

sometimes took a turn sitting in the building's basement with a pair of headphones in order to tune in to the wiretap installed nine floors above him. The listening device was 'very loud and clear', he reported, but the only suspicious note sounded when 'nocturnal noises [made] it clear that Subject was engaged in sexual intercourse, as was often the case, with parties composed of both male and female members'. Clearly this was moral turpitude on Mrs Scheible's part, but it hardly amounted to proof of counterfeiting. The voyeurish insights only fuelled Agent Rubano's determination to get a conviction. 'There is fornication occurring between a large number of people on the premises, and this case raises more criminal possibilities than anything I have seen in a very long time,' he summarised in a report for the personal attention of Homer S. Cummings, the new US Attorney General.

While Lustig was flooding much of the east coast with home-made money, and periodically hiding out with a notorious madam, he also found the time to write devoutly to his daughter at her Catholic boarding school:

> I received your lovely letter and the pictures. Even if they were small, I like them very much. I am sending you some more things this week. When you have time, make a list and let me know your sizes in gloves, dresses, and all other things. It is hard to guess as you are growing like an Indian.

'You say I will be proud of you when you get big,' Lustig continued. 'I think you were wrong. I was proud of you when you were little and am proud of you now. I love you just as you are and always will … I will come to see you sure in June. It is so far away, but don't forget I have made many long trips just to see you, if only for an hour. Someday soon, you and I will have lots of time together.'

Any parent will recognise the essential good intentions of Lustig's last sentence, but it was a promise he was destined not to keep.

There was a curious twist to the way in which Peter Rubano's anti-counterfeiting squad finally made their case against Lustig. For months, the chief and his fifteen subordinates had been patiently sifting through regional police reports of their suspect's relatively petty scores and assorted scams without ever fingering him as 'the arch-criminal … the top of the chain of command [of] those besmirching our currency', as Rubano put it in a report of 2 March 1935. The break in the case came from an unexpected quarter. 'The Good Lord Himself intervened, and showed He has a sense of humor,' Rubano later noted with satisfaction.

On 18 March of that year, a 24-year-old employee of the US Justice Department named Alvar Shell passed between the limestone pillars flanking the front door of the towering Federal Reserve Bank headquarters at 33 Liberty Street in the heart of New York's financial district. The building's designers had aimed for the Italian palazzo look, and the young visitor padded noise-lessly across a multicoloured marble-inlaid floor bathed in the light of six deeply inset bronze windows and a row of cut glass Baccarat Zenith chandeliers. No expense had been spared to convey a sense both of sepulchral calm and fortress-like strength when it came to the business of conducting the flow of the nation's money supply. Shell himself later wrote: 'It was a solemn and stately place. As I approached the door I instinctively softened my footstep … It was like entering a great Cathedral Church. The black-suited men and women seated at their well-polished desks seemed to inaudibly whisper to each other at the arrival of this stranger in their midst.'

Although somewhat nervous to be in such imposing surround-ings, young Shell had come on a relatively routine mission. Each Monday morning, prompt at eleven o'clock, he or one of his fellow juniors would walk down Broadway until they reached what later became the site of the World Trade Center, and then turn up a narrow, winding lane that led to the Federal Reserve. The messen-ger always brought with him a briefcase containing sums of money that might range from a tin box full of assorted coins up to a sealed Manila envelope stuffed with $10 and $20 bills. These represented the funds that well-wishers had sent in from around the country for deposit in a special account designated 'No. 000001- Prisoners' Trust Repository'. At intervals during the year, the proceeds of the account would be added to the general Bureau of Prisons' operating budget in order to bring some small degree of cheer to a particular penal institution or jail. In March 1933, for instance, the fund had been used to help buy 'additional workshop and carpentry supplies' for the inmates of the Lake County Sheriff's House and Keep in Crown Point, Indiana, where it was said 'confined men sit under a leaky mansard roof all day without adequate diversion'. Twelve months later, the bank robber John Dillinger would put these new tools to creative ends when he used them to whittle a sufficiently realistic-looking wooden gun to allow him to escape from custody, before meeting his end one blazingly hot Sunday night four months later in a hail of bullets outside a Chicago cinema.

After depositing the relatively munificent sum of $285.48 that Monday morning, Alvar Shell strolled back uptown to his desk at the local Justice Department building and thought no more of it until three days later, when he received an urgent summons to meet with his supervisor, a Norris Pratt. Pratt showed him a tele-type message he had received from John McCarl, the Comptroller of the United States, one of whose duties was to collate reports of any currency tamperings around the country:

> This Bureau understands that you took funds for deposit in the Prisoners' Trust in the amount specified, representing charitable donations from groups and individuals.
>
> Today the Federal Reserve Bank notified me of a $10.00 counterfeit bill included in that deposit. My associate subse-quently called at the Reserve and gave them a genuine $10.00 bill to replace the phony one, which they surrendered to me.
>
> I have since presented the counterfeit bill to the Secret Service Office, New York, N.Y., and obtained an affidavit from Mr. Peter A. Rubano, Agent in Charge, stating that the bill is associated with his [investigation of] Robert V. Miller, alias Count Lustig.

It seemed that Lustig and his distributors had somehow passed one of their smaller bills to a party who had in turn innocently donated it to a prisoners' welfare charity. As McCarl later observed, the speed with which the Secret Service moved in the matter 'was a measure of the gravity they attached to it'. By the first week of April, Rubano had satisfied himself that 'the bogus 10-spot [had] entered the system [within] a five-mile corridor extending from Guttenberg, NJ, in north to Hoboken, NJ, in south', with Union City lying almost exactly midway between the two points. Even before the blameless Alvar Shell had been called in to be grilled by his boss, Rubano's agents were in motion, driving at speed across the newly opened George Washington Bridge and fanning out to make door-to-door enquiries in the riverfront Hudson Palisades area of northern New Jersey.

Meanwhile, a second Secret Service unit was still watching Billie Mae Scheible's apartment on Manhattan's Upper East Side. There had recently been some technical issues involving the listening post in the building's basement, so Rubano's men moved their operations to a vacant room located two floors above their subject's. James Johnson wrote of this new arrangement: 'Each time the phone rang there'd be a buzz on our earphones, and then we'd hear all the conversation from both ends. We had learned that Scheible had introduced Lustig to her friends as Mr. Frank, so we mentally added that name to all his aliases and settled in.'

It was exhausting and often tedious work, Johnson admitted, although there were sometimes consolations along the way. 'Things were always very quiet until around six each evening and then the phone would be pretty busy until one or two the following morning,' he noted. Some of the transcripts made colourful reading, touching as they did on matters such as the going rate for one of Mrs Scheible's girls ($15 for a call-out, or $25 if she spent the night) and various client preferences, such as the man who 'wanted to call his companion "Mother" while they had congress', and the party – 'a well-known official of the New York court' – who appeared with a box of live cockroaches (of which, then as now, there was no shortage in Manhattan) and watched as his partner crushed them underfoot while wearing a pair of stiletto heels and little else. After reading the first week's reports of his men in the field, William Moran, the morally austere, 71-year-old head of the Secret Service, wrote to Rubano: 'Am not interested in the details of [Scheible's] business. In future, eliminate all material not having to do with counterfeiting.'

★★★

Thanks to the Secret Service's enquiries into the origins of the $10 bill passed at the Federal Reserve, Peter Rubano knew that there was a high-quality printing press operating somewhere on the upper New Jersey shore. His bureau had also compared the design of the bill to that of the forged tender that had turned up nearly ten years earlier in St Louis, and were keen to speak to William Watts as a result. And they further knew that the elusive Count Lustig was one and the same as the client known to the staff of Billie Mae Scheible's establishment as Mr Frank, and that on occasion he was known to visit Scheible herself at her apartment in New York. All Rubano now needed to do to close the case was to find and arrest Frank and persuade him to give up Watts and his money-making apparatus. Lustig 'may believe himself safe and righteous, but with God's help I shall drive him into the light,' Rubano wrote, sounding almost like a revivalist preacher.

At its core, it seemed to be no more than a relatively straightforward surveillance exercise. But identifying Lustig proved to be the most difficult aspect of the entire operation. Men fitting his general description came and went at Scheible's residence at all hours, and as a rule these individuals were not anxious to be recognised. They wore their coats with the collars turned up, and they invariably walked briskly both in and out of the apartment house's front door directly from or into a taxi. One night Rubano was staking out the building from a car parked across the street when he spotted what he described as a 'tall, rangy figure [with] thick ears waving from under his hat', whom he thought might be their man. A call went out to the half-dozen other agents huddled nearby to prepare for an arrest. But when the visitor came out again a few minutes later and paused for a moment on the front step to light a cigarette, Rubano saw to his disappointment that he was 'much younger – perhaps only 28 or 30' than their suspect, and the order went out to stand down.

As all this was going on, Lustig himself was moving freely around the American Midwest, continuing to pull off isolated frauds as he went. Although he obviously did so chiefly for the money, sometimes he seemed to take more pleasure from the clean professional finish of a well-executed scam. In late April, a hard-nosed Chicago banker named Albert S. Snary (commonly known to dissatisfied customers by the acronym formed by his initials) complained that a 'very smooth European character' had stopped him in the street and asked him to sign papers that he understood were a petition to recall the notoriously anti-business mayor of the city, Edward Kelly. In fact he was signing a loan application made out in favour of one Robert Duval. Snary realised his mistake only after the well-spoken stranger had successfully collected his money from the bank later that same day. His second mistake probably lay in reporting the crime to the police instead of making good the loss from his own pocket. The bank's directors soon learnt of the matter and wrote to formally censure their manager for his 'gross laxity' of judgement. To their minds, Snary was as much the guilty party in the affair as Duval was. In time a Detective Lando of the Chicago Major Crimes Squad investigated and concluded that Lustig, whom he knew well, had since left the city and was therefore unavailable for comment, though not 'free from suspicion'. This decision further shifted the blame to Snary, who was fired.

The circumstances leading up to Lustig's arrest are complex and disputed. His daughter Betty saw it almost in terms of Shakespearian treachery, writing that her mother Roberta had 'taken [me] on a little vacation from school to see my father. Doug Conner, Roberta's new husband, had always been jealous of Victor. He tracked [me] down, found out where my father was, and reported him to the Secret Service.'

While plausible, this account may owe something to Betty's tendency to see only the best in her father and only the worst in nearly everyone else. Lustig was seized not in Chicago, as she says, but in New York, and the primary cause of his downfall after more than twenty years of successfully eluding justice around the world was his intimate association with the keeper of a popular brothel. In the end, he was ruined by sex.

There was one further twist to the story of Lustig's demise. It, too, involved what could be called man's lower functions. A note preserved by the US Justice Department remarks that at some stage in the spring of 1935, 'Mrs. Scheible discovered Subject was engaged in carnal relations with another female ... No doubt she was hardened to the world of titillation and sex, [but] she was still not prepared to accept a deception of this sort. In a fit of jealousy she placed a call to law enforcement advising of [Lustig's] location.' If true, it would mean that Scheible performed much the same role as that of Anna Sage – the 'Woman in Red' – in fingering her lover John Dillinger to the feds ten months earlier. According to this version – which Scheible herself always hotly denied – Lustig was undone, as in a Greek tragedy, by a passion that overcame his better judgement, and more particularly by his appetite for women.

Operation Dracula, the overall Secret Service plan to rid society of the degenerate Count and his private mint, reached a climax in the days leading up to Easter 1935. Peter Rubano and his agents were still going door to door around the north New Jersey coast by day, and sitting in or near the apartment building on Manhattan's Upper East Side by night. It had already been over a month since the discovery of the phony $10 bill deposited at the Federal Reserve Bank. 'A lot of manpower, a lot of taxpayers' money, and a lot of time were being devoted to a wire tap at [74th Street] that produced nothing but some racy dialogue,' James Johnson wrote. 'The Secret Service chief in Washington began to get fidgety; our Special Squad chief began to get fidgety; those of us who had to sit in that small room with a pair of earphones clamped on our heads for hours on end certainly got fidgety. The apprehension of [our] suspect and the counterfeiting engraving plates seemed remote.'

It's impossible to know for sure how great a role either Doug Conner or Billie Mae Scheible played in tipping off Rubano's force to Lustig's whereabouts following his return to New York on Thursday, 25 April. It may have been that a combination of outside information and dogged police work played equally vital parts in the outcome. Or perhaps Victor had simply grown weary of running. Unshakeable as he was, he later wrote of what he called the 'hard new tactics' being employed against him. In later years, Rubano himself wrote generously, 'The man known as Count Lustig did more in his mental and physical debilitation than any other agency to bring about his fall.'

On the Monday morning of 29 April, a black car pulled up at an intersection in New York's Little Italy, about 5 miles from East 74th Street. Two Secret Service agents in dark suits and hats suddenly leapt out, seized a man who had been passing by, and bundled him into the back seat. He was a 42-year-old German American bookmaker's assistant and Great War veteran named Josef Gesell, and the authorities wanted to speak to him about counterfeit bills he had apparently been passing around town.

The pick-up did not go quite as planned, however. Gesell put up a struggle in the back of the car, and the end result was that one of the officers pulled his service revolver and shot him through the neck. The suspect was taken, seriously wounded but still alive, to the emergency room of the nearby Bellevue Hospital. By that stage Gesell was delirious. 'These are the men who took me before!' he shouted, as orderlies wheeled him into the operating theatre. 'Sergeant! *Mein Gott!* Help me, I'm falling into their hands again!' – and 'other loud cries in this same vein', to quote the police report, apparently triggered by his experiences in the trenches. Gesell recovered, but was 'not considered a useful witness thereafter', the report concluded.

Three days later, Peter Rubano sent a progress report to his superiors in Washington. In it he lauded the 'very meticulous and patient work' his agents continued to perform in the field. On 4 May, however, William Moran wrote a memo of his own in which he apparently became 'unhinged' and 'made several sharp comments' about the desirability or otherwise of paying government employees to 'loaf around a New York bawdy house' at all hours of the day and night. On 6 May, Rubano was summoned to a situation conference at the new Justice Department building located about a mile down Washington's Pennsylvania Avenue from the White House. As he was ushered in to a large foyer with marble floors, ample natural light, and heavy Italian chandeliers – US federal agencies tended not to stint themselves on their upkeep in the 1930s – Rubano noticed several men in overalls painting a large mural on the back wall above a long row of lift doors. The scene depicted a cowering man on the steps of a courthouse, with a seraphically robed judge, illuminated by a ray of sun, interceding between him and a lynch mob. There was a note of preternatural calm about the Justice Department building as a whole that stood in contrast to the litany of terrible crimes and punishments often under discussion there.

Once upstairs in the conference room it soon became apparent to Rubano that this was not going to be an occasion for constructive, two-way dialogue, nor a convivial exchange of professional courtesies. Instead, William Moran shouted at him for several minutes, and then the Attorney General himself, Homer Cummings, joined the group to emphasise that the government would not waste any further money subsidising men who apparently chose to 'sit around a New York cathouse' without making an arrest. It had all bordered on a 'schoolmaster's bawling-out', Rubano later recalled. He was given a week in which to conclude his investigation or face the consequences.

Four days later, on the afternoon of Friday, 10 May, the headphones crackled in the Secret Service's sparsely furnished hideout on the tenth floor of Billie Mae Scheible's apartment house. Agent Johnson made a shorthand note of the phone conversation that followed. It was an exchange between an unidentified man and a woman named Violet, whom Johnson described as a 'colored maid' employed by Scheible:

Violet: Hello.
 Man: [warmly] Hello, Violet. How are you?
Violet: [coolly] Hello. Ah'm all right.
 Man: This is Mr. Frank.
Violet: Yeah, ah knows.
 Man: May I speak to your mistress?
Violet: Ah don' know iffen' she's not busy.
 Man: Run along and see, like a good girl.

After some more in this same hard-boiled 1930s vernacular, Johnson then quotes Mr Frank as saying he would 'be up [at 74th Street] in about an hour'. Perhaps the government man was simply confused by the suddenly fast-breaking events of the week, however, because literally scores of press reports attest to the fact that the critical visit occurred two days later, on Sunday, 12 May, just twenty-four hours before the deadline imposed on Peter Rubano by his bosses at the Justice Department. As Rubano noted, 'By then it was a case of Count Lustig's head, or my own.'

There was a touch of farce about the particulars of the arrest. At about four in the afternoon of the 12th, Rubano, Johnson and a colleague named Frank Seckler took up position in the doorway of an apartment block across the street from Mrs Scheible's building. 'I had a picture of Lustig in my pocket, and we had studied it on the way uptown,' Johnson recalled. 'It was not a clear picture, and it was at least six years old, but we thought we could make him out all right.'

Agent Johnson's confidence proved ill-placed. Confusion and hesitation reigned as the three lawmen continued to peer up and down the street into the early evening hours for any definite sign of America's most wanted criminal fugitive. As the official assessment of the day's events later noted: 'It was never possible to conclusively identify [the] suspect, although several individuals fitting his general type entered and left the premises. No approach was made, however, as [the agents] might have revealed themselves as federal officers by any premature attempt at seizure.'

Just before six that evening, a well-dressed man with a neatly clipped moustache and holding a black briefcase left the front door of Scheible's building. None of the watching Secret Service men had seen him previously go in. James Johnson, who was then in the process of lighting a cigar, dropped his match to the ground in a moment of shocked recognition. The man was both older and about 20lb heavier than in the mugshot Johnson carried in his pocket. But there was something 'chillingly familiar' about him, and he held himself like someone who was used to avoiding unwanted attention. Moving off at a brisk clip, the man seemed either unconcerned or even mildly amused by the thought that he might now be under surveillance. After weeks of restless anticipation, he was 'striding confidently, looking as happy as if he was going to a ball game,' Peter Rubano later reported. After a block or two, the stranger turned in to a drugstore around the corner on Lexington Avenue. James Johnson followed him there. 'I bought another cigar and then entered a phone booth against the back wall,' he wrote. As Johnson dialled the number of the downtown Secret Service headquarters, 'I looked through the glass panel in the door and directly at [the man's] face. It was Lustig.'

What followed had a touch of the silent film slapstick Keystone Cops as much as of America's most feared crime-busting unit to it. While Johnson excitedly rang his office, Lustig walked quickly out of the drugstore and got into the back seat of a dark-coloured Chevrolet that was waiting at the corner. There was a driver at the wheel and the motor was running. The car took off to the west, then made a screeching right turn and headed north up Fifth Avenue towards Harlem. Johnson hurriedly joined his colleagues in their own unmarked Model B Ford and set off in pursuit. After twenty minutes of zigzagging progress around northern Manhattan the government men, whose car lacked a siren, paused briefly at a red light. As they moved off again, Johnson admitted, 'We looked like chumps.' Lustig's car had pulled far ahead of them and was now nowhere to be seen. 'That man wears a coat of invisibility,' Rubano later insisted he had said, although some of his colleagues would remember their chief having salted his remarks with an intensifier or two that perhaps owed something to his time in the army.

After that, the Secret Service officers drove randomly up and down for a few blocks, but to no avail. By then dusk was falling. 'Finally, with a sick feeling we turned back downtown,' Johnson wrote. For the first time, the agents wondered if their long hours of surveillance had been in vain. The Justice Department historian who later interviewed Rubano, Johnson and Seckler wrote: 'The men were despondent. They believed Lustig had "made" them in their chase, and that they had now lost the day. They were convinced the operation would end in disappointment rather than in an arrest. Chief Rubano voiced the opinion that Lustig would likely be in Canada by the morning.'

About thirty minutes later, the crestfallen G-men again pulled up at the door of Billie Mae Scheible's red-brick apartment building on 74th Street. Their plan was to apprise their colleagues upstairs of the evening's events and then call it a night. On arrival, Johnson recalled:

> We [got out] of the car and stood silent and depressed about our failure on the shadow … As I paused there, immersed in gloom, a vision floated slowly before my eyes. It was a Chevy car and in the front seat Victor Lustig now sat talking animatedly to the driver. I blinked my eyes and looked again. It was no vision. It was reality.

As Johnson and his colleagues watched, Lustig's car drew up and parked only some 50 yards from where they stood in their forlorn conference. There was a split-second of frozen silence like that of a football crowd reacting to a sudden goal, and then the three agents were all moving together in a crouching run down the street, their weapons drawn, towards the parked car. When Johnson reached the right front side of the Chevrolet, he sprang upright and pulled open the door.

'Secret Service!' he said, seizing Lustig by the collar. 'Hands in the air.'

Lustig did as he was told, calmly appraising the faces of the men now swarming all around him, until he noticed Peter Rubano.

'Oh, I remember you,' he said, as Rubano slapped on the cuffs.

The agents took Lustig – who initially told them his name was Robert Wagner, an alias he soon relinquished – downtown, where he was booked on suspicion of counterfeiting. Even then he was still working the angles. Lustig told Rubano and the others that he had been on his way to meet a mark – a millionaire Canadian businessman who was a sucker for the Rumanian Box – and that if they only allowed him to keep his appointment he would return voluntarily for more questioning in the morning. Unabashed by

Federal agents Peter Rubano (left) and Robert Godby finally get their man.

the resulting laughter, Victor added in all apparent seriousness: 'The gentleman has ten thousand dollars that he *wants* to give me. With all his eager heart he will force it upon me. It seems a crime to deny him his wish.'

The Secret Service somehow failed to share Lustig's view that he was practically doing the Canadian businessman a favour by taking his money, and instead led him to an 8ft by 10ft holding cell at the downtown Federal Detention House. The receiving officials allowed him to keep his civilian clothes but searched him thoroughly for any hidden weapons. They pulled a wallet from a concealed pocket in his coat and found a key tucked inside it. Lustig cheerfully agreed that it was his, and that if the officers would only allow him to communicate with his friend Robert Tourbillon, he would show them what to do with it. 'He continued to see himself as running things from jail,' Rubano wrote in his report, 'and seemed eager enough to help with our inquiries.' Lustig may even have believed, though Rubano himself later denied it, that his cooperation was part of a formally negotiated deal that would excuse him from any tedious court appearance. The more reality closed in on him, it seemed, the more he escaped into a fantasy world.

In the morning, the key led agents to the Times Square subway station, where it opened Locker Number 00099. Inside it Rubano and Johnson found $51,000 in phony currency and the plates from which it had been printed. When Rubano brought the money back to the Detention House Lustig bowed, smiled and calmly asked for his coat back. He apparently still thought that that was an end of the matter. 'But we retained him,' Johnson drily noted. On the afternoon of the 14th, Lustig went before a judge to be arraigned for possession and conspiracy. One of Rubano's men saw him stroll past on his way into the courtroom, 'smiling like a boy going off on a holiday', and couldn't restrain himself. 'Count,' he said, 'you're the smoothest con man that ever lived.'

Lustig politely demurred. 'I wouldn't say that,' he replied. 'After all, you've just conned me.'

Few of the major American daily papers failed to splash the story of Lustig's arrest on their front pages. This was hardly surprising, if only because so many of the citizens of their respective towns had suffered from having made his acquaintance over the years. '"COUNT" SEIZED HERE WITH BOGUS $51,000; Arrest of Suave Jail-Breaker Leads to Subway Cache' read the *New York Times*, comparing Lustig to a character out of a racy E. Phillips Oppenheim spy novel. 'Federal Men Arrest Count, Get Fake Cash' the *Chicago Tribune* announced, in a story set higher on the page than the latest news of President Roosevelt's plan for national economic recovery. The *Los Angeles Times* went for irony: 'World's Most Notorious Swindler says Police Ruined his Career'.

Lustig readily admitted to the Secret Service that he knew the master forger William Watts, but that he had no idea where he lived. After a day and a night of continuous interrogation, however, he made a rookie mistake and told his captors that Watts had once mentioned to him that he had 'a comfortable room with plenty of morning sunlight, and that he could look out of his window at the ships bustling around the 57th Street pier just across the river'. It was an uncharacteristic error. For most of the time Lustig was in the Detention House his jailers were struck by 'his complete calmness'. He 'never protested, only smiled coolly' and 'spun an endless variety of tales, entertain[ing] us by demonstrating his street wiles with a pack of cards,' Peter Rubano wrote. On 21 May Rubano went to Lustig's cell for what he called 'an eminently civilised conversation'. At the end of the exchange, the prisoner, who was cuffed and shackled, asked the law enforcement professional if by chance he was missing anything. Lustig had somehow lifted his watch.

Two days later Lustig was moved up from the holding area to the top floor of the jail, where he was given the comparative luxury of his own cell. Although he spoke ruefully about the birds chirping each morning outside his barred window, his life there was passable. The room, number D10, had a wooden bunk, a flush toilet and a wash basin with hot and cold running water under a large vanity mirror, an overhead light bulb in a metal shade, and even an hour of supposedly inspirational choral music piped in over the loudspeaker each breakfast time. Lustig spent most of his first afternoon scrubbing every square inch of his new accommodation with toilet paper. After dinner – a plate of watery stew and bullet-hard carrots, which he ate with a blunt spoon – he repeated the process. Over the next few days he seemed to display an almost fetishistic interest in sanitation and hygiene generally, as a result of which he was issued a mop and broom and assigned to clean the prison day room each morning, when the other inmates were out exercising. According to the Department of Corrections records, Lustig showed a 'solid sense of discipline' and 'none of the usual outbursts of temper' expected of most new arrivals at the facility. 'He was always at [the warders'] command to be of help and service.' When Peter Rubano and some of his colleagues arrived one morning to ask Lustig if he would accompany them outside to recreate his arrest for the invited news cameras, he was happy to oblige. Beaming with pleasure when he was led out to meet the press, 'the Count conversed with them about theater, art, and automobiles – in every respect the picture of a model citizen,' Rubano later wrote of the scene, 'until you [noticed] the irons at his ankles and wrists.'

It may have all been a show, because Lustig privately admitted to an 'utter dejection' during those first few days of confinement. It was 'infernally hot' on the upper floors of the jail, and his nights there were 'difficult' as a result. The pain from his swollen sinuses was so excruciating that he could get little sleep anyway. Visitors were shocked by his appearance. He was grizzled and pale, almost unrecognisable. 'I found him sitting like a frozen thing at the barred window of his cell,' his estranged wife Susan wrote to her predecessor Roberta. Lustig's daughter Betty added that at one stage the Secret Service 'spent 32 hours interrogating [him] and wearing him out. They let him go to the men's room only twice and then under supervision.' Despite this, Lustig seems to have provided no further information about William Watts and his printing press beyond his initial slip about the view from Watts's window. Peter Rubano reported: 'Some of us shouted at [Lustig], while others spoke across the table to him in a friendly voice as if to a sick pet. All our efforts were equally fruitless.'

That Lustig was fit to stand trial was attested by the prison physician, Dr Humbert, who wrote in a special report to the Justice Department on 23 May that his patient had no symptoms of serious disease or mental illness. The doctor, who seems to have had some psychiatric training, concluded, 'He is a generally pleasant person, free of neurosis, although understandably distressed by his present surroundings.' Lustig had an unerring ability to adapt to circumstances, but an equally pronounced need for liberty. 'His adjustment to life here cannot be predicted with any amount of certainty,' the doctor added.

On 27 May, Lustig went before the US Court for the Southern District of New York to be formally charged with 'Unlawful Possession of Counterfeiting Paraphernalia for US Currency' ('Is there ever a lawful possession of them?' he enquired mildly of the judge) and given $50,000 bail, which he failed to raise. There was still some question of whether or not he would ever face trial in an American courtroom, because in July the Department of Labor in Washington again filed an order for his deportation to Czechoslovakia. There seems to be no further surviving paperwork on the subject beyond an internal Secret Service memo of 2 August 1935 saying: 'Subject will not be expelled, due to international situation.' Perhaps the Prague government, preoccupied as it was just then with the matter of its nation's survival in the face of Nazi territorial aggression, simply felt reluctant to welcome back a wayward son and hardened career criminal.

★★★

Lustig made his first, amateurish attempt at escape on Independence Day in 1935. At around 9 o'clock that warm Thursday evening, some of the 'trusty' – or at least non-homicidal – prisoners were allowed up on to the building's rooftop exercise yard to watch the 4 July fireworks. It must have been especially poignant for a man who had enjoyed the same spectacle ten years earlier from the penthouse of a nearby luxury hotel. As the red, white and blue stars burst overhead, Lustig edged backwards towards a funnel-shaped ventilation shaft set up in the corner. In theory a man could have squeezed down this and dropped all the way to the prison's laundry eleven floors below in the basement. Lustig seems to have made no special preparations for his breakout, nor to have planned how to make good his escape from the building itself. Perhaps he thought the guards would be distracted by all the celebrations. He got as far as partially unscrewing the wire grille over the opening of the shaft when he was spotted and unceremoniously bundled back downstairs into his cell. He was put on Number 2 Rations – bread and water – for the next week. 'I had begun to grow weary of institutional life, and felt the need of some fresh air,' Lustig later remarked in a letter to his daughter Betty. At that point the once globetrotting confidence man had spent just fifty-two days behind bars.

Agent Johnson wrote:

> With Lustig in prison, the flow of William Watts's counterfeit notes began to dry up. We guessed that Watts was probably afraid to [operate] because of the past experience of counterfeiters. Several of the better engravers had been kidnapped by gangsters, forced to engrave plates, and when the job was done they were murdered. He must have known this and been reluctant to make new contacts when Lustig disappeared.

Watts's edginess was understandable: Peter Rubano and his men were also closing in on him, having narrowed their search to the stretch of Palisade Avenue between 35th and 40th Streets in Union City, ironically close to the town's main police station. It was now only a matter of time, Rubano assured William Moran, his boss at the Secret Service. 'Our notorious confidence man will have company in jail before Labor Day [2 September],' he predicted.

Lustig spent some of his time that cruelly hot summer writing letters to men high up in the chain of the US government such as President Roosevelt and his Secretary of State, Cordell Hull. He apparently did so not so much to appeal for clemency as to polish his credentials as a great geopolitical thinker by drafting a series of articles on 'Anarchism or Nazism?' in which he argued that Hitler, while bad, at least knew what he was doing when it came to imposing state control over the economy. Lustig remained a staunch believer in national monetary stability. In between these ruminations on the world scene, he was also able to confer twice a week with a visitor to the jail calling himself 'Mr. Tyler', who it later emerged was Dapper Dan Collins in a black wig. Sometimes Tyler was accompanied by a 'buxom young lady [who] wore boots with high heels and a plunging red blouse'. The woman's effect on the sex-starved inmates can be imagined. But generally prison life was as monotonous for Lustig as it was for anyone else. 'The routine numbs you,' he wrote to Betty, only now coming to appreciate what it meant to be locked up for month after month. 'There are no individuals … Everyone's clothes are the same, the cells are the same, the meals are the same. It tears a man down.'

James Johnson could barely conceal his glee at this state of affairs. 'We had Lustig,' he wrote. 'And this was no hick jail in Texas or Indiana. He was in a federal prison. And on a federal rap. He had at last overplayed his hand.'

On Sunday, 1 September, at about 12.30 p.m., the guards let Lustig out of his cell for his scheduled two hours of lunch and unsupervised – or insufficiently supervised – free time. When no one was watching he ducked back into his cell and swiftly shook loose a long, thin object tucked inside his mattress. Then he sidled along the corridor, took the stairs down to the third floor at a bounding trot, picked the lock on a janitor's storage room, and silently closed the door behind him. There was a wire mesh screen covering the room's window, which looked out on the relatively light Sunday lunchtime traffic passing 40ft below on West Street. Victor had a small knife liberated from the prison kitchen in one hand and an improvised rope made up of strips of soiled bed linen in the other. The director of the FBI himself later wrote that there was both 'skill' and 'devilish cunning' involved in Lustig's actions that day. Probably only in America could the head of the nation's domestic security service applaud the spirit of enterprise of one of its most prolific criminals.

At about 3 o'clock that same Sunday afternoon, Peter Rubano, James Johnson and several of their colleagues were hard at work in their room at the top of Manhattan's nearby Post Office building. Rubano had only a few hours left in which to make good on his pledge to capture William Watts by Labor Day, and he was pulling out all the stops. Stretching his legs, the Secret Service man walked across the room to study a large map of New Jersey on the wall, its face studded with coloured pins representing possible leads in the case. By now there were several dozen of them. Words like 'Queer' and 'Socko', along with various addresses and phone numbers, were scrawled in crayon across the top of the map. Sighing, Rubano sat down again. He was about to make a call to one of his agents still out going door to door in Union City when the phone rang pre-emptively next to him. It was the warden of the Federal Detention House. He told Rubano of an unusual occurrence at his facility. When the guards had done their rounds following lunch that day they found a scrap of paper pinned to the bed in cell D10. On it someone had neatly written out these words, addressed to Rubano, taken from Volume 3 of Victor Hugo's *Les Misérables*:

He had allowed himself to be drawn into a promise. Jean Valjean held that promise, and a man must keep his word even with a convict – above all, with a convict. It may give him confidence and guide him to the right path. After all, law was not made by God, and man can be wrong.

There was no sign of the individual who had copied out these lines, the warden added. As a result, it seemed that Agent Rubano would fall short of keeping his own promise about finally breaking up America's most notorious counterfeiting ring. It wasn't just that, with only nine hours to go before Labor Day, William Watts still remained at large. Not for the first time in his career, Victor Lustig had completely vanished.

9

THE ROCK

Just after 11 that Sunday night, J. Edgar Hoover was woken by a phone call from the Secret Service chief William Moran to be told that Lustig had absconded. Moran had deliberately waited several hours before breaking the news to his irascible law-enforcement colleague in the faint hope that the fugitive might be recaptured in the meantime. 'I had no great desire to be the bearer of these unhappy tidings if it could be helped,' he later wrote.

Moran was right to be apprehensive. The 40-year-old Hoover, already in his twelfth year as FBI director, was not pleased to learn that one of America's most notorious criminals had managed to walk out of New York's main detention centre in broad daylight. He wanted answers, he announced, speaking at peak volume, demanding that a report be on his desk by 9 o'clock the following morning. Hoover's anger during their brief exchange had been sufficient for Moran to recall listening to a flow of locker-room language at the other end of the phone 'so furious I had to hold the receiver away from my ear'.

The details of Lustig's escape were both dramatic and relatively easy for Moran to reconstruct. As he sheepishly admitted in his hurriedly prepared report the next morning, 'Several dozen civilians [had] witnessed the inmate's departure.' After removing the wire screen covering the upstairs janitor's room window, it

The third-floor window from which Lustig made his break.

seemed Lustig had tied one end of his improvised rope ladder to a radiator and held tight to the other end in order to swing to earth like a geriatric Spider-Man. To cap a truly bizarre scene, the prisoner had taken a brief time out in mid-descent by pausing to rest on a second-floor window ledge. When a group of 'mildly interested street loungers' had stopped to point up at him, Lustig had calmly pulled a handkerchief from his pocket and pretended to be a window washer. According to one report, 'He lingered there some time, courteously greeting passersby with a wave of his fluttering white cloth.'

Landing on his feet, Lustig then gave a low bow to his audience and walked almost directly past the front door of the Post Office building to Foley Square, where he hailed a passing yellow taxi. Incredibly, he then spent his first night of freedom back with Billie Mae Scheible in the same 74th Street apartment house where he'd been arrested four months earlier. Scheible gave him a change of clothes and some money. In the morning, Lustig took a cab to the Consolidated Transport Terminal in Times Square and bought a one-way bus ticket to Pittsburgh. Scheible had provided him with a dark suit, a straw hat and a pipe, so that he looked like almost any other respectable Labor Day traveller. Although he thought he recognised a Secret Service man standing near the ticket window, Victor recalled that his departure from New York had been 'mostly decorous' and 'quite unopposed by Mr. Rubano'.

The actual means of Lustig's escape from Manhattan's supposedly impregnable House of Detention were harder for William Moran to explain, and various law-enforcement agencies kept up a lively correspondence on the subject for many months to come. It turned out that the kitchen knife he used to cut away the window screen was what Moran called 'a jail heirloom, employed by many prisoners for peeling apples, cutting bologna, etc, and kept secreted behind some pipes in the rear of Cells C11 and C13 for any inmate desiring to use it'. Compounding the problem, as Moran saw it, was both the sorry state of repair of the prison and the laxity of some of its guards. He wrote:

> For a period of years, the windows on the upper floors were allowed to remain in an unsafe condition … No inventory or accurate count was kept by the prison authorities of sheets issued to inmates, and due to the lack of any appropriate system in this regard it was possible for the Count to procure the linen he required … The searches of the cells conducted weekly on Saturday mornings were perfunctory … No system was provided for counting the inmates as they went daily around for recreation purposes between the hours of 12.30 PM and 3.00 PM, and due to this defect, the Count had at his disposal a lengthy period in which to cut the protective wire mesh and make his exit …

In addition to the knife and the bed linen, it seemed that Lustig had also enjoyed the use of a pair of 'high-quality pliers in [his] flight, and that these were conveyed to him by a party or parties unknown'. The suspicion in law-enforcement circles was that this individual was the mysterious Mr Tyler, or his female companion. 'The wire nippers were sharp but compact, and might have been concealed in the woman's natural cavity,' the government report suggested coyly. Hoover wanted further details on this last point. 'Advise if tests are [to be] conducted on feasibility of concealing this item as specified,' he wrote. 'Is it to be directly done, or placed within a tube inserted where you describe?' In the end, Hoover had to be satisfied with a brief Secret Service memo: 'No firm details on the procured wire-nippers, or their presumed receptacle.'

The day after Lustig's escape, Agents Rubano and Johnson made an unannounced visit on Dapper Dan Collins in his suite at the art deco Hotel Belvedere near Times Square. They found him relaxing at noon in a silk kimono, listening to police radio broadcasts on a special scanner 'with a Mint Julep cocktail at his elbow'. Collins suavely told his callers that he knew nothing about any wire cutters, but that if they would excuse him he was expected for lunch at Delmonico's restaurant downtown. 'This man,' wrote Rubano in another memo for Director Hoover's attention, 'lives better than the President of the United States does.'

On the morning of Tuesday, 3 September, the Secret Service belatedly returned to East 74th Street – about twenty-four hours too late to catch their man – to question Billie Mae Scheible. 'She spent the whole time smiling coolly,' said Agent Rubano, finding their hostess 'defiant, crude, and singularly unhelpful', though she had ended the interview by enquiring of the stolidly respectable government operative whether he would like to meet her teenage niece. When Rubano courteously said that he would be happy to do so, Scheible had replied that it would cost $15 normally, but that she would let him have special terms. 'That concluded our parley,' Rubano wrote for the record.

While no one in American law enforcement seethed with pleasure at the news of Lustig's escape, J. Edgar Hoover's reaction shook even those of his inner circle familiar with his explosive moods. It took the form of a furious tirade that left everyone who witnessed it, or even heard about it later, shaken and exhausted. Hoover denounced the incompetence of the Secret Service, shouting that he was surrounded by fairies and cretins. The New York prison officials should themselves be locked up, he added, bringing his fist down on his desk for emphasis. No one had ever seen him lose control so completely. The whole apparatus of the American justice system was a laughing stock, Hoover declared. Heads would roll. In the midst of his raging, Hoover's body was racked by a violent spasm, and one of the FBI director's secretaries unlucky enough to have been present later insisted that she had seen actual foam at her boss's mouth. Long after Hoover's death, while still in office thirty-seven years later, young FBI recruits would marvel at accounts of the scene, passing it down through the generations like old salts recalling a historic hurricane.

Hoover's wrath also took productive form, quickly setting in motion the steps that led to the amendment of Title 18 of the US Code – the nation's main criminal statute – by adding a mandatory five-year penalty for escape from a federal prison: a lasting if unintended legacy of Lustig's actions that Sunday afternoon in 1935.

The Secret Service's James Johnson captured some of the prevailing mood in official circles that September when he wrote:

Lustig's escape created a furor, both at the press and government level … Hoover and the FBI launched a great man hunt. Lustig's picture and description appeared on a Wanted card in every post office in the nation … The governor of New York convened a crime conference in Albany and summoned all high-ranking officials in his jurisdiction. He lashed them for inefficiency and said, 'The report shows that Lustig has been arrested in eleven different states and I cannot find that these many arrests resulted in even one conviction' … Soon Peter Rubano was passing along the heat he got from Director Moran, who was passing the heat he got from [Hoover], who was passing heat he received, no doubt, from President Roosevelt in the White House.

Members of the press were not slow to fan the flames. '"THE COUNT" ESCAPES JAIL ON SHEET ROPE; International Crook Drops 50 Feet in Plain Sight of Hundreds' ran the lead headline of the *New York Times*. Many of the provincial American dailies printed Lustig's quote from *Les Misérables*, criticising the Secret Service for making an apparent deal with a known felon, and then further denouncing them for breaking it. 'They had it both ways,' Johnson later wrote.

Meanwhile, the object of all this attention was 400 miles due west from the scene of his escape, moving between the homes of several of Billie Mae Scheible's employees in Pittsburgh, where Scheible had recently opened a branch of her expanding vice empire, as well as spending a quiet night with a friend in Chicago's Windermere Hotel. Given the circumstances, it wasn't a bad life. None of Scheible's young staff needed much persuasion to take the fugitive in. Lustig was presented to them by their employer as a victim of brutal police persecution, a view readily confirmed by some of the women's own experiences with the law. Besides, he was always a gentleman. In 1986, a Pittsburgh woman calling herself Linda Lamanna, then a grandmother in her late 70s, recalled that she had been one of those to offer Lustig shelter, adding that he had generously dispersed 'lettuce' – cash, real or otherwise – both to her and her co-workers.

Lustig wisely chose not to advertise his presence in Pittsburgh, even so, and Lamanna remembered that he had sometimes gone out on essential errands disguised with a fedora hat pulled down to his nose and a large strip of gauze wrapped round his lower face. The local police seem not to have known what to make of this real-life version of H. G. Wells's *The Invisible Man*, then showing as a popular film in their city. Perhaps they assumed that the heavily bandaged figure was a war hero of some sort, because Lustig recalled that a young officer had once courteously held open a bank door for him, saluting smartly as he did so.

Peter Rubano lived in a frenzy at this time – working all hours, sleeping at the office, spending his nights pumping New York mob figures for information on Lustig and his associates. 'I would have consorted with the devil himself for any such leads,' Rubano reflected later. Some of his contacts came close to that level. There was the dwarfish psychopath 'Choo Choo' Rubin, for instance, the Murcello crime syndicate and a morphine pusher named 'the Stinger' who was rumoured to have already killed three police-men who had interested themselves in his affairs. The Stinger was not pleased when Rubano appeared in his Hell's Kitchen office one night seeking information. He mentioned that the last man to have sought him out in this way had subsequently been found in an alley with his head blown off and a pack of rats devouring what remained of his body. In the end the Secret Service arrested him, anyway, but the Stinger had the last sardonic laugh in the matter. Rather than face trial he hanged himself with his braces one night in his cell, or so the official report stated.

As some of Rubano's men worked the New York underworld, others continued their ever-narrowing search across the river in Union City. Eventually an agent came up with an address that he thought promising: the building was relatively secluded, though with plenty of morning light, and was rented to a man from Omaha named Ramsey who never seemed to go out before noon. At about seven in the morning of 18 September Rubano knocked at the front door. 'Milkman,' he announced. A few seconds later, Secret Service agents were pushing their way upstairs to the build-ing's top-floor apartment, their guns drawn. They found 'a little, mousy and ineffectual-looking' man waiting for them there dressed in his underwear. On the table behind him was a copperplate and a set of etching tools, and the officers' search quickly turned up $60,000 hidden under the floorboards, along with 'piles of spu-rious liquor labels, and United States and Canadian revenue tax stamps'. 'Ramsey' was in reality the master counterfeiter William Watts. He went downtown quietly.

Nine days later, Lustig left his latest suburban Pittsburgh hideout and took a taxi across town to his teenaged daughter's convent school. As we've seen, it had an unusually tolerant mother superior. Betty herself recalled:

> She came to me that evening. 'Your daddy is here,' she said, 'but you must not tell any of the other girls. Go to the chapel and wait there until I call you.'

Lustig spent that night in one of the convent's small guest rooms. He later said that he had been very comfortable, although he had thought it best on first taking possession to thoroughly check the cupboards for any agents who might be hiding there. Before retiring for the night the mother superior had opened a bottle of wine and toasted him; Victor responded. She later told reporters that he had been a perfect Christian gentleman, bringing her flowers and candy, and professed great surprise that the authorities had ever been looking for him.

At about eleven the following morning, Lustig walked out of the convent gates and got into his new Model K Hupmobile touring car, gaudily painted in 'bumblebee' yellow and black and bearing the vanity licence plate number 1N1918. He remained an unlikely cross between the eternal fugitive and the incorrigible showman, almost as if he were taunting the law to catch him. He wasn't wholly unconcerned with security, even so, because he'd changed names – now going by Robert Miller – and lodged in at least five different locations since escaping from jail just twenty-seven days earlier. But despite these precautions someone had recognised him from his Wanted card in the Pittsburgh post office and contacted the local police. They in turn passed on the tip to the Secret Service. Four of Rubano's men followed Lustig's car as he pulled away from the convent that morning, before stopping briefly at a nearby hotel and then driving north across the Allegheny River bridge towards the city's core retail district, close to the site of the modern-day Andy Warhol Museum. Eventually the government men forced Lustig's car to a stop. Three of the agents approached him with their weapons drawn. He was again calm about his arrest. 'Well, boys,' he said, 'here I am.'

The Secret Service men swiftly drove Lustig back to New York, where they arrived shortly before eleven o'clock that same Saturday night. Peter Rubano was there to greet them. A loud cheer erupted from the other residents of the agents' room on top of the Post Office building. They again had their man. The next day, in relating the scene, one New York paper said: 'It was [as though] their team had made a thrilling last-minute win against their opponent, who himself smiled graciously as he was led off to jail.'

Rubano later confided that there may have been more to Lustig's recapture than met the eye. 'The event took shape from a number of factors,' he wrote, adding cryptically that the Secret Service had 'exploited several individual citizens' in their search. It's a story that demonstrates the layers of murkiness in which Lustig typically operated. The US Justice Department later somehow lost their files on the arrest, but Rubano told the *Pittsburgh Post-Gazette* that, far from stumbling on their quarry, the bureau had 'patiently enlisted the assistance of many knowledgeable persons' across America.

Several if not most of these sources appear to have been women. Lustig's associates all knew that he led a baroque love life, his personal and business relationships often overlapping. Could he again have offended even Billie Mae Scheible's morals with his philandering? Frank Seckler of the Secret Service was one of those who believed that the 'shameless but not unprincipled' brothel keeper had now twice betrayed Lustig to the authorities. 'Although the Count was Mae's sweetheart, he had [stolen] her money to take another woman on a trip. We received an anonymous tip … We always thought that Mae Scheible, burning with jealousy, was our informant.' It was, as Peter Rubano added, 'out of restlessness, indignation and grief [at] a sudden loss of affection' that Mrs Scheible 'came to reconsider her feelings [for] Lustig', although Rubano doubted that she personally was the Judas. 'My belief is that she told someone a tale, and that individual then came to us.'

Another theory of Lustig's downfall was that William Watts had given him up and that this act, too, involved a woman. Although the meek and watery-eyed Watts was not known as a ladies' man, at some stage in April 1935 he seems to have taken up with a young New York secretary named Mary Trew. Rubano believed that Lustig had made Miss Trew's acquaintance and, almost out of habit, taken her with him to the Jane Street Hotel in Manhattan, 'where he thoroughly ruined her reputation'. It's hard to know with any certainty whether or not this happened, and if so what William Watts might have done about it. But we know that Watts was in police custody for more than a week before Lustig's own recapture that September. In terms of logic and timing, it makes sense.

Betty Lustig, for her part, long suspected that her despised step-father Doug Conner had played some part in the events of that month, just as he had earlier in the year. 'They caught Victor not by their own strategy, but through an informer who revealed his whereabouts to the police – Conner,' she wrote. This was commendably loyal on Betty's part, but once more it's hard to say whether or not it's true. She also insists that once in custody her father had convincingly feigned tuberculosis by biting into his tongue with such force as to make it appear he was coughing up blood, thus qualifying him for a bed in the relatively cushy hospital ward, and that 'the Secret Service never even knew that he had a wife and child' – both claims refuted by the official record. Other sources point to the mother superior of Betty's Pittsburgh convent as a suspect. Though benign, the theory goes, this lady may have been ambivalent about the prospect of entertaining Lustig as a long-term guest. 'The good woman showed Christian spirit to me, [but] I have come to wonder about her,' he later wrote. 'She has expressed the most extreme views about political matters all over the world.' The mother superior joined the US–German Friendship League later in the 1930s, and at one time travelled around in a specially equipped speaker van in order to spread the Nazi word.

For conspiracy theorists, meanwhile, there was another possible explanation of Lustig's downfall. Had he all along been part of some elaborate government cabal? Perhaps, it was suggested, his pose as a counterfeiter had just been a cover to enable him to gather information about widespread corruption at the highest levels of US law enforcement. Victor had supposedly held out a tempting deal to investigators: he would risk life and limb by going underground to expose official wrongdoing if the federal government dismissed all its charges against him.

If this deal was really struck, it seems the authorities were no longer in the mood for a truce. 'We shall never surrender [our] criminal case against this individual,' J. Edgar Hoover wrote in October 1935. During a later interview with the FBI, Lustig was said to be 'especially vindictive against the Secret Service and Operative Peter Rubano in particular ... Alleges Agent Rubano is a crook and that one Eddie King, who has a criminal record and who is a government informant, is a "collector" for him,' the file went on. In a further twist, Lustig claimed to have been working with William Moran, the head of the Secret Service, on a sting operation to trap Rubano. The FBI report concluded:

Lustig guaranteed us that he could prove that Operative Rubano was crooked and proposed to us the following scheme: that we, without Rubano's knowledge, should cause the latter to arrest some counterfeiter, any counterfeiter, and that he, Lustig, would guarantee, although in jail, to bring about the release of such a counterfeiter through the payment of money to Rubano.

Although this story may have had substance, it seems more likely to have been the crazed diatribe of a man desperately seeking to avoid a lengthy prison sentence, and also to suggest that Lustig and his principal adversary were now mutually obsessed with each other. A memo sent up the line to Chief Moran asking if he would like to take up Lustig's request for a personal interview came back with the one-word stamp: 'Rejected'.

Perhaps the final judgement on Lustig's course of action, or inaction, in September 1935 is his daughter Betty's comment on the matter: 'He just gave up,' she concluded sadly. After escorting him back to New York, the Secret Service locked him up in a cell at the Tombs (despite its uncompromising name, actually an eight-storey tower block in French chateau style, if with no pretensions to comfort) in Lower Manhattan. The nearby House of Detention was a model of refinement by comparison. In three successive nights Lustig had gone from lodging in a prostitute's apartment, a girls' convent school and now New York's most notorious jail, which surely says something about the unusually wide and often contradictory extremes of his life as a whole.

Similarly, the idea that Lustig would choose to spend many of his waking hours diligently studying the Bible might well have struck many of his victims as a ludicrous or even incredible notion. But he now did so. Lustig told his benefactor Alexander Hadden that the Psalms particularly moved him, though he loved the 'bold, militant tone' of the Old Testament in general. It seems to have inspired him to take up his pen, because in late 1935 he told Hadden: 'A memoir is good exercise. I want to write about myself while I can. After all, why should anyone object? It's not history, it's just one person's view of the life he's led.' Lustig proposed giving his book the subtitle *The Story of Why I Couldn't Go Straight*.

On 19 October 1935, Lustig was formally indicted for the possession and passing of counterfeit currency. He also became the first person to be charged under the newly amended Title 18 of the US Code, which provided an extra five-year penalty for anyone escaping from federal custody. He received the first part of the arraignment in silence when it was read out to him in court, but was not pleased to learn of the secondary complaint. Soon his voice was rising: 'I consider this an act of retribution against a

Lustig has his day in court.

foreign national, and as such a violation of your constitution, and therefore I refuse to accept it. I did no more than seek to make my way back to my homeland. You may charge me today if you wish, but I categorically protest. It is Mr. Hoover who should be wearing prison stripes, not I.' The judge had to gavel down the laughter. 'May we proceed?' he asked gruffly.

Lustig seems to have made no special attempt to prepare a defence, telling several correspondents that he was resigned to his fate. 'It's all in vain,' he grumbled in a note to his ex-wife Roberta. 'My efforts are useless. They'll lock me up and throw away the key, or they'll bury it so deep there'll be no trace of it.' By contrast, Lustig's co-defendant William Watts would make an unusual request of the authorities. 'Watts asked to be allowed to return to his room in Union City in the company of our agents,' James Johnson recalled. 'We took him there, and when we arrived he opened the oven door, dismantled the temperature gauge, and inside it was folded a thousand dollars in genuine hundred-dollar bills. We impounded it with red faces, but it was later used for his defense.'

On 4 December 1935, Lustig and Watts jointly stood trial in the United States Courts and Postal Building in New York, located just nine floors below the headquarters of the task force that had brought about their arrests. Even by the somewhat makeshift standards of 1930s American jurisprudence, it was a curious spectacle. Lustig was charged under his arrest alias of Robert V. Miller, and the court formally recorded both that he was 44 years old, not 45, and unmarried. The principal defendant still wore the crisp blue suit in which he had been captured, although he was now shackled at the ankles and wrists. The *Herald Tribune* wrote, 'Once known for his suavity, continental accent and perfect poise, the Count arrived in court dejected, a bit greyer, and with none of his old flamboyance.' Other observers agreed about Lustig's age, but not about his lack of spirit. On the second day of the proceedings he appeared in the dock wearing a 'jaunty white linen number' that Peter Rubano half-admiringly remarked 'made it seem as though he would shortly be strolling down to meet Mr. Harold Vanderbilt for a day's yachting'.

On Friday, 6 December, Watts took the stand as both one of the accused and star witness for the prosecution. He told the court that Lustig was the brains behind the whole counterfeiting operation, which he modestly believed had pumped well over $5 million in bogus money into the American economy. He, Watts, had been nothing but a hired mechanic in the enterprise, he insisted. James Johnson of the Secret Service was in court. 'Throughout Watts's opening statement, Lustig slumped in his chair,' he wrote. 'On his face a variety of emotions took turn; there was defiance and sullenness, and self-pity. But there was no pride.'

After listening to Watts's testimony for half an hour, Lustig turned to the lawyer sitting next to him at the defendants' table and said, 'Let's get it over with.' Later that day he stood up and formally pleaded guilty to all the charges against him. The following Monday morning (these were the days before lengthy psychiatric evaluations or victim impact reports), Judge Alfred Coxe announced the sentences: ten years for Watts and fifteen years for Lustig on the counterfeiting charge, plus the further five years the latter had earned for his escape. The politically outspoken judge (he once wrote in *The Atlantic* that the Wall Street crash was the work of Communists) remarked that it had been a 'monstrous conspiracy against the United States', and that he was in no doubt 'the prisoner Miller' had been the 'primary actor' involved, having made it his business to 'freely visit various cities and places throughout the nation for the purpose of negotiating for the distribution of the notes manufactured, heedless of any results this might have on the workings of the legitimate financial cycle'. As well as the twenty years, he handed Lustig a $1,000 fine for his offences.

The convicted man, so wrote Coxe in a privately published memoir he characteristically called *If the Bolsheviks Come*, then promptly announced that he would pay up in 'foreign bank notes, as these were the only funds still left available to him by the government'. While the judge was silently pondering this unusual idea, Lustig continued, 'And just think, sir, what prospects such a proposal would afford the court to make a little extra from procuring a beneficial rate of exchange.' Once more, the judge had to gavel down the mirth. The record shows that Lustig's government-appointed attorney later paid in '265 British pounds sterling, [and] this was accepted in full reparation'. The prisoner made no trouble as he left the court, although Agent Johnson wrote: 'While he was being led out in handcuffs, the convicted man muttered that he would again escape, but it was a hollow boast. Even he didn't believe it. It was a pose out of the past.'

That night Lustig was locked up in the federal penitentiary at Lewisburg, and in due course transferred 1,000 miles west to the maximum-security prison at Leavenworth, Kansas, a facility where hangings took place on a regular basis. Although he made no attempt to abscond, he admitted to being uneasy that he might find himself in the same confined space as one of his aggrieved former marks, who 'may take the opportunity to revisit certain of those outstanding questions which lie between us'. There was the disgraced ex-Sheriff Richards, for instance, who was still serving a lengthy sentence for passing counterfeit bills that had come into his possession while supervising the town jail in Grove, Oklahoma, ten years earlier. 'Even now I have the distinct feeling that the man wishes me ill,' Lustig wrote, accurately enough.

A Justice Department report on the new inmate remarked that 'Miller alias Lustig' might yet face 'sundry additional charges and indictments', and that if convicted on these he was liable to serve a possible eighty-two years behind bars. Under the section headed 'Give details of offenses committed, including any aggravating circumstances', an unknown government official found himself pressed for space. 'Continued on separate sheet', he wrote, after beginning his account of this 'Counterfeiting King, [also] known as a confidence man who has many aliases'. There were three final questions on the form put by John McGohey, the Assistant State Attorney General for New York:

Q: Was prisoner of assistance to the Government?
A: No.

Q: Additional comment which shows the extent and intensity of public injury:
A: Miller very freely admits that he swindled many people.

Q: Your opinion relative to parole?
A: I recommend against it.

A subsequent stark note from Lamar Hardy of the Department of Justice reviewed Lustig's extensive criminal record, before concluding: 'In view of the above, the length of the sentence and the background of the offender, I respectfully recommend that he be incarcerated at Alcatraz.' This was the newly opened island fortress located in San Francisco Bay, reserved for an initial batch of 137 of the nation's most hardened convicts. 'He is definitely regarded as a menace to society,' Hardy added.

Just before being shipped to the Rock on 2 March 1936, Lustig wrote a pitiful note back home to a 14-year-old Betty:

> Received your letter, and also five dollars. Thanks very much. I hope you will not think I have forgotten you. When you have time, think of me as I think of you … You can come and see me this month … I close with all my love and a million kisses. My best to the folks.
>
> Always your daddy.
>
> Robert V. Miller
> (48065).

On arrival at Alcatraz, Lustig was stripped, searched and thoroughly hosed down with icy bilge water. After that he was issued a pair of khaki overalls and a blue pea coat, and told that henceforth he was to be known as Inmate 300. 'He is somewhat superficially humiliated,' his entry card notes. 'Asserts that he is accused of everything in the category of crime, including the burning of Chicago.' Victor later complained that for several days he had been crammed with seventeen other new arrivals in a receiving cell designed for six. It was early March, and the cold was reported to be more intense

The Rock.

than in the deep freeze of a meat-processing plant. The prisoners slept on their sides, and were packed so tightly next to one another that in order for any of them to change position they all had to turn over in coordinated waves. Lustig said that his fingers and toes were a 'throbbing blue' when at last he stumbled out to eat his first breakfast in the mess hall.

Six days later, filling out the prison's required admission card in his best italicised handwriting, Lustig noted that he expected to receive visits in custody from his wife and daughter, and that it was immaterial to him whether he slept in a single or a shared cell, provided that he could 'breathe air at night'. Other than that, he 'consider[ed] it unnecessary to bother much with such petty arrangements'. The last question on the form asked what sort of work the inmate proposed to do at Alcatraz, and he answered: 'Bookkeeper'.

Although Lustig put on a brave face for the authorities, he experienced the full gamut of horrors of life at Alcatraz, beginning from the moment he was herded off the prison boat, shackled to another convict, and marched up the fog-shrouded jetty into the harsh sodium lighting of the main cell block. He later told his wife Susan (apparently better disposed to him now that he was behind bars) that it had been the single worst moment of his life, adding: 'There's no lower fate than being led down a dark passage, smelling of all the most ghastly things on earth, knowing that men in uniform with clubs in their hands await you at the far end.'

Lustig's official medical evaluation called him a 'quiet, responsive man, without any underlying feelings of hostility to society'. This made him an exception to the general Alcatraz population. His IQ was thought 'slightly below normal', but set against this he showed a 'fair degree of aptitude'. The prison doctors recommended him for 'close to medium custody' and approved him for schooling and trade training. Poignantly, Lustig soon went on to request a 'better-paying manual job whilst in residence, so that financial aid may be given to family'. Since an Alcatraz inmate typically earned between 5 and 8 cents an hour for sewing mailbags in the prison work-shop, this could have been of little material comfort to Betty or her stepmother. The resident chaplain, Wayne L. Hunter, thought Lustig 'very courteous in interviews, and showed a good attitude to the educational program', although, like others, he suspected Victor was more cunning than narrowly intellectual. 'He always has some grand idea, you know, some scheme.' In time the guards even nicknamed him 'the Thinker'.

Although a now-enfeebled Al Capone was housed in a 9ft by 5ft cell just down the central aisle – known as Broadway – Lustig seems to have avoided any trouble with his fellow inmates. The prisoners were naturally fractious, and their feuds in the pressure cooker of Alcatraz had a malice all of their own. One cold Monday morning not long after Lustig arrived, a convict named Henri Young fatally stabbed the occupant of the next-door cell, Rufus McCain, with a sharpened spoon. Young never explained his

The cell where Lustig spent several years.

motive, but the official report on the matter concluded that he had simply 'lost his reason' and was 'punch-drunk [after] an extended period of solitary confinement'. Despite incidents like this one, Lustig told his wife that he was reconciled to life on the Rock. 'I eat three meals a day, and at night burn a small candle and read in my bunk when the guards aren't looking.'

While Lustig managed to escape mentally in this way, the Department of Justice finally wound up its investigation of his actual breakout from the jail in New York. There had been serious lapses of protocol, the report noted, and one of the guards suppos-edly on duty that day had been 'consort[ing] in the basement with an unauthorized female guest instead of tending the roof'. The man in question had now been transferred, the file concluded, 'but beyond that we have no further recommendation of a discipli-nary nature to make'. Nonetheless, complaints continued to rain down on Lustig from police departments across America about offences committed in their cities. Whether known as Lamar, Duval or Baxter, he was wanted everywhere from Concord in New Hampshire to Tacoma in Washington. There was also still intermittent talk that he might be deported. The problem lay in finding a country willing to take him. 'Possible destination for Miller so far remains unknown,' the Justice Department was forced to admit.

Several sources – including the prison's warden James Johnston, an elderly white-haired ogre of funereal aspect, habitu-ally dressed in black, whose teeth gleamed with gold bridgework that he exposed on the rare occasions he smiled – insist that Lustig made no serious trouble on Alcatraz. 'The silence of the tomb surrounded him,' Johnston wrote, with perhaps just a touch of hyperbole. Betty Lustig quoted a letter from her father in which he remarked that he sat outside whenever he could in order to 'watch the boats and a lot of airplanes – when I see a plane leaving in the daytime, I wish the pilot luck, even though he can't hear me'. Victor's main call on the prison authorities was in filing an impressive total of 1,192 medical requests during his years there, at a rate of roughly one every three days. Other than that, Warden Johnston recorded only a series of relatively minor transgressions of the rules. Lustig was punished for 'Leaving cell before count' in one report, 'Participating in food strike' in another, 'Destroying government property (a pair of socks)' in a third. The only hint of the old schemer came one morning in May 1942, when a guard found 'four pieces of torn blanket concealed in Miller's cell, [although] he explained that he had been in the hospital for treatment, and had torn these pieces of cloth to shine his shoes'.

Betty Lustig later wrote of a distressing scene when she had first gone to visit her father on Alcatraz. After being thoroughly searched and 'humiliated in every way', the teenager was ushered into a long, darkened room. 'There he was, standing up,' Betty wrote, 'his face pressed against the glass with a wire mesh inside. I couldn't touch him. He picked up a phone and motioned me to pick up the other one on my side … I started to cry when I heard his distorted voice come over the line.'

Lustig invariably told his daughter that it was all right, he would be out again soon, and that he would take her away to Europe with him. He may even have believed it. One fine day, Victor added several years later, something would change the entire situation. The Allies would need men of proven ability and experience to administer the post-war world, and he would put himself at their disposal. Lustig also confided in Betty that he had plenty of money waiting for him on the outside, which she assumed might have involved a deposit box held at a downtown Chicago bank, but if so his family never saw it. It's possible that by then he was slowly losing his mind, succumbing to a combination of boredom and oppression, as so many Alcatraz inmates did. One day Lustig presented the authorities with an elaborate chemical formula for the manufacture of a low-priced ink. The Prison Bureau rejected this 'as it [was] contrary to policy to permit a convict to commercialize any invention or patent'. In 1942 Lustig informed the warden that he had a foolproof plan to finally eliminate Hitler from the scene. If the Allies would just drop him by parachute in a wooded area he knew around Zürich, he would make his way from there over the German frontier and in short order insinuate himself on to the kitchen staff of the Reich chancellery building in Berlin. According to this 'grandiose program', as Warden Johnston called it, Victor would lace Hitler's favourite teatime pastries with cyanide, and 'await the inevitable developments'. This proposal, too, came back with a one-word official stamp: 'Refused'.

Somewhere around this time, following a visit to his cell by the FBI, Lustig wrote to his brother Emil:

> Received your letter, also money, and thanks. I wish I could do something for you. If you go to Kansas City, don't see my ex-wife, you know how she is.
>
> Yesterday Chief Callahan came to see me with two others. He told me that when the time comes he would like to help me about deportation. At first I talked to him alone, but then the other gentlemen came in, and wanted to know what happen [sic] 6 or 7 years ago. I saw they did not come here to comfort me, only to complain that so much counterfeit money, supposed to be mine, are [sic] being circulated. They seemed to have very good information … I hope they did not intend to bring any charges but as I stated I don't trust them fellows. I told the Chief I don't want to use any more lawyers to defend me, and, again, that I don't know anything about the money … It is a shame how they have treated me.

Not surprisingly, Lustig's own finances were a persistent source of worry to him while on Alcatraz. By late 1939, the international con man who had once employed a household staff of five, with a fleet of Rolls-Royces at his disposal, was writing to his brother: 'Thank you for the $20, but please do not send any more unless you have some left over.' He got another $15 from his ex-wife and $7 from his daughter, but he needed more. Lustig must have written to a contact in Chicago, because Warden Johnston intercepted a return letter addressed to Victor from the downtown branch of Wells Fargo Bank, advising him that they were unable to send him the funds he requested. By May 1941, Lustig was forced to appeal to the US Treasury Department in Washington: 'Enclosed you will find fifty dollar Bond, No. 11198J, [which] I have held since 1938.

The reason I am sending you this is because I would like to get the money for it, and because it is against the rules in this institution to handle Bonds.'

By then Lustig was writing a long article about the war in Europe that he modestly entitled 'Cultural-Military History of Mankind'. He had one of those minds capable of the sweeping geopolitical overview, which he used to confound experts and impress the gullible. Although he lacked not only humanity but the capacity for critical appreciation, he was eminently qualified as a judge of character. Lustig wrote that 'Stalin [will] surely dictate the peace. He has taken his country from 90 percent illiteracy to 90 percent literacy … It is he we will have to deal with in future.'

This set the scene for Lustig's magnum opus of November 1943, in which he expounded at length on his vision for the post-war world. It is hard to say if this was brilliantly perceptive or just the obsessive meanderings of a mind that was nimble enough, particularly in its grasp of human psychology, but completely lacking in objectivity and reason. The answer is probably a bit of both. At times Lustig's screed seems to contain an almost pre-hippyish appeal for universal brotherhood:

> The people of all the nations in the world shall be responsible to uphold the harmony of man … [I] propose the establishment of an international group whose duty would be the policing of the globe and the enforcing of peace. Whereas the Atlantic Charter specifies freedom of speech, International Law could forbid the agitation of war, just as most nations would forbid such abuses of free speech as the public teaching of methods of robbing a bank.

In time, J. Edgar Hoover personally took possession of this document, his pleasure at reading it seemingly well contained.

Lustig wasn't quite ready to go gentle into the night, however. His self-image was too bound up with the idea of successfully extracting other people's money to allow him to adopt the role of the benevolent elder statesman. On 7 June 1944, as Allied troops were still struggling ashore on the beaches of Normandy, Victor again wrote to Emil, tailoring his language for the prison censor, to ask whether they might not 'take succor' from the developing situation in Europe. Once again Lustig relied on his uncanny flair for smelling out a good business opportunity. The essence of the scam involved selling a row of luxury Paris townhouses, sight unseen, to the American high command for their use following the liberation of the French capital. The non-existent homes were meant to be an old Bourbon-Busset family asset, and they were being made available to the American brass at a giveaway cash price. Of course, Victor couldn't use words such as 'racket' or 'fraud' in his letter, so he resourcefully gave his proposals a series of innocuous-sounding code words, at one point suggesting, 'You should arrange suitable shelter for the migrating flock who will soon arrive …' But for once the whole thing seems to have fallen through, because both Lustig brothers died effectively penniless.

Even as Lustig was pondering ways in which to profit from the war, Warden Johnston would write of him: 'He gave us little trouble at Alcatraz. Perhaps on occasion he bent the rules. But for the most he was polite, open, compliant and quiet-spoken.' Even so, a lifetime of restless travel and almost continuous personal reinvention had left their mark, and caused Lustig to develop what the prison psychiatrist called 'an obsession with escape and flight in every sense'. When not busy filing one of his frequent medical transfer requests, Victor spent the war years continuing to write to senior government officials, asking them to intervene to have him paroled or at least deported. Most of the letters went unanswered, while others came back to him with the curt notification that there was no such person at that address.

Lustig also wrote weekly to his daughter Betty, always assuring her that he was in good spirits and that they would be together again soon. As a rule, the letters were signed: 'With all

Though poorly educated, Lustig had exquisite handwriting right up to the end.

my undying love, your papa, #300 Robert V. Miller.' Victor told Betty in June 1943 that he believed he would already have been released but for the war. 'Yet I can't complain,' he added. 'With all the people suffering in Europe one cannot think of oneself.' The 22-year-old Betty married the next year, and her father wrote to her: 'I have been planning that as soon as the hostilities are over I want you and your husband to see all of Europe. I should be able to be your guide. There will be a lot of people going, and I want to show you all the places you want to see ... I will be released in 38 months, even if the war is still on. I know it is still a long time but it is the best I can do.'

This was wishful thinking on Lustig's part. The Justice Department had made it clear that his earliest possible parole date was December 1952, marking seventeen years from the time of his original sentencing, and that even then 'Inmate will face additional charges from U.S. municipal jurisdictions, New York, Chicago, Boston, Spokane, San Francisco, etc.' As the world entered the atomic era, Lustig was still answering for the sins of his Jazz Age youth. 'You would think the [authorities] would be more concerned about the futures of their own folk,' he told Betty, adding wryly, 'You may kill a man and be forgiven, but dupe the government and they will pursue you unto the grave.'

A surprising number of Lustig's old circle nonetheless survived to enjoy old age. William Watts did his time in federal prison and then disappeared back to live quietly under an alias in his native Omaha. Nicky Arnstein, with whom Lustig had worked the Atlantic liners at around the time of the Great War, died only in 1965, aged 86, having kept out of trouble for the last forty years of his life. In retirement, Arnstein preferred not to speak about matters such as loan sharking, extortion, or otherwise chiselling the public. Lustig's old flame Ruth Etting moved out of the house in Los Angeles where her former husband had once menaced her with a gun, married her pianist Myrl Alderman, and settled with him on a ranch in Colorado. She died there in 1978, aged 81. Towards the end, Etting wrote to a friend that most of the old Hollywood crowd had been 'louses' and 'morally, just this side of an oil slick'. But she admitted that Lustig had been 'a real man'.

Billie Mae Scheible was arrested when the FBI raided her establishment in Pittsburgh, following a tip-off that 'Relations between men and females other than their wives' were regularly occurring there. The agents' midnight visit revealed no fewer than 'fourteen fully congressional couples, and two others in an advanced pre-coital state' on the premises. The bureau's report added, almost coyly, 'It would seem that unchaste conduct was involved.'

Scheible was charged with tax fraud and breaking the terms of the White Slave Act, which made it a felony to transport 'any woman or girl for the purpose of prostitution or debauchery, or for any other lewd act' across state lines. She made the most of her day in court. 'Six guards were called to clear the corridors,' it was reported, 'as the crowd of men all but tore the doors off their hinges to get inside, where [Scheible] and her rouged and silken-clad former inmates were telling the story of their lives.' These were not the normal scenes of a criminal trial in 1930s America. Scheible asked that the press photographers shoot her 'from a slen-derizing angle' and that they accentuate her 'upholstery'. She spent five years on a work farm in Michigan, before returning to her old life after the war. The FBI arrested her again in 1962, but even then, J. Edgar Hoover's men described her in largely positive terms. 'Of small stature and not unrefined features, with a good taste for clothes, she makes a fairly attractive appearance, speaks with a very sweet, girlish voice and affects a pleasing attitude when she wishes to impress.' Scheible appears to have retired from the position she liked to call 'Public Hostess No. 1' only around 1970, when she was in her mid-seventies. Her lawyer later remarked that 'the male population of Pittsburgh [were] very thankful that the card-index file Mrs. Scheible kept did not emerge in print incident to her investigation and trial'. In December 1935 Scheible had appeared dressed in a floor-length mink coat and a red pillbox hat trimmed with butterflies outside the courtroom in New York as the guards led Lustig away to start his twenty-year sentence. 'He did me wrong,' she informed reporters. They did not meet again.

Lustig had already been in Alcatraz for more than three years before his old associate Dapper Dan Collins was brought to jus-tice. Even then it was in a bizarre set of circumstances. Collins, whose youthful criminal adventures had included running a load of bootleg liquor into Miami from the Bahamas with five women as his crew, had taken to impersonating a US Customs officer and clipped $200 from the wife of an illegal Jewish immigrant. When he went back for more the real feds were waiting for him. He was sentenced to serve between fifteen and thirty years. 'I've been around, but now I'm just an old reprobate,' he told reporters. 'The only way I'll get out of jail again is feet first.'

He was right. Although Collins was described as a model prisoner, working tirelessly to help educate his fellow inmates, it did not do him much good: he died in custody in 1950, aged 70. The government knew of no relatives, and he was given a pauper's grave in the penitentiary grounds at Attica, New York, survived only by 'an unpublished memoir, his many victims – and the Eiffel Tower,' wrote the satirical magazine *Awake!*

There was some doubt among Warden Johnston and his staff at Alcatraz whether or not Lustig was justified in filing quite as many medical requests as he did. They came even more often in 1946 than before, at a rate of roughly one every other day. Could he be faking? Johnston thought his prisoner 'inclined to magnify physical ailments and to expect much medical treatment, which indeed he receives … He is constantly complaining of real and imaginary ills.' Was it all part of some elaborate scheme to get himself shipped out to a civilian hospital, and then to again make his escape? Did he believe, a visibly diminished man of 56, that he still possessed the strength or the nerve to carry it through? Or was the truth that Lustig had no such plan in mind, and wanted only to be transferred from what he called 'devil's island' back on to the American mainland, where he could at least hope to see his beloved daughter more often?

Before events could provide the answer, Lustig was dead. On 29 November 1946, Dr John Robinson, the Alcatraz medical officer, wrote to Warden Johnston: 'Miller appears to be in pain and there is slight unexplained swelling at left side of forehead.' Although the doctor noted that 'X-Ray, sedation and penicillin are all indicated', even then he was left to wonder if 'inmate's illness is real, or [to] what extent his symptoms are due to his stated wish [to be] moved from Alcatraz'. Dr Robinson was at least concerned enough to call in a specialist from San Francisco to perform exploratory surgery on his patient. In the starkly clinical words of the report that went to Warden Johnston's desk: 'Incision & drainage of Frontal Sinus carried out … Opening was made along left eye-brow. Orbital plate of frontal sinus was exposed. Left frontal entered through drilled opening.'

As a result of this procedure, Lustig finally got his wish to leave Alcatraz. After waiting nearly eleven years, it was not the release he would have chosen for himself. On 27 December, two armed guards escorted him off the Rock to begin a four-day road and rail journey to the US Medical Center for Federal Prisoners, located 2,000 miles away in Springfield, Missouri. This was the same town where, posing

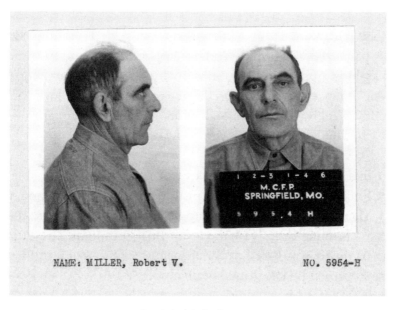

Lustig in his final captivity.

as a New York chemicals tycoon, Victor had once clipped the manager of the local savings bank for $10,000. 'The inmate was rather weak, and no special trouble from a custodial point of view,' it was now reported. At one stage the party was forced to wait several hours for its connecting train in Kansas City, and Lustig was temporarily lodged in the town jail. He'd been there, too, in the past, always managing to talk his way out of trouble. Now he was a spindly little man weighing less than 90lb, and escape was no longer possible. The official report noted: 'Miller is afflicted with a potentially dangerous disorder, and it is well that he is confined in an institution [Springfield] where constant medical care is available.'

Two months later, Betty Lustig opened a reverse-charge official telegram, dated 3 March 1947. It read: 'Your father, Robert V. Miller, Reg. No. 300-AZ, remains at the US Medical Center and is considered critically ill.' Betty had just turned 25, and now had a daughter of her own. Her cross-country visit to Springfield was never going to be pleasant, but she later remembered it in especially sombre terms:

> When [I] saw my father I knew that I had waited too long. He was paralyzed and could not talk … I took his hand in mine and gently tapped on his palm as I whispered in his ear 'Morse Code'. I tapped in code in preference to whispering. 'I love you, Daddy.' Feebly, with a strained smile in those large, expressive eyes, he tapped back, 'I love you, too, Skeezix.'

After that Lustig drifted in and out of consciousness, unable to speak, for several days. He died at around eight o'clock on the night of 11 March 1947, having agonisingly spelled out the word 'L-o-v-e' on a hospital orderly's hand as his final comment. The official cause of death was listed as 'Pneumonia – Due to Hemiplegia, probably caused by left frontal brain abscess'.

Betty collected her father's body two days later in Kansas City. 'He arrived from Springfield in a pine box, with an orange makeup on his face and a celluloid collar stapled in such a way that one end of a staple had penetrated the flesh of his face.' She dressed him in a new suit and had him buried at the local Mount Moriah cemetery. Victor's ex-wife Roberta sent a cellophane-wrapped spray of roses. Other than Betty, there were just two Prison Bureau observers in attendance at the funeral, as if to confirm that the elusive 'Tricky Vic' truly was dead.

When Roberta herself died from a prescription drug overdose in 1969, Betty had her father disinterred and laid her parents to rest side by side at Davis Memorial Park, near her current home in Las Vegas. Perhaps it was a fitting comment on the Lustigs' marriage and subsequent relationship. They had always seemed to be woefully incompatible and yet utterly inseparable. Betty reports that during the war years Roberta sold off her valuables in a bid to get Victor moved from Alcatraz. It was all in vain. 'She disposed of her jewellery; expensive pieces which Victor had given her through

the years, and amassed $70,000. She went to see James Bennett, the Director of Prisons, who was in Los Angeles. She came home and wept. $70,000 was not enough to free her Victor.'

Emil Lustig eventually leaked the news of his brother's death after he in turn had been arrested on a counterfeiting charge. It was part of a long interview he gave the Associated Press, apparently in the hope that it would serve his cause with the authorities. Emil's account, unreliable in most aspects, rightly surmised that Victor 'was too intelligent not to know that he would be pinched in the end'. It was perhaps the most perceptive comment of an otherwise unexceptional life, largely spent in his brother's shadow. Betty wrote of Emil: 'He passed his last days with friends or relatives, living off their bounty and straining their efforts at charity.'

Betty herself was successively divorced and widowed, raised two children, took a medical course, and for some years supported herself as a secretary in a Los Angeles doctor's office. She died in her early sixties of cancer. Those who knew Betty in her final days agreed that the disease failed to blunt her independence of spirit ('The nurse came to my room with a pan, and what I told her to do with it is still spoken of in hushed tones,' she reported), and that she never wavered in her lifelong devotion to her father. Towards the end she was heard to utter, 'Let the whole world hate me, as long as Papa loves me. No child was ever as blessed as I was.'

Lustig himself went on to enjoy a sort of professional afterlife. Since no one in authority announced the news of his death, scores of police departments around the world continued to enquire about him long after Betty had lowered his coffin into the ground at Kansas City. Not untypical was the letter from John Grosch, the sheriff of New Orleans, written in October 1949 to the warden at Alcatraz: 'Will you please forward to me information as to whether Victor Lustig, alias "Count" Lustig, is still confined in your institution – we are keen to confer with him'; or from the police chief of Dallas: 'Miller left this town at an increased rate of speed, and we would welcome his return.'

Lustig also lives on today as a template for the kind of endearing villain we never seem to tire of either in print or on screen. Whether it's the wheeling-dealing Arthur Daley in *Minder*, insidious rascals such as Simon Templar and Tom Ripley, or *Breaking Bad*'s slippery lawyer Saul Goodman, the appeal seems to be the marriage of a certain feline charm to an agile exploitative brain, alongside a rabbity turn of speed when the need arises. Although Lustig perfectly captured the giddy, materially acquisitive spirit of the 1920s, he's also achieved a sort of immortality in coming to define the role of the unprincipled but essentially warm-hearted male rogue. He's the type of character who somehow exudes a kind of winning honesty, no matter how contrived and devious his actions. Every dodgy car dealer puffing a Panatela cigar – that's Lustig. Every plausible chancer to appear over the horizon with his foolproof get-rich-quick scheme – that's Lustig. The aristocratic spiv, the diamond geezer, the disdain for what's commonly referred to as respectable behaviour, the fast buck or the 'nice little earner' merchant – Lustig. He's a timeless example of unscrupulous conduct, and of the art of almost getting away with it.

Meanwhile, one of the most extraordinary figures in the history of twentieth-century crime died with just $93.09 in his only known bank account. On 27 March 1947, the warden at Alcatraz wrote to Betty Lustig to itemise her father's other remaining possessions:

2 scrapbooks
1 Winston Simplified Dictionary
1 File marked 'Peace Plan'
1 Folder containing numerous personal letters from wife and daughter
1 Family photograph album

1 Pair of glasses
1 drawing of boat in crayon

It wasn't much to show for more than thirty years as an international criminal mastermind, but it was matched by the modesty of Lustig's death certificate, which gave his occupation simply as 'Apprentice salesman'.

SOURCES AND CHAPTER NOTES

The following pages show at least the formal interviews, published works, and/or primary archive material used in the preparation of this book. Although it necessarily lacks the direct, first-hand input either of Victor Lustig or any of his contemporaries, I was lucky enough to have a number of Lustig's notes, as well as his lengthy records from the US Bureau of Prisons, at my disposal. I'm grateful to Douglas Williford for much of this information. I should also particularly acknowledge the memoir *From Paris to Alcatraz*, as cited in the bibliography, co-written by the late Betty Jean Lustig and Nanci Garrett; the reader will see that I've once or twice attributed quotes from this book to Ms Lustig alone simply for economy's sake, and that in certain cases I've slightly edited these quotes for sense.

Chapter 1: The Age of Illusion

There are a large number of sources relating the adventures of Arthur Gregory and his ilk, among them A.F.L. Deeson's *Great Swindlers* and Kathryn Lindskoog's *Fakes, Frauds and Other Malarkey*, as noted in the bibliography. The quote beginning, 'He had an enormous limousine built specially …' appears in Deeson, p.122. Victor Lustig's line beginning, 'I have a consuming thirst for knowledge …' appears in *From Paris to Alcatraz*, also as cited in the bibliography, p.21. A request to the FBI Freedom of Information Division will yield data on most or all of the criminals mentioned in this chapter, if little or no direct material on Lustig himself. Again, I made use of the US Bureau of Prisons archive on Lustig; it contains not only his lengthy arrest record but a variety of correspondence to, from and about him covering the years 1912–47. In order to reconstruct events as Lustig saw them, I tried to critically scrutinise certain informal reminiscences of his friends, relatives and adversaries. Their accounts are often partial, in Betty Lustig's case fiercely partisan, and above all chronologically imprecise. Nonetheless, they provide important insights into Lustig's modus operandi during what might be called his glory days of 1920–35. A systematic reading of the British and North American daily press of the period helped to picture Lustig as a child – in some ways a leading representative – of those rackety interwar years.

Chapter 2: Bohemian Rhapsody

Reliable information on Victor Lustig's youth is notoriously scarce on the ground. Not only was record-keeping in the central Europe of the 1890s a more haphazard affair than it is now, but in later life Lustig himself frequently adapted the facts to meet the circumstances of his current criminal enterprise. The account I've given here is based in large part on the tireless research of my friend Albert Clinton, who was himself born and raised in the same area, and in broadly similar circumstances, as Lustig, if subsequently taking a markedly different course in life.

The lines beginning, 'He carefully raised the instrument …', 'There, for two months, he lodged in various quarters …' and, 'Victor [now] knew six languages …' all appear in *From Paris to Alcatraz*, as cited, pp.21–22. The account of Lustig's physical examination of December 1935 appears in his US Bureau of Prisons file, p.71. The quote on Lustig beginning, 'His greatest ability was to change tack …' appears in James Morton and Hilary Bateson, *Conned*, as cited in the bibliography, pp.2–3.

The family of the late Karl Harrer kindly put his unpublished memoir at my disposal. I should also particularly acknowledge the assistance of the Daudet family, as well as James Johnson's and Floyd Miller's book *The Man Who Sold the Eiffel Tower*, as cited in the bibliography. While perhaps labouring under the prevailing US federal law-enforcement idiom of the day, with a full quota of stoolies, snitches and wise guys, it's an invaluable account of the authorities' sometimes admirably dogged, sometimes comically inept, pursuit of their man.

Chapter 3: A Mask to Show the World

I'm grateful to the archive of the *New York Times* for much of the contemporary coverage of that city's criminal underworld around the years 1914–19. The Woodrow Wilson Presidential Library and Archive in Staunton, Virginia, an engagingly modest affair compared to the neon shopping mall-like enterprise of many of Wilson's successors in office, was also invaluable in establishing the social and political climate of the day. The US Bureau of Prisons again kindly put many of their contemporary records of Lustig's arrests, and his surprising avoidance of almost any official retribution, at my disposal.

The line beginning, 'One of Lustig's minor swindles was of girls …' appears in James Morton and Hilary Bateson, *Conned*, p.89, as previously cited. The line beginning, 'Victor Lustig came to America looking around for contacts …' and the line describing Lustig as 'an habitué of Paris and the leading European cities …' both appear in *From Paris to Alcatraz*, also as cited, p.13. The brief description of Lustig's 'pocketbook scam' follows in part the same account given in Jeff Maysh's excellent *Handsome Devil*, as quoted in the bibliography. The passage beginning, 'DUVAL, alias Miller, always possessed a very poor reputation …' is extracted from Lustig's US Bureau of Prisons file, courtesy of Douglas Williford. The first Mrs Lustig's line protesting, 'I'll throw myself in the ocean and let the fish eat me …' appears in *From Paris to Alcatraz*, p.16. The family of the late Karl Tuke kindly put some of their ancestor's unpublished memoirs of post-First World War life in New York at my disposal, as did the Spivack family of Joliet, Illinois.

I'm also grateful to the Office of the Clerk and Recorder of Denver, Colorado, and to the Omaha, Nebraska, City Clerk, responding to a request filed under the Nebraska Public Records Statute 84-712, for information concerning Lustig's activities in their respective jurisdictions.

Chapter 4: The Private Mint

For all the shortages of documentation, the FBI Freedom of Information Division holds important files on the general criminal backdrop to 1920s America, particularly in its details of the FBI's newly formed General Intelligence Division and its growing interest in Victor Lustig. The archives of the US Treasury Department similarly hold a wealth of material on that body's attempts to counter the widespread counterfeiting operations of the day. I'm also grateful to the volunteer historians of the Saratoga Race Course of Saratoga Springs, New York. The US Justice Department also proved responsive to a request for information on Lustig's known activities in and around St Louis, Missouri, in 1921. As I did in an earlier book on the strange relationship between Arthur Conan Doyle and Harry Houdini, I was again able to profitably search the back files of the Society for Psychical Research. I visited both Springfield, Missouri, and Butte, Montana, where I was lucky enough to inspect both those towns' municipal records of the 1920s. The successors of the Western Savings Bank of Salina, Kansas, also kindly put their archives at my disposal.

The report of Dr Ritchey of the US Public Health Service is contained in the US Bureau of Prisons file on Lustig, p.574. The line beginning, 'My father, spotting [the agent], looked around …' appears in *From Paris to Alcatraz*, p.46. The line beginning, 'It was so beautifully and painstakingly crafted …' appears in James Johnson and Floyd Miller, *The Man Who Sold the Eiffel Tower*, p.95, as cited in the bibliography. The line beginning, 'At home or in a locked hotel room …' appears in *From Paris to Alcatraz*, p.34. The description of 'Dapper Dan' Tourbillon beginning, 'He was bright enough…' is taken from James Johnson's field notes on the Lustig case, many or most of which he then incorporated into his co-authored book *The Man Who Sold the Eiffel Tower*. The line beginning, 'The bankers were more than ready …' comes from that same source, as does the line beginning, 'He had to go to his wife, a gentle elderly woman …'

The Bundesarchiv (State Security) Collection in Berlin also fills out the story of some of Lustig's arrests and subsequent trials, if any, of the period. The Paris police prefecture archives describe his activities in that city with a variety of intelligence reports, after-action files and personal memoirs, although with few if any surviving photographs of their subject. I am grateful to archivists from all these collections for their assistance in retrieving and advising on documents.

Chapter 5: French Connection

It was one of the inescapable obligations of the book to spend several pre-lockdown days in a well-appointed Paris hotel, and I should thank the estimable ASAP Travel accordingly. My friend Valya Page also very kindly visited and photographed the Hôtel de Crillon on my behalf, and I'm warmly grateful to her for her help. The archives of the Paris police prefecture were also useful in establishing the known facts, as opposed to the widespread speculation, concerning Lustig's activities in their city in the spring of 1925.

The line beginning, 'She never wanted for anything …' appears in *From Paris to Alcatraz*, as previously cited, p.65. The line of reported speech beginning, 'No. That's the way it takes him …' appears in Ernest Hemingway's *A Moveable Feast*, p.149, as cited in the bibliography. The line about the Paris Exposition remarking that 'almost everywhere the will to modernism dominated …' appears in John Baxter, *The Golden Moments of Paris*, p.142, as cited in the bibliography. The line beginning, 'The city had no more permanent fixture than the shabby guide …' appears in the same book, p.148. The excerpted speech beginning, 'You had him eating out of your hands, Victor …' is closely adapted from the version reported in *The Man Who Sold the Eiffel Tower*, p.82. The line beginning, 'An expression of relief came over Monsieur Poisson's face …' similarly appears in that book, p.85.

Bookshelves are sagging under the weight of the secondary literature on Paris in the 1920s, but any author should of course pay tribute to the always supremely readable, often deeply insightful and occasionally also lewdly catty *A Moveable Feast*. After all, Hemingway was there. Jill Jonnes's book *Eiffel's Tower* and John Baxter's *The Golden Moments of Paris*, both as cited in the bibliography, are excellent core reference texts for the time and place. I should also particularly acknowledge the help of the UK General Register Office, the US Library of Congress and the Manuscripts Reading Rook of the University of Cambridge. Without them there would have been a very different Chapter 5, or no chapter at all.

Chapter 6: Conning Capone

It's a great pleasure to again acknowledge the resources provided by the Manuscripts Reading Room of the Cambridge University Library, where I spent rather longer in the course of two days than in my three years as a Cambridge undergraduate, and of the Rare Books

Room of the British Library. Every effort has been made to comply with the copyright provisions involved. I am also indebted for material included in this chapter to the archival Collections of the Chicago Public Library, the City Archives held at the Ronald Williams Library at Northeastern Illinois University, to the Oklahoma State University Library, and to the Margaret Herrick Library in Los Angeles.

The line beginning, 'His wife was gone, taking his child …' appears in *From Paris to Alcatraz*, p.69, as previously cited. The description of Lustig's interview with Al Capone, in which he extracted $5,000 from the notorious gangster, closely follows the account given in *The Man Who Sold the Eiffel Tower*, p.116. The line beginning, 'The banker had sent innocent friends to prison …' appears in *From Paris to Alcatraz*, p.60. The line describing the 'steel skeletons of sky-scrapers rising everywhere to give Miami …' appears in Frederick Lewis Allen, *Only Yesterday*, p.226, as cited in the bibliography. The line beginning, 'In 1926, [we] were in New York …' and the line beginning, 'My mother married Doug Conner …' both appear in *From Paris to Alcatraz*, p.88. The line beginning, 'Lustig was most co-operative …' appears in *The Man Who Sold the Eiffel Tower*, p.33. The line beginning, 'Murdoch began to speculate in stocks …' appears in that same book, p.118. The direct speech beginning, 'Dear Sir, I was arrested in Paris …' is quoted, in slightly modified form, in *From Paris to Alcatraz*, p.109. The line beginning, 'I saw a woman in a white nurse's uniform …' appears in that same book, p.86.

I also made extensive use in this chapter of Lustig's surviving FBI file, and more particularly his extensive US Bureau of Prisons file, courtesy of Douglas Williford.

Chapter 7: Going South

On an institutional note, I should again acknowledge the help of the US Bureau of Prisons, the FBI Freedom of Information Division and the Public Archives of the US Justice Department, as well as that of The National Archives of Mexico (AGN) and its IT director Erick Carduso. I only wish I had been aware of this last facility at the time I wrote my small biography of Steve McQueen twenty years ago. I also enjoyed at least limited access to the records of the US Census Bureau of 1930.

The line beginning, 'Cash was a problem for Lustig …' appears in *The Man Who Sold the Eiffel Tower*, p.126, as previously cited. The line beginning, 'In the 1920s he ran a Nebraska drugstore …' is from that same book, p.159. The line beginning, 'My father [Lustig] visited me often and became a good friend …' appears in *From Paris to Alcatraz*, as previously cited, p.91. The line attributed to the *New York Times* reporting, 'Little more was known about them …' is quoted in Jeff Maysh, *Handsome Devil*, as cited in the bibliography. The line beginning, 'Rubano opened an envelope and removed a hundred-dollar bill …' appears in slightly modified form in *The Man Who Sold the Eiffel Tower*, p.153.

Among other newspapers and periodicals, I consulted the back files of the *Denver Post*, the *New York Times*, the *Seattle Times*, the *Spectator*, the *Spokesman-Review* of Spokane, Washington, and *The Times*.

Chapter 8: Escape from New York

I should particularly acknowledge the papers I made use of in this chapter lodged at The Collections of the Chicago Public Library and at the Vital Records Department of the Cook County Clerk's Office. I also consulted the files of the *Chicago Tribune*, the *New York Times*, the *San Francisco Chronicle*, the *Spokesman-Review* and the *Washington Post*. I visited the site of the old Wilbarger Hotel in Spokane, and also made use of that same city's District Court and Municipal Court records. The family of the late Edith Keep very kindly put her unpublished memoir at my disposal.

The line beginning, 'Whereas … Hon. Justin F. McCarthy of the Municipal Court of Chicago …' forms part of a criminal complaint against Victor Lustig contained in Lustig's US Bureau of Prisons file, p.710. The line beginning, 'We were all races and creeds …' appears in *The Man Who Sold the Eiffel Tower*, p.151, as previously cited. The line beginning, 'His quick wit helped him out …' appears in A.F.L. Deeson, *Great Swindlers*, p.69, as cited in the bibliography. The line beginning, 'I began to make the rounds of bars and restaurants …' appears in *The Man Who Sold the Eiffel Tower*, p.157. The passage of reported speech beginning, 'I received your lovely letter and the pictures …' appears in *From Paris to Alcatraz*, p.99. The line beginning, 'Each time her phone rang there'd be a buzz …' appears in *The Man Who Sold the Eiffel Tower*, p.167. The line recalling that Roberta Lustig had 'taken [me] on a little vacation from school …' appears in *From Paris to Alcatraz*, p.92. The line beginning, 'A lot of manpower, a lot of taxpayers' money …' and the transcript of the phone call beginning, 'Hello … Hello, Violet …' both appear in *The Man Who Sold the Eiffel Tower*, p.174 and 175 respectively. The line insisting that the US Secret Service 'spent 32 hours interrogating [Lustig] and wearing him out …' appears in *From Paris to Alcatraz*, p.94. The line beginning, 'And this was no hick jail in Texas …' appears in *The Man Who Sold the Eiffel Tower*, p.190.

For accounts of Lustig's arrest and detention I again consulted his US Prisons Bureau file, as well as secondary sources including the *Chicago American*, the *Denver Post*, the *Detroit News*, the *Morning Post*, the *New Republic*, the *New York Evening Journal* and the *Philadelphia Inquirer*. I'm also grateful to the archivists at the British Library, the FBI Freedom of Information Division, the General Register Office, the UK Public Record Office and the US Department of Justice.

Chapter 9: The Rock

The lengthy excerpt beginning, 'For a period of years the windows on the upper floors …' appears in Lustig's bulky US

Prisons Bureau file, which is in the public domain but was kindly retrieved and supplied to me by the Bureau's Douglas Williford; I'm extremely grateful to him for his help in the matter. The line beginning, 'Lustig's escape created a furor ...' appears in *The Man Who Sold the Eiffel Tower*, p.202. The line beginning, 'She came to me that evening ...' appears in *From Paris to Alcatraz*, p.95, as previously cited. The line beginning, 'We took him there, and when we did he opened the oven doors ...' appears in *The Man Who Sold the Eiffel Tower*, p.214. The line beginning, 'Throughout Watts's testimony, Lustig slumped in his chair ...' appears in that same book, p.215. The passage of reported speech beginning, 'Received your letter, and also five dollars ...' appears in *From Paris to Alcatraz*, p.105. Victor Lustig's letter to his brother of 18 January 1939 beginning, 'Yesterday Chief Callahan came to see me ...' appears in Lustig's US Prisons Bureau file. Lustig's 'Proposed Peace Plan by Prohibitive International Law (November 1943)' appears in the same file. The lines beginning, 'I have been planning that as soon as the war is over ...' and, 'When [I] saw my father I knew that I had waited too long ...' both appear in *From Paris to Alcatraz*, p.107 and 113 respectively.

Victor Lustig's death certificate is available from the offices of the Missouri State Records Department. I visited Alcatraz.

SELECT BIBLIOGRAPHY

Allen, Frederick Lewis, *Only Yesterday* (New York: Harper & Brothers, 1931)

Baxter, John, *The Golden Moments of Paris* (New York: Museyon, 2014)

Bohlen, Charles E., *Witness to History* (New York: Norton, 1973)

Deeson, A.F.L., *Great Swindlers* (New York: Drake Publishers, 1972)

Hellman, Lillian, *Scoundrel Time* (Boston: Little, Brown, 1976)

Hemingway, Ernest, *A Moveable Feast* (New York: Scribner, 1964)

Johnson, James, with Floyd Miller, *The Man Who Sold the Eiffel Tower* (New York: Doubleday & Company, 1961)

Jonnes, Jill, *Eiffel's Tower* (New York: Viking Penguin, 2009)

Lindskoog, Kathryn, *Fakes, Frauds & Other Malarkey* (Grand Rapids, Michigan: Zondervan, 1993)

Lustig, Betty Jean, and Nanci Garrett, *From Paris to Alcatraz* (Bloomington, Indiana: Author Solutions/Xlibris, 2011)

Maysh, Jeff, *Handsome Devil* (Kindle Single, 2016)

Milgram, Stanley, 'Behavioral Study of Obedience', *Journal of Abnormal and Social Psychology* 67, No. 4 (Washington, D.C.: American Psychological Association, 1963)

Morton, James, and Hilary Bateson, *Conned: Scams, Frauds and Swindles* (London: Portrait, 2007)

Moss, Norman, *The Pleasures of Deception* (New York: Reader's Digest, 1977)

Pizzoli, Greg, *Tricky Vic* (New York: Viking Penguin, 2015)

Sparrow, Gerald, *The Great Swindlers* (London: John Long, 1959)

Stone, Irving, *Earl Warren: A Great American Story* (Englewood Cliffs, New Jersey: Prentice Hall, 1948)

Trager, James, *The New York Chronology* (New York: HarperResource, 2003)

Tugwell, Rexford Guy, *A Chronicle of Jeopardy* (Chicago: University of Chicago Press, 1955)

Winchell, Walter, *Winchell Exclusive* (Englewood Cliffs, New Jersey: Prentice Hall, 1975)

INDEX

ABOUT THE AUTHOR

Christopher Sandford is a regular contributor to newspapers and magazines on both sides of the Atlantic. He has written numerous biographies of music, film and sports stars, as well as *Union Jack*, a best-selling book on John F. Kennedy's special relationship with Great Britain, described by the *National Review* as 'political history of a high order – the Kennedy book to beat'. His book *The Final Innings: The Cricketers of Summer 1939* was the joint winner of the 2020 Cricket Society/MCC Book of the Year Award. Born and raised in England, Christopher currently lives in Seattle.

ALSO BY CHRISTOPHER SANDFORD

FICTION

Feasting with Panthers
Arcadian
We Don't Do Dogs

PLAYS

Comrades

MUSIC BIOGRAPHIES

Mick Jagger
Eric Clapton
Kurt Cobain
David Bowie
Sting
Bruce Springsteen
Keith Richards
Paul McCartney
The Rolling Stones

FILM BIOGRAPHIES

Steve McQueen
Roman Polanski

SPORT

The Cornhill Centenary Test
Godfrey Evans
Tom Graveney
Imran Khan
Keeper of Style

HISTORY

Houdini and Conan Doyle
The Final Over
Harold and Jack
The Man Who Would be Sherlock
Union Jack
The Zeebrugge Raid
The Final Innings

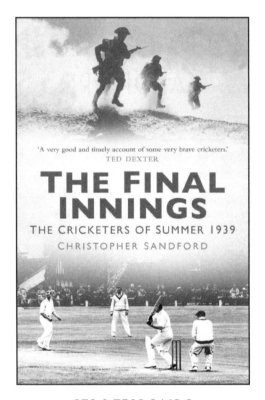